THE GEORGE GUND FOUNDATION
IMPRINT IN AFRICAN AMERICAN STUDIES

The George Gund Foundation has endowed
this imprint to advance understanding of
the history, culture, and current issues
of African Americans.

*The publisher gratefully acknowledges the generous support of
the African American Studies Endowment Fund
of the University of California Press Foundation,
which was established by a major gift from the
George Gund Foundation.*

Race, Place, and Suburban Policing

Aerial view of Meacham Park, 1965. This aerial picture captures Meacham Park in its original size—prior to the 1968 highway construction of Interstate 44 and the 1991 annexation to the City of Kirkwood. Credit goes to the Kirkwood Historical Society, who afforded me unlimited access to donated Meacham Park photos and memorabilia.

Race, Place, and Suburban Policing

TOO CLOSE FOR COMFORT

Andrea S. Boyles

UNIVERSITY OF CALIFORNIA PRESS

University of California Press, one of the most distinguished university presses in the United States, enriches lives around the world by advancing scholarship in the humanities, social sciences, and natural sciences. Its activities are supported by the UC Press Foundation and by philanthropic contributions from individuals and institutions. For more information, visit www.ucpress.edu.

University of California Press
Oakland, California

Library of Congress Cataloging-in-Publication Data

Boyles, Andrea S., author
    Race, place, and suburban policing : too close for comfort / Andrea S. Boyles.
        p.   cm.
    Includes bibliographical references and index.
    ISBN 978-0-520-28238-4 (cloth, alk. paper) — ISBN 978-0-520-28239-1 (pbk., alk. paper) — ISBN 978-0-520-95808-1 (electronic)
        1. Police—community relations—Missouri—Kirkwood.
    2. African Americans—Missouri—Kirkwood—Social conditions.
    3. Police—Missouri—Kirkwood.   4. Racism in criminology—Missouri—Kirkwood.   I. Title.
    HV7936.P8B69   2015
    363.2′30896073077865—dc23   2014045122

Manufactured in the United States of America

24   23   22   21   20   19   18   17   16   15
10   9   8   7   6   5   4   3   2   1

In keeping with a commitment to support environmentally responsible and sustainable printing practices, UC Press has printed this book on Natures Natural, a fiber that contains 30% post-consumer waste and meets the minimum requirements of ANSI/NISO Z39.48-1992 (R 1997) (*Permanence of Paper*).

And yet her legacy lives...
*I dedicate this book to my late mother, Brenda, who embodied
immeasurable resilience through life and death, and to my
children, Prentis, Jr., Anaiah, and Faith, as the next
generation of hope, determination, and accomplishment.*

CONTENTS

ILLUSTRATIONS

FIGURES

TABLES

In *Race, Place, and Suburban Policing,* Andrea S. Boyles presents a gripping and at times, alarming depiction of police-community relations in Meacham Park, an African-American enclave of Kirkwood, Missouri. Boyles skillfully demonstrates how both race and community context help shape Meacham Park residents' overall perceptions of and experiences with the police. While an abundant body of research reveals that urban blacks often bear the brunt of unwelcome police contacts (e.g., pedestrian and/or vehicle stops, physically intrusive searches, and arrests), there is considerable debate about the role of place in influencing their disproportionate police encounters. For example, some scholars suggest that race is often confounded with disadvantaged neighborhood context in studies of inner-city African-Americans' negative police interactions, such that attributions of racial bias actually result from officers' preconceived notions of ecologically dangerous and/or suspicious places.

Few studies have been able to disentangle the impact of race from that of disadvantaged community context in explaining dubious police practices, because the urban disadvantage found in African-American neighborhoods is often ecologically unmatched. Simply put, researchers have found it quite difficult to identify inner-city, lower-class white communities for comparison to similar black communities. *Race, Place, and Suburban Policing,* however, enjoys a research design advantage over many prior neighborhood-based, qualitative examinations of police-minority citizen interactions. Specifically, Boyles situates her work in a suburban community context and as a result, the book is uniquely positioned to make several important contributions to the growing body of literature on race, place, and policing.

There are a small number of published monographs and collections investigating African-Americans' experiences with racially biased policing, despite this issue being an important national and local policy concern. While previous scholarship has advanced our understanding regarding how members of poor minority communities simultaneously experience under- and over-policing, what clearly distinguishes *Race, Place, and Suburban Policing* from its contemporaries is its focus on race and suburban community context. In particular, Boyles' trailblazing research trains the spotlight on the suburbs, drawing attention to an important, novel, and commonly overlooked research setting. Her project parallels the migration patterns of many African-Americans, who, like their counterparts from other racial groups, have long considered the suburbs a refuge from harsh, urban living conditions (e.g., physical decay, social disorder). Boyles offers a compelling set of study findings, challenging the conventional wisdom that suburbia insulates blacks from potential harms once faced in the inner city, including heavy-handed and unwarranted policing tactics.

Race, Place, and Suburban Policing is especially timely given the recent and well-publicized civil unrest in Ferguson, Missouri—a nearby St. Louis County suburb. Frustrated community residents and civil rights leaders held several days of protests after an unarmed black male teenager was shot to death by a white Ferguson police officer. The subsequent global media coverage chronicled recurrent clashes between police officers clad in militarized tactical gear and impassioned demonstrators, casting light on long-standing tensions between black Ferguson residents and the police. Boyles' research precedes the Ferguson incident and emphasizes the importance of examining how disadvantaged blacks residing beyond the city limits make sense of their personal and vicarious adverse police experiences.

Boyles spent approximately two years conducting painstaking fieldwork, adeptly using qualitative research methods to systematically compile and later analyze a wealth of incredibly rich data. Her investigation yielded detailed renderings of Meacham Park residents' lived experiences. Furthermore, Boyles interviewed thirty adult respondents at length, and so she was able to identify a number of salient themes. For example, she reveals that study participants were steadfast in their belief that following annexation (and its injurious by-products), Meacham Park had been besieged by police. In fact, many of Boyles' respondents recounted being harassed and mistreated by Kirkwood officers.

The book's subtitle, *Too Close for Comfort,* apparently emerges from important conceptual and theoretical frameworks (i.e., race-and-place effect, group and racial threat perspectives). Throughout the monograph, Boyles gradually and cleverly brings the title's relevance into sharper focus. For instance, she asserts that "blacks have historically been situated, segregated, and policed in places based on proximity to whites." Accordingly, Meacham Park residents attributed their chances of being arrested to arbitrary police decision making, undeniably influenced by race and/or community context rather than by legitimate legal factors. Finally, Boyles' respondents expressed grave concerns about the long-term life consequences resulting from what they considered highly unethical police actions.

Boyles succeeds in presenting a sobering account of how both race and disadvantaged community context shape suburban blacks' general assessments of police. Thus, she grants readers keen insights into the social world of individuals who are principally studied as offenders but rarely have their own perspectives at the center of social inquiry. For example, Boyles masterfully presents respondents' unsettling descriptions of poor treatment at the hands of police. Some readers of *Race, Place, and Suburban Policing* will undoubtedly reject study participants' disconcerting accounts of police wrongdoing. This is understandable, as most citizens, due to their social status and access to mechanisms for redress, will seldom experience the kinds of police misconduct intensely captured in this book.

Furthermore, the literature aptly demonstrates that citizens sometimes misinterpret officers' behaviors and intentions. What is most relevant for the current study, nonetheless, is precisely *how* Meacham Park residents came to understand their experiences with and perceptions of the police. Given that efforts to improve police legitimacy are often predicated on the input of community members, speaking with those individuals most likely to experience involuntary police contact provides important insights for better understanding their impact. In the end, Boyles offers a holistic examination of how the interactions of race and place helped shape Kirkwood officers' decision making. Boyles also effectively uses the case-study approach to underscore the cumulative impact of negative police experiences. In particular, her careful analysis of circumstances preceding "two nationally profiled" deadly shootings of Kirkwood police officers by Meacham Park residents (i.e., Kevin Johnson and Charles "Cookie" Thornton) helps situate both tragedies within everyday milieus.

Race, Place, and Suburban Policing is written and organized in a way that highlights and takes full advantage of study participants' detailed narratives of their adverse police encounters. Few studies on police-minority interactions have drawn from in-depth interview techniques, which provide unique opportunities to examine not just the context and circumstances of emotionally charged events, but also their meanings for study participants. The monograph will likely be of particular importance for anyone interested in studying the interactions of race and neighborhood disadvantage. While *Race, Place, and Suburban Policing* has several strengths, there are three main reasons that Boyles should be applauded: (1) for undertaking this arduous and pioneering research, (2) for providing concrete strategies for improving police-community relations, (3) and for her efforts to give historically marginalized people a much-needed voice.

Rod K. Brunson
Rutgers University

PREFACE

Weeks after the shooting death of eighteen-year-old Michael Brown, Jr., by police in Ferguson, Missouri, the events leading up to his death and immediately following remained ambiguous. How did a brief encounter between a young, unarmed black man and the police lend itself to such a brutal killing? Furthermore, how did concerned citizens come to experience militarized policing from countless local and state jurisdictions—where they were tear gassed, shot with rubber bullets, and arrested—in pursuit of answers and perceived justice? I myself was there, in this now internationally recognized St. Louis suburban community, witnessing and documenting much of what transpired in the wake of this incident. Perhaps the answers lie in a range of unexplained black citizen-police incidents; there is an undeniable pattern of dubious encounters and outcomes driving dissention between blacks and law enforcement.

For example, roughly a week prior to the Mike Brown incident, news broke that the untimely death of Eric Garner—a forty-three-year-old black father of six from Long Island, New York—had been ruled a homicide. How could a man lose his life during a police confrontation over his alleged selling of loose cigarettes? More directly, how could he fall prey to an NYPD chokehold at a time when controversial policing policies and practices, ranging from racial profiling to stopping, questioning, and frisking, are at the forefront of national debates? Similarly, who could have imagined that Marlene Pinnock, a black great-grandmother, would receive a barrage of punches from a California Highway Patrolman, straddled atop her in broad daylight, alongside a Los Angeles freeway? Has there not been enough attention called to police improprieties, thereby necessitating video and cell-phone footage of bystanders to serve as wake-up calls? My answer is no; there can never be too much coverage or attention yielded to a persistently overt continuum of police aggression toward blacks.

Race, place, and policing research can be challenging. We need the police. And policing practices need to be protected and sometimes even covert because full transparency may at times compromise a mission. Still, do private citizens not have the right to critically assess police services and hold them accountable?

Further, how can I as an outsider—a black female academic who has never served a day on the force—shed light on problems within police culture above what its own members are free to do? My position has been to defer to the populations most likely to encounter these problems. Who can better account for policing than the citizens subject to the policing?

For this project, the citizens are those of Meacham Park and the city of Kirkwood, Missouri. Recent policing events within these neighborhoods illuminate often unaccounted-for dimensions of disparity and backlash faced by people of color and perpetuated by the police, and they allow us to closely examine spheres of racial divide in hope of achieving policing that is just. As an embodiment of social progress—teaching and conducting research from what I recognize as privileged space compared to most study participants—I believe that at the core of two adversely adjoined, fractured communities exists very real possibilities for social sensitivity and justice.

Apart from drawing attention to the violence inflicted on Brown, Garner, Pinnock, and others discussed throughout this book, and apart from Meacham Park residents' experiences that this book brings to light, innumerable instances of heated, even deadly exchanges between blacks and law enforcement officers have not been—and will never be—documented. Therefore, I am even more resolved today to further race, place, and policing dialogue than I was five years ago when this project began. My hope through this study has been to advance the human condition and quality of life in all communities and, as a catalyst for social change, to afford uninterrupted space for true social examination and criticism, thus precipitating social improvement.

Andrea S. Boyles
August 30, 2014

ACKNOWLEDGMENTS

Writing a book must be one of the most intimidating yet rewarding experiences ever. I entered this process excited and extremely humbled, recognizing it as an amazing milestone, and it is in this spirit that I finished it—nervously hopeful, but mostly lowly and grateful. Therefore, it is with immeasurable gratitude that I extend thanks to the following people. It is through their contributions, personal and professional, that I was motivated to write this book, while simultaneously remaining committed to and able to endure life's complexities alongside of it.

For starters, I would like to thank Dana Britton, Spencer Wood, and Robert Schaefer for supporting me. Dana provided me with safe space and mentorship while at Kansas State University, and thus, I learned a lot while there, academically and otherwise. I absorbed a lot from Dana—her instruction and intuitiveness with navigating and climbing the Ivory Tower. More directly, I am appreciative of her support for my project and for helping me think about my data comprehensively and, in its infancy, deliver it intelligibly. Likewise, I am grateful to Spencer for always taking time to recognize and celebrate my endeavors, for always having recognized me as a skilled student, and projecting me to be even more accomplished, as a colleague. And lastly, Robert . . . where should I begin? Thank you for believing in me and mentoring me well beyond the doctoral program. I appreciate your availability, your willingness to offer advice and guidance as I ventured into the world of book publishing. You can never know what your involvement—your excitement about it all—has meant to me. Students can all but hope for high regard and professional validation from former professors. Yours continuously resonated loudly and clearly for me. Thanks, Dr. Schaefer.

I would also like to extend thanks to Rod Brunson and Jody Miller. My work is an extension of theirs conducted in the City of St. Louis, and I wholly respect their contribution to race, place, and policing research, as well as urban, gender, and criminological literature entirely. It has been through their efforts that I found space to make my stake in the field. Not to mention, it was Jody who first suggested that I take a closer look into the policing of Meacham Park and the City of Kirkwood. She has always been supportive, available, and congratulatory of the project. Likewise, Rod certainly looked out for me. We frequently talked shop before I completed my doctoral degree and afterward. Hence, he totally backed me on pursuing the project as a book, unequivocally becoming my first avid reader. I will always be grateful for the depth to which he supported me and his tireless commitment to reading, rereading, scrutinizing, and critiquing each chapter intensely. At times, writing or rather synthesizing my thoughts proved tedious, but he hung tough, helping me to balance ideas and approaches most sensible to the work. Thus, I am appreciative of his insightfulness and dedication to time management and humor, all traits that helped me stay intellectually engaged, fervently working, and in touch with my humanness.

Moreover, I am very grateful to my editor Maura Roessner and Jack Young—my lifelines at the University of California Press. Thank you both for fielding countless questions and working out the kinks for me, and especially you, Maura, for taking a chance on me and my work, calling and knowing precisely what to say to calm my raging storms (nerves). You are awesome!

Additionally, I would like to thank my Lindenwood University-Belleville family, for colleagues, graphic artist Lennon Mueller, and students alike who recognized, respected, and fully supported my research—my goal and its role in contributing to the betterment of people, particularly at the disadvantaged end of the social spectrum. These lessons are ripe for instruction, well beyond the scope of classrooms, and it has meant a lot having you realize their broad implications.

All of life's lessons should not and cannot be limited to the confines of a classroom, and thus, those most endearing and enduring for me came from my mother—Brenda L. Richardson. My mother battled cancer, nine out of my last twelve writing months, and it was through her journey—her extraordinary perseverance—that I came to truly understand *who I was* and *what I was capable of* as her daughter. Thus, her unfaltering zeal and determination as she faced the most unfathomable of circumstances became infectious. She refused brokenness, and as her caregiver, daughter, and legacy, I had to do the same. We hung tough together, with me caring and writing, and her sharing and celebrating my accomplishments with doctors, nurses, family, and friends, while resiliently fighting to live. I will forever be indebted to my mother for teaching me how to win when life leaves you dangling on the fringe. Thank God! I did it, Mom! And after having arrived at such an incredible end, or rather beginning, I can now only hope and pray that the next generation, my children, Prentis, Jr., Anaiah, and Faith, will make good on their inheritance—a deeply entrenched spirituality and an uncanny ability to attain the impossible. I am ever so grateful to the three of you for being patient with me. I chase dreams—as in this book—because I do not want *you* too afraid to. I pursue social justice and change for and as an example to you.

As for the rest of my family, I love them dearly. At times, some of them bypass my name and nickname, referencing me as "Dr. Granddaughter," "Dr. Niece," "Dr. Mom," and so forth. They are funny and amazing; I am thankful for the times where they uniquely said and did things in support for me. I appreciate it. I had to juggle a lot, mostly loss. As fate would have it, my grandfather and mom passed two weeks apart, in the heat of writing season. Consequently, I was forever working on campus, at home, at various libraries—mostly before daybreak and late at night—stealing time when things were calmer. But I managed, thanks to timely prayers, phone calls, texts, and coverage I so desperately needed in different places, at different times. So thank you, Dad (Daryl Mensey, Sr.) and stepmother, Sam, for checking on me and covering for me especially at home, when I was pulled in countless directions. I appreciate my grandmothers, Annie Thorpes and June Florez, who called often reminding me that I needed to eat and rest. Their calls never waned but increased following the passing of my mother; I really needed it. To my late grandfathers, James Thorpes and especially Jim Florez— who in his final days said, "Don't worry, I'm okay, I understand. I'm proud of you, take care of your mother, work, and come when you can." I will always be grateful. And for my aunts, Maria and Beverly, who also covered for me, and uncles like Mack and Aaron, who in their own way, at very critical stages, also encouraged me, thank you as well.

Likewise, Mr. Will did the same. Thanks for picking up the slack, when I was trying so desperately to provide care, to work—teaching, and writing, among countless other things. Furthermore, I am grateful for Queen Ford, who told me I would be an author long before pursuing both master's and doctoral degrees. Ha, go figure! For Jacqueline "Jackie" White, Lorez White, and Laura Logan for always making me feel like a *she*-ro: I beg to differ, but because I am forever trying to make good on that, this book is the result.

Finally, I am thankful to the Kirkwood Historical Society and even more so indebted to the residents of Meacham Park. This book could not have been possible without your willingness to share and entrust your historically rich community and most intimate stories with me. With nothing more than sheer humility, I thank them, and more importantly, I wholly thank God.

Introduction

I don't trust cops and I don't know many Black people that do.

LZ GRANDERSON 2012

A STARTLING TURN OF EVENTS

My interview with Brian, fifty-eight years old, was scheduled for seven o'clock in the evening. I went by his house, rang the doorbell, and knocked. No answer. I then called Brian on the phone, with no answer. Thinking that he was just late getting home or that there was some other logical explanation for his absence, I circled the neighborhood and eventually parked at Kirkwood Commons, the neighboring shopping plaza. Again, I attempted to call Brian, and finally, he answered the phone and asked if I was still in the community. I told him yes. He apologized for being late and anxiously asked if I could still meet him at his house. I said yes, told him I was on the way, and we hung up.

It took less than two minutes to get back to Brian's house. As I pulled up, I saw two Kirkwood police cars parked on the sidewalk in front of his house and a couple of white male officers, but I did not see Brian. Needless to say, I was puzzled and somewhat disconcerted to find the police at his address. After all, Brian and I had just spoken, with no mention of them. I parked across the street from Brian's home; immediately, an officer walked to my window. With a serious tone, he said, "I'm not sure what you're over here to talk to Brian about, but I need you to stay in the car for a minute. We're talking to him about some things." It was then that I spotted Brian in the back seat of one of the squad cars. Given the scene and the officer's directive, I was alarmed. Two things were clear: one, the officers were there to address a problem involving Brian; and two, he had obviously alerted them of our appointment. I pondered leaving, but instead I stayed. Here was a good opportunity for observational research of black citizen–police interaction in Meacham Park.

Roughly five minutes later, the same officer returned, explaining that Brian had several warrants and that they were taking him in. He also stated that Brian wanted me to secure his home. Brian yelled, "Please, lock up my house," from the police car. He repeatedly called my name, apologizing and begging for my help: "Ms. Boyles, will you PLEASE go inside my house, get my keys, and lock up my front door for me?" At this point, Brian was refusing to cooperate or leave with the police without first seeing his home get locked, and he clearly did not want the officers to do it.

Given his belligerence and obvious distrust of the police, I worried that the police would become less patient and more forceful. After all, research shows that citizens' demeanor can influence officers' treatment of them.[1] To prevent escalation, I reluctantly agreed to lock Brian's front door and asked for his keys. Brian wanted to go inside with me to find them but he was not allowed. "The keys are on the kitchen table, I think ... they might be in my bedroom ... I don't know where I put them, that's why I need to go in and look for them." As I proceeded toward the front door, so did an officer, stating, "I'll help her find them." Immediately, Brian panicked: "NO, I don't want them in my house. Ms. Boyles, will you PLEASE look around for my key. I don't want them [police] in my house, going through my stuff, planting stuff."

Finally, I went inside, found his keys on a table, immediately locked his front door, and with the officers' permission, returned his keys to him. Brian calmed down, apologized for having involved me, and, along with the officers, thanked me for assisting. They immediately pulled away.

I could not help but wonder how much of their patience and restraint with Brian, despite his antagonism, was motivated by my involvement. Local officers were aware of my neighborhood inquiries and research. It is also possible that Brian adjusted his behavior accordingly; he too was familiar with my research. It is plausible that he may have behaved adversely, thinking that the police would not do anything harmful with me there as a witness.

Nonetheless, the tense exchanges and distrust in Brian's situation represent those of many black citizen–police interactions, particularly in disadvantaged communities. Black citizen–police encounters are often negative, often unexpected, and often include physical restraint or even altercations. Brian's experiences were direct, but indirect experiences with the police—in the form of being an observer—also shape black attitudes and distrust toward police.

Race, Place, and Suburban Policing accounts for actual, everyday black citizen encounters with police and an all-too-often ambiguous "to protect and to serve" response by police. This book explores black sensitivities to, interactions with, and perceptions of the police, irrespective of criminality and place. The reality is that bad encounters between black folks and the police take place, not only in the well-documented inner city, but also in perceivably upscale, secluded, and thus, "safe" communities in the suburbs. That said, this research takes as its place of focus Meacham Park—a disadvantaged black neighborhood located in the heart of one of St. Louis's most exclusive suburbs.

AN ALL-TOO-FAMILIAR RECAP

On March 4, 1991, the world awakened to an amateur video clip that not only rocked the City of Los Angeles but also inflamed the nation and thrust issues surrounding race, policing, and the criminal justice system onto the national stage. The roughly two-minute footage transported us to a dark, suburban street in San Fernando Valley, where twenty-five-year-old Rodney King was repeatedly stunned, kicked, and beaten by four police officers, leaving King "with eleven skull fractures, a broken eye socket, and facial nerve damage."[2] With each airing of the horrific images, racial tension and frustrations mounted. Most were unaware of King's history with the criminal justice system: he was on parole for an armed-robbery conviction, had a history of drug and alcohol abuse, and had just led police on a high-speed chase. Similar to Brian's behavior in Meacham Park, King was initially noncompliant, and it was somewhere between the chase and officers' restraint that his resistance became an excuse for immense police aggression. Hence, all we saw was a seemingly defenseless black man being viciously brutalized by four, armed, white police officers. This incident divided the nation along racial lines and exploded into a three-day riot that left fifty-five people dead, over two thousand injured, and roughly $1 billion in property damage.[3] Recently deceased but still a well-known name, Rodney King has become nearly synonymous with police brutality.

Years later, in February 4, 1999, the shooting death of twenty-two-year-old Guinean immigrant Amadou Diallo by officers reignited fury and national conversations surrounding police brutality and intensified black citizen–police relations. Unlike King, Diallo had no criminal history and certainly had not just spurred a high-speed chase. As they would later recount, the officers confronted Diallo because he resembled an armed serial rapist believed to be at large. According to the officers' testimony, Diallo ran when confronted and ignored their orders to show his hands. Even though Diallo was unarmed, the officers mistakenly assumed a reach for what later would be discovered his wallet was a reach for a gun. The officers responded with forty-one shots, nineteen of which hit Diallo.[4]

Diallo was posthumously cleared of any criminal culpability, which leaves one to question why Diallo fled. His fleeing likely suggested guilt to the police and thereby spurred them to more serious action: if he had nothing to hide, why run? It is not too much to surmise that, as a black man, Diallo assumed the police would not believe he was innocent; he may have thought that he was going to be subjected to a negative police encounter either way, whether he stayed or ran.

Similar to the King beating, this shooting came to symbolize racially biased brutality, a pattern of officers appearing to resort to excessive use of force in restraint of black suspects. Such ready—even anticipatory—violence appeared to stem from negative assumptions of race and place, or more specifically, a suggestive black criminal nature or the appearance of criminality among young black men from disadvantaged communities.

With each incident, citizens' perceptions of racially biased policing intensified, particularly among blacks. It is no wonder, then, that the 2006 police shooting of twenty-three-year-old Sean Bell set off yet another race-related firestorm. Bell was killed, and his two friends injured, after his bachelor party at a Queens strip bar.[5] While the details leading to the shootings remain unclear, it is undeniable that none of the men were armed and the officers' fifty shots were unwarranted and excessive. As did the King and Diallo cases, the shooting death of Sean Bell resulted in numerous protests and marches, casting further light on persisting police brutality and excessive use of force with black suspects.

As is evident in all four cases (Brian, King, Diallo, and Bell), the least bit of perceived resistance can, in a split second, create volatile black citizen–police exchanges. Such encounters can trigger impulsive, unjustifiable, and potentially deadly acts of police aggression, irrespective of criminality and place. Yet, despite what the public, particularly blacks, believed to be overwhelming evidence of police brutality in the three nationally profiled cases, all officers involved were initially acquitted. For many, the acquittals indicated not only injustice for the victims but also institutional protection and license for aggressive policing tactics and differential treatment targeting and endangering minorities. Protests driven by hurt and fear demanded changes in verdicts and law enforcement policies detrimental to minority communities. National discourse surrounding the cases were riddled with questions:

Why did this happen? Is this really indicative of racial biases among officers, police departments, and the criminal justice system altogether? Should we grant officers the benefit of the doubt, given their stress and risk? If racial bias is a factor, how do we recognize it as such and then adequately address it through effective policy change and training? How do we prevent the discriminatory practice of conflating blackness and criminality?

Discussions and debates surrounding the role of race and profiling in policing, the criminal justice system, and society at large again commanded the national spotlight with the February 26, 2012, fatal shooting of unarmed seventeen-year-old Trayvon Martin by George Zimmerman. While Zimmerman was not a commissioned officer, he acted as such in his role as a neighborhood watch volunteer, and, like the officers in the King, Diallo, and Bell cases, is believed by many to have exerted excessive and unwarranted force, acting on assumptions and fear indicative of a broader problem: differential policing that presumes blacks, particularly young men, are inherently deviant, and thus, suspicious and criminal in nature.

The widely held belief that the Zimmerman-Martin confrontation began because of racial profiling stems from Zimmerman's 911 call describing Martin as "a real suspicious guy" looking "like he's up to no good."[6] The fact that Zimmerman was not initially arrested after Martin's death further stoked public perception that this case was about race. Authorities' protection of Zimmerman based on Florida's "stand-your-ground" self-defense law did not resonate: Zimmerman had just killed an unarmed teenager, so Zimmerman's protection seemed more about disregard for Martin's life and race-based differential treatment than about justified self-defense.[7] Following weeks of outrage and nationally organized protests, marches, candle-lit vigils, and online petitions, the Florida State Attorney's office arrested and charged Zimmerman with second degree murder and launched a full investigation, but in July of 2013, Zimmerman was acquitted. Thousands spoke out, demanding reevaluation, not only of the stand-your-ground legislation, but also, more broadly, of racially motivated law enforcement policies and even racial discrimination in general.

HOODLUMS WEAR HOODIES

That the Martin case brought so much attention to broad societal issues of race and discrimination is due in part to covert suggestions that Martin himself, the victim, bore responsibility for looking suspicious. Heraldo Riverio's candid assertion on Fox that the "hoodie" worn by Martin the night he was killed was attire that a "hoodlum" or "gangster" would wear, and, by implication a voluntary contribution to his suspicion and eventual death, outraged Martin supporters and raised important questions: Does wearing a hoodie make a person a hoodlum? What does attire and its accompanying stereotypes mean for other young black men, and is this standard equally applied across races? Should Martin have "known better" than to wear a hoodie in an affluent, white neighborhood? Is that even a fair or relevant question?

The notion that blacks bear responsibility for drawing suspicion is not new. Accordingly, as reporter Jesse Washington explains, a sort of black male code permeates black culture, a code aimed at preventing black men from seeming suspicious.[8] A set of "safe" and educated directives for how to respond to and compensate for the social construction of black male suspicion and its effects, the "code" includes paying close attention to one's surroundings, especially if one is in an affluent neighborhood where few or no black folks live; and understanding that not being a criminal might have little bearing on people's suspicions or assumptions, especially if one is wearing certain attire. However, while pragmatic and maybe even necessary for safety, the compensatory nature of such a code does not address the real issue. It absolves any harm done to a suspicious-looking-but-innocent person and blames the victim for not knowing better than to take precautions against looking suspicious—a subjective determination at best. Emphasizing the need to anticipate and compensate for negative stereotypes takes the focus away from the real problem: the negative stereotype itself and the resulting persistent racial discrimination in policing.

When Martin supporters took to wearing hoodies in protest of the contention that Zimmerman was justified in his actions because Martin "looked" suspicious; when President Obama commented, "If I had a son, he'd look like Trayvon"; and when other prominent figures, such as black male legislators, wore hoodies and carried bags of skittles or a can of tea to the floor of their respective capitols, the message was clear: this could happen anywhere to anyone with characteristics similar to Martin's, which means current law enforcement policies and practices are not working.[9] Instead, these policies and practices leave black citizens, especially young men, vulnerable to racial biases and excessive use of force—a vulnerability that deserves serious attention.

It is somewhere between "hoods" (neighborhoods) and "hoodies" (appearance) that blacks, especially young men, come to be suspected of wrongdoing. As such, police scrutiny and aggression are not based solely on place *or* race, but they occur at the intersection of the two. Consequently, race, place, and policing cannot be understood as separate from one another. They must be recognized as overlapping forces that produce a set of often unavoidable circumstances for blacks. Blacks, especially young men, by virtue of where they are and what they look like, can fall prey to criminal biases when found within predominantly black communities, and perhaps even more so, when found within predominantly white ones.

Because poor black neighborhoods, or "the hood," often have high crime rates, they are deemed by police as "hot spots" and are thus subject to aggressive forms of policing.[10] This kind of proactive policing is not generally deemed necessary in more advantaged white communities, where, rather than proactively and anticipatorily patrolling suburban areas as a policing strategy, reactive policing is more common: officers respond upon request.

An exception to this proactive versus reactive policing pattern occurs when a white community is adjacent to a black community, as Kirkwood, a white community, is to Meacham Park, a black community. Brian is from the "hot spot" neighborhood of Meacham Park situated in the seemingly safe, crime-free suburb of Kirkwood. His location called for the police to *re-race place,* deferring to proactive policing as a result of a neighboring black enclave instead of the usual reactive strategies employed in predominantly white locations. Such policing tactics work to contain or remove racial minorities where they threaten to disrupt nearby white comfort—when blacks are within close proximity to predominantly white locations or black-white overlap occurs in certain places.

While Amadou Diallo and Sean Bell were found in "hot spots," or locations known for criminal activity. Rodney King and Trayvon Martin were not; they were in areas where police would not be routinely patrolling or would be doing so infrequently by comparison. They experienced the "race-and-place effect": an increase in surveillance such as tailing and other behaviors motivated by suspicion.[11] Despite King's criminal history and the chase leading up to his beating, the "crime" instigating the incident seemed to be traveling into a predominantly white community, the suburbs of Lake Terrace. Martin, on the other hand, had no criminal history, and was guilty only of being a young black man traveling after dark in a hoodie through the Retreat at Twin Lakes, Florida, a gated, predominantly white community. What ensued, particularly with Martin, was bias, harassment, and excessive use of force from pseudo-law enforcement in a pseudo-safe location.

Differences between the four cases notwithstanding, the salient commonality is aggression by law enforcement officers toward young black men. Notably, the crime scenes included both hot spots (overtly disadvantaged minority communities where anticipatory policing is common), and more advantaged, predominantly white areas. This illustrates how factors of race and place work together rather than independently.

MY OWN PLACE AND RACE

Walking to church one evening when I was young, my mother and I witnessed a drive-by shooting that killed an older gentleman just paces ahead of us. Officers sought details from us as paramedics worked unsuccessfully to save the man, but because everything happened so fast, we were unable to provide much information. I remember being relieved that the police were working to gain information and evidence that might lead to the shooter's capture. However, I also remember being skeptical that they would catch the shooter and worried about what that might mean for my mom and me. Would the shooter remember us as witnesses and try to apprehend us later? Is the shooter watching us talk to the police right now, seeing us as threats? I felt vulnerable and scared and wanted to get away from the scene as soon as possible. Even as a child, I doubted entrusting the situation's resolution to the police.

Growing up in a disadvantaged, troubled community in St. Louis, I was no stranger to police. They were extremely visible in my neighborhood, and witnessing police stops, frisks, drug busts, and arrests was commonplace. I can recall many negative interactions between police and my neighbors concerning shootings, domestic disputes, drug-related offenses, and so forth. Based on what we heard and saw, many of us, especially the teenagers, could identify officers by name and as "good" or "bad." I accepted tense citizen-police exchanges as the norm because I felt powerless to provoke change.

As I grew up, I became interested in studying criminal justice, and more specifically, police-citizen relationships. I wanted to better understand the nature of such relationships, how they emerged and how they persisted.

Ultimately, I wanted to improve police-citizen interactions in my community and others like it.

The high-profile cases of Rodney King, Amadou Diallo, and Sean Bell increased my concern and desire to contribute to change. With each incident, the media portrayed the nation as divided along racial lines, and increasingly, I wanted to be a part of those national discussions. Like others, I deeply wanted to understand the contentious concept of racial profiling and its role in excessive use of force and brutality and blatant police misconduct that was often exonerated. Using my own experiences, thoughts, and ideas regarding police in disadvantaged, black communities, I hoped to extend race, place, and policing dialogue in ways that would work toward improving police-citizen relationships.

While the King, Diallo, Bell, and other high-profile police-brutality cases brought concerns about police-citizen relations to the national stage, I more personally confronted these issues by following two lower-profile tragedies in a suburban St. Louis community near my childhood home. Three police officers were killed in two separate racially charged incidents in 2003 and 2005, prompting me, by then in a doctoral program, to begin my contribution to the dialogue on police-citizen relationships with my research. It began with a very basic question: "How do blacks feel about the police?"

RACE, PLACE, AND POLICING

Race, place, and policing research has provided greater insight into how blacks experience policing, how policing differs by population and location, and how the policing agenda particularly is shaped and influenced by dominant forces. While this research has been beneficial, it has been limited in several ways. First, apart from a few studies, researchers generally account only for attitudes toward the police (ATP) rather than the experiences that created them.[12] ATPs do not emerge in isolation; they are the effects of experiences with the police. Therefore, it is crucial to race, place, and policing dialogue to account for the chronology of negative black-citizen perceptions: experiences first and attitudes second. Otherwise, the uninformed become misinformed and are left to conclude that "black folks just don't like the police."

Second, race, place, and policing dialogue has not given sufficient attention to the policing of race in a variety of places. It has typically addressed black disadvantaged, inner-city "hot spots," neglecting to account for the policing experiences of blacks in other locations. Consequently, the tenets of race, place, and policing have been somewhat weakened; its contributions to the larger black citizen–police platform have been minimized and depreciated by consistently covering the same ground, the inner city. As it stands, current race, place, and policing research involuntarily suggests the following: (1) that black places are exclusively urban areas; (2) that blacks do not have contentious experiences with the police in other locations, and if they do, the most salient of black experiences rest in the inner city; (3) that arguments and analysis situated around differential policing can be produced only in urban places; and (4) that the implications of racialized policing hold true only in the inner city.

By default, urban experiences have become the template for what black citizen–policing relationships look like, consequently giving the impression that negative black experiences outside of the inner city are simply the exception to the rule. However, *Race, Place, and Suburban Policing* calls attention to the biases of place and attends to other locations inhabited by blacks— specifically, the suburbs. This book recognizes that the suburbs do not necessarily provide better social experiences for blacks than does the inner city, but perhaps similar or worse experiences. As Douglas Massey and Nancy Denton have stated, "Often black 'suburbanization' only involves the expansion of an urban ghetto across a city line."[13] Consequently, *Race, Place, and Suburban Policing* calls into question the practice of routinely attributing certain places as unambiguously "bad for blacks" and other places as good or better. In this book, I argue against one-dimensional notions of disadvantageous black places and experiences—but only to the degree that I acknowledge and avoid partiality to certain locations, thus making race, place, and policing analysis more "race-and-space inclusive."

Research has suggested that black experiences are similar irrespective of place. If by the social construction of race alone, the totality of black life, even when seemingly embedded in accomplishment and privilege, is riddled with the effects of "difference" and racialized treatment. Likewise, research suggests that it is with respect to place that differences emerge as a result of perceived measures of threat. Group-threat theory argues that predominantly white populations perceive an economic and political threat by large groups of minorities living within close proximity;[14] therefore, because black populations are often perceived as threatening, they are viewed with suspicion, as are the places they occupy.[15] Hence, a fear or suspicion of black presence and their motives then gives way to more aggressive police tactics, particularly as feelings of "racial threat" increase with them living near or within a white community.[16] Furthermore, the "race-and-place effect" suggests that black experiences with the police are worse when blacks travel closer to or through predominantly white places.[17] They fall under suspicion, prompting increased police inquiries (e.g., tailing, running plates) and stops.

In the broader sense, this project hinges on the interactive effects of race, place, and policing. However, with respect to suburban policing, this project tests group- and racial-threat theories in analyzing interactions and exchanges between police within the predominantly white location of the City of Kirkwood, and blacks in neighboring Meacham Park. Under examination is whether blacks in Meacham Park experience the "race-and-place effect," which would hold that close proximity to the white Kirkwood area makes blacks in Meacham Park more susceptible to increased police scrutiny than blacks in urban settings.[18]

In an attempt to extend race, place, and policing dialogue, this book first pays attention to black citizen–policing experiences. While this study began with a basic inquiry into how blacks felt about the police, the more salient question became how blacks *experienced* policing, and more specifically, how they experienced it in suburban contexts. Underlying this question were still others: Should we *expect* black experiences with urban and suburban policing to differ? How and why? *Are* the experiences similar/dissimilar? Again, how and why? And therefore, what are their perceptions of the police? Are they similar/dissimilar as well? These are all crucial questions regarding race, place, and the police.

Second, this study challenges the status quo by calling attention to "taken-for-granted" presumptions of place. It exposes the limited analyses of the past and forces future race, place, and policing data to account for black places and experiences beyond the scope of urban locations. It aims not to propose, conduct, or implicate research which assumes that the worst of black social experiences, particularly with the police, occur only in inner-city neighborhoods.

The uniqueness of this study lies in the following: (1) It recognizes and dispels subtle suggestions of black life as synonymous with urban life and likewise for black experiences. (2) It turns a critical lens on the misconceptions of race and place by challenging and discrediting notions of the inner city as an inherently bad place for blacks and the suburbs as inherently good. (3) With black-citizen experiences of the police in the forefront, it tells a full story of social injustice and the ambiguity of black life, ranging from land grabs to the retaliatory shooting deaths of police and city officials. (4) This study is all-inclusive with regard to race, place, and policing, and to broader social issues, by showcasing similarities in black experiences irrespective of place and dissimilarities in their experiences associated with place. And finally, (5) it makes data readily available whereby the rigidity of race and class, as well as possibilities for poor black-rich white cohesion, can be analyzed and measured through the most acrimonious and tragic of circumstances.

While this book does not offer absolutes for resolving differential treatment across broader social spheres, it does discuss possibilities by paying homage to previous urban-based studies and through suburban analysis. After all, it is in urban locations that race, place, and policing gained respectability in social science. As a testimony to this, this project seeks to further the framework by strengthening its credibility in uncharted territory—the suburbs. Its influence and ability to propel social change heavily depend on the depth to which it is willing to go in producing contemporary analyses of evolving experiences. Otherwise, race, place, and policing research undermines its mission, becoming as guilty as stereotypical dominant ideas in furthering black uniformity and exclusion—and even more so, for having done so under the guise of social justice and awareness.

THE PLACE

Well, it's pretty much an African-American community ... a poor part, a community that now has been annexed with Kirkwood. But to those who are not familiar with the area, it's Kirkwood. But to us [Meacham Park residents], and the police, and everybody that was born and raised in Kirkwood, it's still Meacham Park.

LOLA, FIFTY-NINE

While the City of Kirkwood, also known as West County St. Louis, is predominantly white, dubbed the "Queen of the St. Louis Suburbs," the adjacent Meacham Park is an annexed, low-income black enclave.[19] Though originally classified as an unincorporated area of West County St. Louis, Meacham Park was annexed to the City of Kirkwood in 1991, thus expanding Kirkwood's borders politically, economically, and geographically. Annexation can be likened to colonialism: the most powerful, dominant region, the City of Kirkwood, commandeers unattached, disadvantaged territory, Meacham Park, establishing complete ownership and governance, as well as use of its public services. This is the story of Meacham Park and how its poor black residents came to gain Kirkwood citizenship, that is, Kirkwood residency rooted in class conflict and racial divisiveness.

Despite sharing suburban status, Meacham Park is extremely segregated and thought of as somewhat of an "enigma" to many Kirkwood residents.[20] Its property values are low, and a significant number of its residents fall below the poverty line, receiving low wages or welfare benefits. Meacham Park is characterized as the ghetto—a shadowy, crime-and-drug-infested community only a couple of miles from Kirkwood's more elite sections. There exists a history of racial tension between the two communities, inflamed most recently by the shooting deaths of Kirkwood city officials and officers in two separate incidents, in which both of the shooters (Kevin Johnson and Charles "Cookie" Thornton) were black men from Meacham Park.

Any inquiry into how blacks experience policing in suburban contexts must begin, of course, from within a specific community. Community context matters; it is in such locales that citizens and police alike define as well as interpret one another.[21] Accordingly, my research commenced while in attendance at a mediation forum between Meacham Park and the City of Kirkwood. There, I observed and familiarized myself with Kirkwood city officials and residents, residents of Meacham Park, and the politics of both communities. Following that mediation forum I came to know about the Meacham Park Neighborhood Association and was later invited to attend a meeting where I introduced my project and reasons for why the Meacham Park neighborhood was an ideal location for race, place, and policing research.

SUMMARY

Thus began two years of close interaction with thirty adult Meacham Park residents, ages eighteen to eighty, acquired through neighborhood association meetings and snowball sampling. Open-ended interviews afforded cathartic and safe opportunities for participants to discuss their perceptions of Meacham Park, the City of Kirkwood, and the police, as well as to provide detailed accounts of vicarious and direct contacts with the police inside and outside of their neighborhood.

In general, Meacham Park residents suffered ridicule and stereotypes for the tragic actions of Johnson and Thornton, so their stories have been muffled, lost, and in some instances, completely ignored by the media. *Race, Place, and Suburban Policing* draws on these compelling stories of disadvantaged, suburban blacks, whose policing experiences are unaccounted for in the broader race, place, and policing literature.

Since blacks have historically been situated, segregated, and policed in places based on proximity to whites, chapter 1 provides a template and a timeline from which black citizen–police relationships emerged in U.S. history. This chapter traces the history of differential policing by chronicling the functions and persisting effects of the slave patrol, Slave Codes, Black Codes, and Jim Crow laws. Also, this chapter delves into the growth and policing of segregated urban and suburban areas by providing a historical analysis of black citizen–police interactions in so-called sundown towns—white towns off-limits to blacks after sunset. Additionally, I review literature on the current state of suburban segregation, black citizen–police interactions as understood through racial profiling, and data accounting for citizens' attitudes toward police. Finally, I review studies that have relied on interview and ethnographic studies to assess the community context of policing and the responses of black citizens.

Chapter 2 describes the process and experience of annexation, as the unincorporated community of Meacham Park transitioned to being a disadvantaged neighborhood within the affluent suburb of Kirkwood. This chapter communicates experiences and attitudes of Meacham Park residents regarding the loss of land, homes, and overall displacement due to eminent domain brought by the building of a strip mall over half of the Meacham Park land acquired through annexation. It also discusses residents' overall perceptions of their new local government and its role in the annexation process, as well as the role played by police in ensuring their compliance to new ordinances.

Chapter 3 provides insight into involuntary police contacts faced by the participants. Blacks in Meacham Park gained new residential status through annexation; this chapter accounts for aggressive policing experienced by them under a new, stricter jurisdiction. Additionally, this chapter calls attention to the significance of race and place and how the stereotypical idea of black criminality in the neighborhood of Meacham Park gave way to contentious police encounters in the forms of harassment and misconduct. Furthermore, this chapter accounts for the everyday experiences of blacks that work to shape negative attitudes toward police.

Chapter 4 delves into the lives of Kevin Johnson and Charles "Cookie" Thornton, two black men from Meacham Park, and their contentious interactions and relationships with Kirkwood city officials prior to two separate high-profile shootings that rocked residents of both Meacham Park and Kirkwood. In 2005, Johnson shot and killed a police sergeant, and in 2008, Thornton went on a shooting rampage in Kirkwood City Hall, injuring the mayor, the city's attorney, and a newspaper reporter, and killing two police officers, two city council members, and the city's director of public works. Thornton was killed at the scene by responding officers, and months later, the mayor died from shooting injuries and complications from cancer. This chapter also accounts for how Meacham Park residents came to perceive the police prior to and following the two shootings, and how, through vicarious contacts, both shooting incidents came to be characterized by many participants as a result of police negligence and harassment. Additionally, this chapter describes experiences gained by Meacham Park residents with multiple police agencies. Lastly, this chapter discusses some participants' grappling with what they believe to be preexisting stereotypes of them now having been exacerbated and confirmed by the actions of their neighbors, Johnson and Thornton.

Chapter 5 addresses misconceptions regarding blacks' attitudes toward the police and their willingness to partner with them in the community. Subsequently, this chapter lends itself to the possibility of reconciliation in the City of Kirkwood by accounting for voluntary contacts with the police whereby participants came to have not only negative encounters with them but positive ones as well. This chapter also explores the mediation process, and how improving relations through federal intervention became muddled with approval from some and dissent from others.

This book's conclusion summarizes key findings regarding black citizen–police interactions in Meacham Park. Additionally, this chapter examines the mediation process and agreement leading to a 2010 mandate issued by the U.S. Department of Justice between Meacham Park and the City of Kirkwood. Finally, this chapter offers suggestions and possible solutions for improving police-community relations, locally and nationally, based on positive policing experiences shared by some Meacham Park residents and a review of outcomes from the mediation agreement. The book concludes with ideas for future race, place, and policing research.

ONE

Race, Place, and Policing in the United States

RODNEY KING, AMADOU DIALLO, SEAN BELL, TRAYVON MARTIN, and countless other black citizens who have experienced and experience racialized policing do so in the context of long-standing differential policing strategies aimed at controlling and monitoring the locations and behaviors of blacks. Race-based differential policing practices and negative black citizen-police interactions do not occur in isolation or apart from the broader structural establishment of policing, but rarely do national debates address them within that context.[1] Instead, incident by incident, conversations take place wherein the media, politicians, political analysts, activists, and other interested parties chronicle, compare, and propose amendments to policies that would address differential policing practices. As such, these race, place, and policing debates often fail to call attention to policing agencies, policies, and strategies as structurally prejudicial, and thus, discriminative.[2] In the end, there is no real accountability or change, other than continuing to publically acknowledge persistent differential treatment of blacks in the criminal justice system. Acknowledging differential treatment is to see only the symptoms of the problem rather than the cause: inherent structural prejudice and discrimination.

To gain insight into how this institutional racism developed, one must understand the historically discriminative structures and trends that paved the way, and must have a clear picture of the current reality of black citizen-police relationships. In other words, the legacy of race and place is significant and should not be discounted or lost in contemporary discussions. Otherwise, we address problems on the surface rather than at the root, and risk losing opportunities for reform and social change. Furthermore, as the experiences of the past and present are interwoven and often understood and discussed as such by black citizens, likewise should this be the case with broader plat-forms. Take Terrance and Mark of Meacham Park, for instance. Terrance, thirty-eight, described his present experiences by linking and attributing them to his knowledge and understanding of the past:

> When I grew up, I aspired to get a job and retire and be able to pull my truck and my car up on the lot and be able to sit with the old men and drink my drink, sit by the fire. Wasn't any troublemakers, [just] grown men that raised families, and they [the police] call that standing out on the street. You know, just being out congregating, and now that lot's gone, those old men got pushed off of it. Even people in their thirties, forties, fifties were waiting to get on that lot like I was and now there's no place to go. That's history, but police and Kirkwood look at it as hanging out on the streets, but I'm talking about grown men that worked at Chrysler, Ford. Just a place to sit, a whole bunch of chairs, they had their can [trash barrel] out there and yeah they got loud, but they were grown men.

What Terrance laments is a disruption of culture, a breakdown of cama-raderie that once existed among hardworking, well-respected black family men in his community. Frustrated by the lack of regard for life lessons and of laughs earned and shared by these men in ways unique to their environment, Terrance feels disadvantaged and robbed of socialization processes that once gave him and other local young black men something to aspire to: exemplifi-cation of accomplishment by those most like him (black men)—something far more valuable to a disadvantaged black community than persistent police control and subjective criminalization. Similarly, Mark, fifty, discussed his experiences from a historical perspective:

> When you can finally back up and look at what happened in Meacham Park, to me, it's a sin, but it's something that's gone on in our history as far as black people for hundreds of years . . . to be able to take our property systematically or the policing habits that they had.

In this account, Mark is frustrated as well and describes a history of what he believes to be the routine manipulation of blacks. Like Terrance, Mark felt robbed, though his anger came from the loss of personal property rather than the loss of community property. He lost land through eminent domain, dur-ing the annexation phase, and continues to fear and fight for remaining prop-erties in Meacham Park.

Terrance and Mark, along with others, could not tell their stories without incorporating history. It seemed the only way they could make sense of and cope with their experiences was by recognizing the plight of blacks before them. Accordingly, this project mimics the approach of the respondents. As they conceptualize their experiences by giving significance to historical parallels, I aim to do the same out of respect for the gravity of what they face and the depth of their feelings. Therefore, this chapter (1) chronicles black citizen-police relationships throughout U.S. history, providing a template and timeline from which negative interactions between the two groups first emerged; and (2) considers the current state of negative black citizen-police interactions—within the context of residential segregation—as illuminated by the present body of research examining policing's differential treatment practices.

This chapter's first focus, an overview of historical policing of blacks, opens with an examination of the precedence for differential policing set by the slave patrol. Attention is next given to how the discriminative ideas and expectations of blacks set by the Slave Codes, Black Codes, and Jim Crow laws further legitimized race-based differential policing. Then, a chronicling of situating, restricting, and the policing of blacks in particular places provides clarity into the growth and persistence of segregated urban and suburban areas. The chapter's second focus, the current state of negative black citizen-police interactions, includes a review of racial profiling and attitudes-toward-police (ATP) research, which provides further insight into interactions between black communities and the police. Finally, a look at research relying on interviews and ethnography helps assess the community context of policing and the responses of black citizens.

POLICING AND THE EXPERIENCES OF BLACKS IN U.S. HISTORY

Centuries of contentious black citizen-police relationships can be traced to the intersection of race, place, and policing during the transatlantic slave trade. As oppression and cruelty of slaves became institutionalized, the possibility of slave revolts and insurrections significantly increased. Slave rebellions proved extremely threatening to white populations. Whites also feared freedmen, whom they believed to be supporters of and sympathizers with slave revolts.

Fear and suspicion of both slaves and freedmen fueled an increasing desire for surveillance and social control of slaves, giving rise to the creation of the slave patrols—officers designated to police slave populations. The establishment of slave patrols became the driving force behind enacting and encouraging the application of laws such as the Slave Codes, Black Codes, and later, Jim Crow segregation.

The Slave Patrol

History suggests that the slave patrols were among the first organized police forces in the United States and were formed by local and state militias, court-appointed local committees, and state legislators.[3] Their mission was to keep both the slaves and freedmen "in place," physically and figuratively. In the *physical* sense, slaves and freedmen were required to "know their place" and were relegated and segregated to certain locations and to specific behaviors within those locations. Policing of slaves and freedmen aimed to restrict and monitor the movement of slaves and freedmen.

Policing slaves *physically* was merely one part of the mission; the patrols also sought to police in the *abstract*—to control attitudes and beliefs through intimidation in order to reinforce safe, less-threatening behavior, comfortable to whites. Slave patrols were threatening sights, visual reminders of slave's and freedmen's inferior status in relation to white superior status.

Slave patrol duties included frequent searches for runaways, the apprehension of slaves or freedmen caught outside of plantations or designated areas, the prevention of all slave gatherings and meetings, and searching slave quarters and the homes of white citizens suspected of assisting slaves to escape.[4] Slave patrols were also present and expected to keep order at markets, funerals, festivals, and various other activities and events. In essence, their mission was to harass and intimidate slaves.[5]

Slave patrols were designed to provoke fear and submissiveness among the slaves. Patrolmen went about on horseback both day and night, armed with guns, whips, and ropes.[6] Slave patrols were prohibited from killing slaves, especially as slaves were investments for whom the state would have to reimburse the legal owners. Nonetheless, inflicting bodily harm on slaves was common. Slaves were terrorized and brutalized: women were sexually abused, captured freedmen faced being sold into slavery, and slaves were frequently threatened and received flogging, whippings, mutilation, and their few valuables were taken from them.[7]

Slave patrols and specialized militias were appointed, paid, or in some instances called upon to volunteer by local and state militias, court-appointed local committees, and state legislators.[8] Additionally, "the laws . . . established a militia, requiring every [white] man between sixteen and sixty years of age" to serve.[9] Many poor whites ultimately became slave patrollers because, unlike wealthier whites, they were unable to buy themselves out of patrol duty.[10] As a result, Slave Codes—differential laws for blacks—especially created a rift between slaves and poor whites.[11] The enactment of the Slave Codes affirmed racial inferiority for blacks and superiority for even poor whites. Furthermore, where slave control and regulation had primarily been the slave owners' responsibility, by the late seventeenth century, it had become the responsibility of the entire white population.[12]

Hence, police harassment of blacks in the present should not be discounted as mere complaints by disgruntled blacks or as isolated incidents that periodically occur across time and departments. Rather, the police harassment of blacks should be understood, analyzed, and addressed as one of the agency's first mandates and as a significant component in the institutionalization of persisting discriminative practices.

Formalizing Restrictions: The Slave Codes, Black Codes, and Jim Crow

As slave patrols enforced restrictions and policed the behavior of slaves, these restrictions were formalized in Slave Codes.[13] Slave Codes were laws put in place to govern slaves as chattel or property. After all, slaves were investments and the Slave Codes served to protect masters' interests legally. The codes were subjective in nature; they varied among locations and periodically changed depending on the threat level. For example, they changed depending on the influx of new slaves, rumors of plots, and insurrections in other locales, thus making all slave and freedman actions suspicious and punishable at whim.

Similarly, Black Codes were postemancipation laws enacted to regulate free blacks. Their purpose was to regulate the locations and behaviors of emancipated slaves, and more importantly, to monitor and mandate their continued employment. Since southern planters and former slave owners depended on slave labor, following emancipation, they feared a loss and shortage of laborers. Realizing that freed blacks were important to southern agriculture, planters worked to negotiate and bargain contracts with them. Some blacks agreed to stay on and work, while others fled the plantations, leaving a shortage of field laborers.[14] Free blacks migrated to cities and towns, away from the plantations that were a reminder of slavery. southern white land owners, unable to retain or force freed blacks back to the land, turned to the Black Codes as a means of doing so. White southerners pushed for laws that would force blacks back to field work or other menial labor. In 1865, the first Black Codes were officially enacted.

Under Black Codes, black populations continued to face racialized policing along with ordinances that were not applicable to whites. Generally, these laws were "designed to drive Negroes back to the land and compel them to work."[15] In the event of noncompliance, blacks faced vagrancy and loitering violations.[16] They could be punished by fines, imprisonment, and slavery for up to twelve months. Vagrancy statutes were particularly broad—blacks could easily be convicted for the appearance of idleness; immoral conversations, behaviors, and actions; unwillingness to sign work contracts or to commit to some form of labor; and so forth.

The Black Codes attempted to legally reimpose a version of slavery. They extended the control and policing of black populations mostly by criminalizing idleness or what was believed to be unproductive actions. Likewise was the case with the subsequent enactment of the Jim Crow laws, which advanced the criminalization of blacks, exacerbating it by codifying the separation of the races.

Jim Crow laws solidified white supremacy and black subordination and came from a climate of "economic crisis, political opportunism, and racial fears."[17] While white populations had previously been motivated by fear of revolt, southern whites were especially intimidated by the black vote and place in politics. Consequently, segregation served as a way to nullify and disenfranchise blacks politically, and to further restrict blacks in all facets of social life.[18]

Jim Crow laws included complete separation of the races in businesses, hospitals, schools, the military, transportation vehicles, cemeteries, restrooms, elevators, residential areas, hiring practices, entrances and exits of most facilities, penal institutions, and all other locales. Jim Crow laws also barred interracial dating and marrying.[19] Under Jim Crow, no black person was exempt from surveillance, scrutiny, accusation, and the abuse of white persons who felt justified in doing so through white superiority. This left southern blacks defenseless, particularly as the police upheld, supported, and in many instances, inflicted brutality upon blacks individually and collectively.

Jim Crow laws gave way to policing black life not just by police but by any white citizen. With the implementation of Jim Crow and other, similar rules and regulations, black populations began experiencing policing and fear that harkened back to pre-emancipation days. A black man in the text below recalls being confronted by the police in the Jim Crow South:

> Negroes who have lived South know the dread of being caught alone upon the streets in white neighborhoods after the sun has set. . . . The color of a Negro's skin makes him easily recognizable, makes him suspect, converts him into a defenseless target. Late one Saturday night I made some deliveries in a white neighborhood. I was pedaling my bicycle back to the store as fast as I could, when a police car, swerving toward me, jammed me into the curbing. "Get down and put up your hands!" the policeman ordered. I did. They climbed out of the car, guns drawn, faces set, and advanced slowly. "Keep still!" they ordered. I reached my hands higher. They searched my pockets and packages. They seemed dissatisfied when they could find nothing incriminating. Finally, one of them said: "Boy, tell your boss not to send you out in white neighborhoods after sundown." As usual, I said: "Yes, sir."[20]

The legacy of controlling space and place with regard to black populations in the United States is deeply rooted, and extends beyond the deep South. The vulnerability and susceptibility of blacks to segregation in the Midwest and the North can be understood best through a look at all-white neighborhoods or "sundown towns."[21]

Sundown Towns in the Midwest

Restricting blacks to certain locations occurred far beyond the South to states such as Missouri, Illinois, Ohio, Michigan, Indiana, California, Oregon, and others, and sundown towns played a significant role in these confining practices. A sundown town is "any organized jurisdiction that for decades kept blacks or other groups from living in it and was thus 'all-white' on purpose."[22] Sundown towns were off limits to blacks, particularly after dark. Loewen (2005) extends the term *sundown* to "sundown neighborhoods,"[23] "sundown states,"[24] and even "sundown nation."[25]

The emergence of sundown towns has been tied to the northern migration of southern blacks. The North and other regions reacted by restricting or prohibiting this migration.[26] However, during and following the Civil War and Reconstruction periods, race relations began improving in the North. As a result, legislation changed, extending national and state citizenship to blacks.[27] However, as always, change was met with resistance and the institutionalization of Jim Crow remained visible, especially in organized efforts to prevent blacks from living in white places while strategically shuffling them into urban ghettoes. This was certainly the case in Missouri and the neighboring state of Illinois. Blacks generally migrated to cities such as St. Louis and Chicago, avoiding all-white areas, where they were clearly not welcome. And in instances where blacks did venture into or near to white areas, the Ku Klux Klan (KKK) and other white-supremacist groups were successful in chasing them out.

Blacks were subject to a variety of obvious cues, signs, and threats in an effort to create or maintain sundown towns. Such towns could easily be identified by the total absence or extremely small population of black residents. Many towns went to great lengths to make black exclusion clear. Mike Haas, a historian, recalled signs posted well into the 1980s in Sunman, Indiana, that stated, "NIGGER, DON'T LET THE SUN SET ON YOU HERE."[28] In fact, signs were common and can be recalled as having been posted in most, if not all, sundown areas (e.g., train depots, main roads).

Residents of Tamaroa, Illinois, were referred to as "rock throwers," because they threw rocks at blacks passing through, even to the point of stoning them to death.[29] In Anna, Illinois, the word *Anna* came to be interpreted as "Ain't No Niggers Allowed";[30] the continued use of this acronym was affirmed as recently as 2001.[31] In Sheboygan, Wisconsin, in the early 1960s, a police officer was assigned to meet blacks at the train station, warning them against staying.[32]

In Missouri, particularly in the Ozarks (near the Arkansas border), vigilante whites were known to post signs, brandish weapons, throw stones, and refer to sundown areas as "gray towns."[33] The lynching of a black man in police custody in Monett, Missouri, has been noted as the start of such violence throughout all the Ozark counties.[34] In Joplin, whites "helped foment an ideology of ethnic cleansing that made most of the Ozark Plateau a sundown region."[35] White mobs rioted through black neighborhoods, looting and burning their homes. Subsequently, additional lynchings took place in Pierce City and Springfield.

Even after the civil rights era and legislation barring racial discrimination and segregation, off-the-record discriminative practices and the threats associated with them continue to thrive. But perhaps worse is the legacy's continuation in more formalized and strategized forms: (1) residential seclusion that keeps blacks restricted to certain places (e.g., disadvantaged, urban) and with limited access to white ones (e.g., affluent, suburban); and (2) policing practices (e.g., racial profiling) that are advantageous to white interests, particularly in white places, while disadvantageous to those of blacks.

People have always resided in urban, suburban, or rural places, irrespective of race, ethnicity, and social class, though at various junctures, race and class distinctions became more apparent in certain locations. Likened to sundown towns, the formation of U.S. suburbs hinged on exclusion, and by design, barred blacks and Jews.[36] Contemporary characterizations of places and the people that occupy them can be traced to the progressive movement of the early twentieth century, which fueled white suburban segregation, and to the increase of the black middle class in the 1970s, which led to black flight from the inner city and to what was initially perceived as a push toward suburban integration.[37]

Motivated by progressive messages and ideas, urban whites sought social advancement by retreating from big cities, considered dirty places as a result of large immigrant and black populations.[38] In the suburbs, whites believed they could have the best of both worlds: they could maintain close proximity to the city and simultaneously enjoy comfortable separation from the poor and from blacks. They could separately and freely take pleasure in the luxuries of prime real estate and amenities without being impacted by the "vice and pollution" of blacks.[39]

Meacham Park could have been thought of as a preferred place to live for whites. It is situated near two interstates and enveloped by a plethora of predominantly white, West St. Louis County suburbs. Dorothy, fifty-seven, has lived in the vicinity for most of her life. In fact, she was one of few blacks to integrate into an area elementary school. She realizes the geographical advantages of Meacham Park:

> This [Meacham Park] sits right at highways 44 and 270 and then it's surrounded by Sunset Hills, DePeres, Ladue, Webster Groves and Crestwood. So this is really prime real estate.

Dorothy's description points to Meacham Park as a locale within comfortable reach of the city, where there are buffers that keep it separate from undesirable characters/characteristics of the city.

Likewise, Terrance, thirty-eight, commented on the benefits of living in Meacham Park, though he sees the community's ideal location as the cause of its inevitable annihilation. He stated:

> We're at the crossroads of everything and everybody. We're fifteen minutes from downtown, we're fifteen minutes from Illinois ... location, location,

location [*chuckles*]. The interstate, it pushes all money so I mean, if you look at it, where you at? Look at how you got here and where you gone be at twenty minutes after you leave here. I mean some people not seeing it like that, they want to brush this off . . . but twenty years, thirty years from now, these houses [in Meacham Park] won't be here.

Meacham Park has already lost a significant number of businesses and homes as a result of two annexations, one in 1957 and another in 1991. Terrance, along with others, believe it is only a matter of time before the last section of Meacham Park succumbs to redevelopment projects for the larger, white, affluent Kirkwood. If this happens, the City of Kirkwood will have successfully managed to do two things: (1) secure, or rather, extend what is perceived to be an ideal suburban location, far enough from the hub of the inner city and yet close enough to access it at will; and (2) strengthen and protect the predominantly white status of surrounding suburbs by eliminating the only sizable population of blacks in the area.

Hypersegregation and Models of Causation: Spatial Assimilation and Place Stratification

> Despite generations of urban experiences and substantial geographical distance from the urban core, blacks in the suburban fringe still live in ghettoes.[40]

Blacks tend to experience the greatest amount of residential isolation. Studies show blacks as persistently living "hypersegregated" from whites, meaning they experience isolation from whites in multiple areas: (1) *evenness*, or the degree to which minorities evenly reside across communities; (2) *exposure*, or the likelihood of contact between black and white groups; (3) *clustering*, or the degree to which minorities live adjacent to one another; (4) *centralization*, or the distance from which minorities live to the center of an urban area; and (5) *concentration*, or the amount of physical space inhabited by minorities.[41] Interestingly, of the countless segregated metropolitan areas nationwide, St. Louis is one of twenty-nine persistently hypersegregated metropolitan areas in the United States.[42] Blacks in St. Louis experience residential segregation in *four* of the five dimensions: evenness, exposure, centralization, and concentration.[43] Hence, Meacham Park—a black enclave situated in predominantly white suburban St. Louis (Kirkwood)—is not only hypersegregated; it is also reflective of black-white segregated patterns nationwide.

Since the white flight of the early twentieth century, studies show urban communities as being mostly black and suburban communities as being predominantly white.[44] Camille Charles characterizes suburban communities as made up of "nearly 60% of Asians, 50% Hispanics, and 40% of Blacks . . . compared to 71% of whites."[45] While such figures may appear indicative of residential integration, largely, they are not. Rather, they show blacks, along with other ethnic minorities, as likelier than whites to integrate and into predominantly white communities. However, even when minorities live in predominantly white suburban communities, they still remain separate; they create enclaves, or geographical spaces—such as Meacham Park—distinct to their cultures. In such instances, integration is more theoretical than practical. The communities still maintain a predominantly white status. Thus, suburban places reflect continued residential segregation, with or without ethnic enclaves. Consequently, suburban segregation deserves further analysis, and therefore, examining the causes of such only adds credence to the significance of race and place as it shapes distinct interactions across the United States.

In efforts to understand residential segregation, and more specifically, black-white suburban segregation, researchers have focused their attention on various social factors ranging from age, income, and educational level to racial/ethnic inequality and discrimination. Moreover, researchers have examined the causes of suburban segregation from two, complementary perspectives: spatial assimilation and place stratification.[46] It is through these two models that the present research carefully considers possible causes of residential segregation, and develops evidence-based ideas about the persistence of nationwide racial and residential segregation, especially as it relates to Meacham Park and the City of Kirkwood.

The spatial-assimilation model attributes minorities' ability to integrate into predominantly white suburban neighborhoods to personal achievement, or rather, as depending on both their socioeconomic status (i.e., income, educational attainment, occupational prestige) and cultural assimilation (i.e., length of time spent in the United States, English proficiency).[47] As studies show positive correlations between income, education, and suburban residency at the individual level, the inference is that people tend to live in communities most reflective of their social class.[48] The result is economically stratified neighborhoods, which tend to be disproportionately urban spaces for minorities and suburban places for whites. Spatial assimilation posits that as minorities disproportionately have less education and lower-paying jobs than their white counterparts, they are likelier to reside in segregated, disadvantaged communities. However, as minorities progress in social status, thus increasing their education and income levels, they become more likely to move away from their less advantaged, minority communities into more affluent white ones—the suburbs.

Like all perspectives, spatial assimilation has its limits. It cannot fully account for the hypersegregation of blacks, despite socioeconomic or cultural achievement. Of all racial/ethnic minority groups, blacks persistently live in extreme isolation from whites, even when they have comparable income and despite being English-speaking, U.S.-born citizens.[49] Consequently, place stratification complements spatial assimilation by calling attention to the discriminative effects of race on place, and how racial bias and ideas about locational status and prestige can interactively mean residential inclusion for some and exclusion for others.

The *place stratification* model focuses on the complexities of racial/ethnic prejudices; it brings us full circle in examining the past-to-present relegation and segregation of blacks to certain places (e.g., sundown towns and predominantly white suburbs). It calls attention to social forces that police people and space devoid of law enforcement. So, while it is often assumed that blacks do not live in predominantly white suburbs simply because they cannot afford to, place stratification reminds us of the nuances of racial/ethnic discriminative practices.[50] In lieu of spatial stratification, place stratification examines the ways by which many blacks come to disproportionately reside in nonwhite, marginalized locales, even when they can afford to live in more affluent, predominantly white ones.

While black families do reside in predominantly white suburban communities, the place-stratification model argues that many do not because the costs are greater for them to do so than they are for whites.[51] Likewise, place stratification infers that whites reside in the suburbs, in part, to maintain distance from large concentrations of minorities—particularly blacks.[52] Therefore, blacks face institutional barriers such as "racially segmented housing markets," differential consideration among financial institutions, and other like practices that prove costly as they attempt to reside in such communities.[53] Consider home ownership, for instance. Though home ownership is an individual variable associated with spatial assimilation, it is also indicative of differential housing practices. Blacks face differential lending practices, being disproportionately denied mortgage loans; and when they *are* approved for loans, they are offered lesser amounts or higher interest rates than whites. Blacks are less likely to own homes than whites are, negatively affecting blacks' suburban residency.[54] The process toward home ownership becomes a form of policing in that it inadvertently monitors, regulates, or restricts the movement of blacks.

Additionally, along with dual housing markets—one for blacks and another for whites—place stratification contends that inequitable political processes, such as redlining, are at work against community development.[55] As a result, even when blacks reside in the suburbs, they typically do so in predominantly black, segregated ones, where they are closer to the urban hub than whites and there are "few jobs, poor governmental service, and high tax rates" (as is true in Meacham Park).[56]

Where spatial stratification contends that suburban integration will increase as minorities' acculturation matches that of whites, place stratification argues that even when it does, suburban segregation remains intact due to racial/ethnic inequality, thus, becoming more distinct. This has certainly been the case for the residents of Meacham Park, pre-annexation and post-annexation. Meacham Park is a community that has been persistently characterized by economic disadvantage, racial discrimination, and residential isolation. Consequently, the tenets of place stratification are most applicable here, given this model works best when accounting for groups of minorities. Spatial assimilation, on the other hand, proves most compelling when examining minority individuals, or rather, individual characteristics and attributes that lead to acculturation.[57] In either case, both spatial assimilation and place stratification are credible and work in attributing achieved and ascribed statuses to residential mobility, and more specifically, the persistence of suburban segregation.[58]

As social location gives way to residential mobility, likewise, it extends itself to socially constructed ideals about who people are and the way they live. Beyond recognizing the social forces that often determine accessibility to the suburbs, it is important to note how people process the composition of their communities, meaning, who they feel least or most comfortable and compelled to live with and why. This is crucial to race, place, and policing, especially as it is in such attitudes that citizens shape local political and, by extension, policing agendas, and in turn, come to be influenced by them. In this light, let us briefly turn our attention to residents of Meacham Park. The participants in this study frequently saw their role as providing what they believed to be all-too-often-muffled black commentary about their community, which contradict frequent, indefensible, publicized white remarks.

Kim, sixty-two, a lifelong resident of Meacham Park, offered an optimistic description:

> It's [Meacham Park is] an open community. There's some crime, but basically I like it because it's open. You can see people all the time, kids playing. Yeah to me, everybody's out, it's a living community, you don't see people like locked up in their houses. People are out walking their dogs, kids playing, riding their bikes, neighbors knowing neighbors. I like the togetherness of people, how they come together any time, doesn't have to be a tragedy for people to know people. Basically, everybody knows everybody. People are willing to help.

Meacham Park has suffered from neighborhood deprivation, two controversial annexations, years of racial tension, and crime—specifically, two high-profile murder cases. Seldom has the neighborhood been characterized as a "living community." Like other participants, though, Kim acknowledged problems within her community but accentuated its positives. She described her community as one of "togetherness," where people were free to live harmoniously, despite widespread concerns about safety and lawlessness.

Lola, Rodney, Keith, and Francis also spoke encouragingly of their community. They took great care in highlighting good things to make clear that "it's nothing like what's been described in the news" (Lola, fifty-nine). Likewise, Rodney, fifty-five, stated:

> It's a nice community, you know. You got your bad scenes, you got good scenes. It's not a bad community, it's just that we have a few bad people out here, you know what I'm saying, that's all.

Keith, twenty-two, described the community of Meacham as

> a really close-knit community, everybody pretty much knows everybody. Tragic events happen everywhere so it's not like Meacham Park is any worse or any better.

In each instance, when asked to describe their neighborhood, most participants did so intending to counteract the negative reports and perceptions of those who did not live in Meacham Park, did not know its history or residents, and generally lacked sensitivity or appreciation for its culture. As Francis, sixty, put it,

There's a lot of love shared, it is a plus for us [the blacks in Meacham Park]. The culture in this neighborhood is warm and welcoming.

Francis and others believe such details to be small, yet vital characterizations of their neighborhood. Accordingly, my introduction to the community was not one of denial or negligence regarding its persisting problems, nor was it one of exaggerated negativity. Rather, my first acquaintance with the community was one of balance and optimism in the midst of a racially divisive climate. I encountered residents longing to be heard, hoping for change, and subtly clinging to my assurance that this project was designed to do both. Participants needed reassurance that I would share their experiences in the spirit of fairness, that their accounts would be prefaced, read, and understood in lieu of subsequent, perhaps negative information gleaned through this project or otherwise. With these sentiments in mind, let us now account for attitudes toward integration that extend beyond Meacham Park residents.

Attitudes toward Suburban Integration

So long as whites believe that blacks lack a work ethic, are prone to criminal activity, and are less intelligent than whites they will disparage them as neighbors.[59]

Meacham Park, as a black suburban enclave, is not an anomaly. Rather, it is merely one of many racial/ethnic enclaves nationwide, where minorities live separately while having a preference for and residing within close proximity to predominantly white locations. In such cases, residential integration is more idealistic than realistic. Ideas about people and the places they inhabit are entrenched to the point that they impede true integration. So while some minorities may live in predominantly white communities, many of them do so in isolation of their white counterparts (e.g., blacks in Meacham Park). Accordingly, in this section, I review literature detailing current attitudes toward suburban integration, especially as it relates to blacks and whites. It is through such perceptions that we gain greater insight into black-white suburban expectations and the role of racialized thoughts and beliefs in meeting them.

While some theorists contend that residential segregation is a by-product of class segregation, they cannot discount the role of race—and more specifically—racialized stereotypes when examining the hypersegregation of blacks from whites.[60] As Reynolds Farley and colleagues stated, "If residential segregation were a matter of income, rich blacks would live with rich whites and poor blacks with poor whites."[61] That this is not the trend, that blacks, apart from other racial/ethnic minority groups, have historically and persistently lived in extreme isolation from whites, extends the narrative well beyond one of social class. Similarly, the narrowing gap between blacks and whites, educationally and economically, further pushes the analysis beyond one of socioeconomics. The fact that blacks are making tremendous strides academically and earning higher incomes forces us to revisit the role of stereotypical ideas, thoughts, and feelings about blacks and why they continue to live separate from whites in less advantageous communities, even when they have the means to live elsewhere.[62]

As predominantly white suburban communities often project nicer homes, schools, and other like amenities, researchers find minorities aspiring to live in them.[63] Minorities perceive suburban integration as indicative of achieved economic success while simultaneously gaining racial/ethnic inclusion. Incidentally, residency in predominantly white suburbs becomes the measure by which minorities see themselves as "having arrived," and thus, they embrace and prefer residential integration. More specifically, blacks tend to prefer suburban integration where there is fifty-fifty black and white residency.[64]

Meanwhile, whites have been documented as regarding the suburbs as places exclusively for them.[65] When shown pictures of neighborhoods with black and white households, whites became increasingly uncomfortable with the prospect of living with increasing numbers of blacks.[66] Whites expressed concerns over depreciating property values and personal safety. Hence, suburban communities that are open to blacks are generally undesirable to whites. As such is the case, despite affordability and desire, blacks are leery about moving into all-white communities for fear of white hostility. They are willing to be one of several black families living in such a place, but certainly not the first or only.[67]

Theorists such as Reynolds Farley and colleagues extend the suburban-integration dialogue through the following discoveries. One, both blacks and whites perceived blacks as being able to afford comparable suburban locales.[68] Two, blacks prefer suburban integration over residing in predominantly black places.[69] Consequently, in-group preferences among blacks do not shape residential segregation, but rather, it is whites' in-group preference that does. In fact, the tipping scale for predominantly white neighborhood integration is 70 percent white and 30 percent black.[70] Therefore, as black percentages increase and white decrease below that margin, white flight ensues and consequently racial segregation does as well.[71]

Similarly, the literature suggests that blacks are perceived as the least desirable neighbors.[72] Relying on the 1992 Los Angeles County Social Service Survey (LACSS), where 1,869 respondents (625 white, 483 black, 477 Latinos, and 284 Asians) were questioned regarding their attitudes toward residential integration, 34 percent of whites said they would be opposed to living in a community where half of their neighbors were black, compared to 22 percent opposition for Asian neighbors and 25.6 percent opposition for Hispanic neighbors.[73] While the percentages seem modest and again suggest some willingness among whites to integrate, they show their levels of openness as fluctuating depending on the group.

Like whites, minorities fluctuated in their preferences when considering other minorities as neighbors. Similar to whites, Asians and Hispanics least preferred integrating with blacks.[74] However, minority groups in general differed from whites in that overall they embraced the idea of living in a racially/ethnically diverse community. Each of the minority groups showed very little opposition by comparison for living with whites and actually preferred them over one another.[75] In sum, research aimed to examine attitudes toward residential integration based on class differences, in-group preferences, and racial prejudice.[76] Theorists found no significance with regards to in-group/out-group preferences and economic status.[77] Rather, they discovered whites as influenced by racially stereotypical ideas and prejudices, that is, attitudes consistent with racial and group threat theories[78]—where whites perceive minorities as threats to their dominance and privilege.[79]

When accounting for attitudes toward suburban integration, several things are clear: (1) as minorities—particularly blacks—advance in social status, analyses of class segregation become increasingly inept at explaining persisting residential segregation; (2) minorities are generally receptive and show a preference toward residential integration, while whites are resistant by comparison; (3) blacks are the least-desired minority group to live among; and (4) stereotypical ideas, thoughts, and perceptions of blackness, black spaces, or blacks in white places run so deep that they conflate subtle prejudices with progress.

The limitations of research on attitudes toward suburban segregation often lie in the ambiguity of explaining citizens' residential preferences. Generally, studies discuss residential segregation/integration through a myriad of convoluted factors based on census data. As a result, citizens' true thoughts and feelings regarding residential integration can be lost by simply deferring to conventional explanations. For instance, as blacks are the least desirable neighbors among whites, it would be especially interesting to know why that holds true for other minority groups (e.g., Asians, Hispanics).[80] Simply attributing it to socioeconomic factors or questions such as "Would you sell to a black?" does not explain such attitudes.[81] It is through critical examinations and pushing the limits of acceptance that we might better understand the evolution of racially biased, stereotypical ideas as they are extended beyond dominant-minority relationships into minority-minority ones. Therefore, it would be more advantageous to the discussion to account for citizens' attitudes by relying more on ethnographic analysis.

CONTEMPORARY SOCIAL CONTROL AND THE POLICING EXPERIENCES OF BLACKS

While the slave patrol, Slave Codes, Black Codes, Jim Crow, and the overtness of sundown towns no longer exist in today's society, the ideologies that gave rise to them remain visible through current policies and subtle practices. Blacks continue to be relegated and segregated to particular places, and as a result, they are differently policed while traveling in and out of those locations. Take racial profiling, for instance—particularly of blacks. As the subject of many studies, its contribution is significant. It provides insight into current differential policing as motivated by race and place. To that end, it is worth looking at the aggressive, proactive policing experiences of blacks today as explained through (1) research on racial profiling, (2) ethnographic studies, and (3) their attitudes toward the police (ATP).

Racial Profiling: Police and Self-Reporting Citizen Data

As the suspicion of black populations persist, this section highlights different yet well-balanced assessments of the continuance of racialized policing. Quantitatively and qualitatively, as communicated by officers and citizens, racialized policing has been analyzed and confirmed through the use of three sources. Let us turn our attention to the first: police ride-alongs and observations.

Police ride-alongs provide an excellent opportunity to engage police as *they* see and understand citizen-police interactions. This is essential to the larger race, place, and policing discussion, particularly since the thought of people being policed differently often results in empathy and public outcry for citizens and their experiences rather than giving similar consideration to officers and theirs. By drawing from the perspectives and experiences of the officers themselves, police ride-alongs and observations benefit the literature in the following ways: they provide answers in the heat of citizen-police interactions; they provide balance by minimizing or eliminating room for criticizing the lack of police voice; and more importantly, they corroborate the persistence of racial profiling—from the officers themselves—in that race and place are significant factors in policing for blacks compared to whites.[82]

Police suspicion, discretionary power, and behaviors can be influenced by nonbehavioral factors, meaning officers have been directly observed and documented as being suspicious of black citizens and aggressively responding to them, even when they did nothing to warrant it.[83] So, if blacks, contrary to their white counterparts, are facing police tailings, stops, and other like behaviors without having done anything to provoke them, what are the reasons?

Police suspicion and aggression can be aroused simply when police see black male drivers driving newer-model vehicles in disadvantaged communities.[84] Newer cars are often perceived to be possible "drug cars," and thus, indicative of criminal activity. Consequently, after a hundred hours spent noting the differences in exchanges (e.g., stings, traffic stops, serving warrants) between officers policing in black places versus white, William Chambliss found officers actively looking for black male drivers and newer-model vehicles.[85] In such instances, the driver, the vehicle, as well as the community gave way to officers' suspicion rather than considering the actual citizen's behavior.

This certainly seemed to be the case with Rodney, a lifelong resident of Meacham Park. An expensive car in a disadvantaged neighborhood, driven by a perceivably poor, young black man—Rodney clearly understood the implications of that combination. He recalled a time, as a younger man, when his flashy vehicle elicited suspicion.

> I inherited some money when my grandparents passed. So back then with a Cadillac, navy blue, gold trim, you know I was flashing so they [the police] thought I was a dope dealer and every time I pulled a load [drove the car], I got pulled over. Police wanted to search the car. I started telling them, "Man, look here, if you don't smell any marijuana or anything like that you don't have any reason to search my car. If I ran a light, then give me a ticket and let me go ... all that 'can I search your car' stuff ... No, you [police] can't search my car!" Then when you say no you can't search my car, now that's when the

problem come in. See now you got another car that pulls up. So now they want to provoke you. If I go to jail they can search my car cause now they gone [going to] tow my car.

Rodney is now fifty-five years old; this was one of many accounts he shared concerning his experiences with the police. He has had quite a few—many of which have been very contentious—ranging from what he believes to be sheer racial profiling to admittedly bad-mouthing officers, and having unpaid traffic tickets and subsequent warrants. The story of the "flashy car," however, is one of his earliest recollections, one where he had done nothing wrong. It is because of this encounter and others like it that Rodney would develop negative perceptions and distrust of officers. The incident of the "flashy car" was the start of what would later become a volatile relationship, filled with years of heated verbal exchanges, tazing, and arrests between a young black man and the local police. While this is just one of many documented instances, others consisted of officers issuing unprecipitated threats and warnings to black citizens in instances where there were no drugs, weapons, or offenses committed.[86]

Such findings are crucial in an effort to gain well-balanced insight into officers' regarding minorities as suspicious, since the findings come directly from the officers themselves rather than from presumably disgruntled black citizens. After conducting 132 random police ride-alongs, researchers found: officers eight times more likely to be suspicious of individuals driving certain types of vehicles, four times more likely to be suspicious of black citizens, and to be particularly suspicious of citizens in troubled neighborhoods.[87] Moreover, Geoffrey Alpert and colleagues found race to be the most significant factor in the forming of officers' suspicion, and place, most salient in actual police stops.[88] Generally, officers were found to be suspicious while patrolling in disadvantaged neighborhoods—irrespective of criminality. Since most communities are racially segregated, it is likely that race and place gave way to one another. Their interactive effects guided the formation of officers' suspicion and their decision(s) to act on their suspicion.

Likewise, Albert Meehan and Michael Ponder found race and place to be significant determinants in officers' suspicion over actual behaviors.[89] After 240 hours of police ride-alongs and twenty-five interviews with officers of every level of command over a four-year period, the researchers found that blacks were twice as likely to be surveilled as they traveled out of black places into white places, and consequently, police were twice as likely to run their plates, despite the drivers having committed no offenses.[90] Differing from previous ride-alongs, this study is particularly interesting in that it captured officers' behaviors—at various stages of escalation—while citizens were in motion. Consequently, there is a precedent for comparing and analyzing officers as they are moved to suspicion, particularly with desegregated driving: driving that integrates typically racially segregated places. This is a predicament that Travis, forty-five, knows all too well, as a black man frequently pulled over while driving in white locations.

> *In general, how many times have you been stopped by the police?*
> Oh maybe a hundred times I imagine.
>
> *For traffic violations?*
> No, driving while black.
>
> *You think so?*
> Yeah, I'm being honest, yes. The majority of times, it's not for running a red light or stop sign or anything like that. A few times, I know it might have been, but for the most part, just being in the wrong neighborhood at the wrong time.

While Travis may have overexaggerated the number of times stopped, he spoke matter-of-factly about them. It was as if he had become accustomed to them and was somewhat puzzled by my possible disbelief. What is clear and significant about Travis's situation is that police stops have occurred enough for him that he expects them and identifies most of them as not being traffic violations, but rather attributes them to his being in certain places that act as a red flag to police. Terrance's situation is indicative of the subjectivity of police suspicion and discretionary power. Despite criminality, officers' suspicion and their decision to act upon them can manifest not only as blacks drive within their own communities, but also—if not more so—as blacks are found driving outside of them.

Along with ride-alongs, the second source of information for racial-profiling studies is police databases. Researchers have accounted for differential police behaviors, ranging from running plates to actual stops, by analyzing the following: information compiled from police mobile data terminals (MDTs) and mandatory forms completed by officers following each stop.[91] Like police ride-alongs, this approach is significant to race, place, and policing dialogue in that it provides insight into policing behaviors as reported by the officers themselves. Again, this increases the voices of officers in analyzing differential policing rather than relying solely on that of citizens.

Through data collected from MDTs, blacks were found two times likelier to have their plates run (i.e., proactive queries) compared to whites, regardless of their location.[92] Researchers also found such queries to significantly increase as blacks moved farther away from black areas and closer to white areas;[93] black motorists were then three times more likely to have "unwarranted" checks run on them compared to whites. Additionally, forms completed by officers following pedestrian stops confirmed a pattern of aggressive policing toward blacks. Based on officers' reported stops and the detailed factors that led to them, Andrew Gelman and colleagues found that blacks and Hispanics were 2.5 and 1.9 times, respectively, likelier to be stopped for violent crimes and 1.8 and 1.6 times likelier to be stopped for weapons crimes compared to whites.[94] However, though blacks and Hispanics were *more* likely to be stopped, they were *less* likely to be arrested; 1 in 7.9 whites stopped were arrested, compared to 1 in 8.8 Hispanics and 1 in 9.5 blacks. Moreover, blacks and Hispanics are stopped with less probable cause than whites.

Information logged into MDTs by officers, as well as data reported by them following pedestrian stops, are advantageous to differential dialogue in that (1) race and place are confirmed as significant factors; (2) it is further determined that minorities are likelier than whites to be stopped in any location; (3) the likelihood for minorities to be stopped significantly increases when they near or enter into white places; and (4) minority stops tend to lead to fewer arrests compared to whites, suggesting that at least some stops are driven more by police suspicion and unwarranted surveillance rather than by criminality.[95]

Of course, there are also disadvantages to soliciting information from police databases. As they communicate data, officers have some measure of discretion in what they actually report. Therefore, crucial information may be withheld, somewhat limiting the findings. As police are likely motivated to minimize any appearance of discrimination, such studies may plausibly underestimate the extent to which discriminatory patterns of policing occur.

Self-reporting data (e.g., surveys)—as a third source—differs from police-reported data in that the information gained reflects the voice of citizens as they experience and perceive their interactions with the police. Drawing on 2,830 self-reporting surveys, Patricia Warren and colleagues estimate racial disparities among police stops from local and state police in North Carolina.[96] Richard Lundman and Robert Kaufman draw from 7,034 respondents, accounting for both stop patterns and citizens' perceptions.[97]

In both data sets, race and place emerged as significant factors, individually and collectively, in stop patterns as well as in influencing citizens' perceptions of law enforcement. For example, with Warren and colleagues, being black proved to be salient with *local* police stops, while place was significant with *state* police stops.[98] In other words, race decreased in significance with highway patrol as place increased. Drivers were more likely to be stopped in suburbs and rural areas as opposed to cities. Hence, as in Alpert and colleagues, it might be that race gives way to place and vice versa since places are racially segregated.[99] Additionally, it might be that drivers are traveling at a faster rate on the highway, thus, making race not as easily identifiable. Nevertheless, when accounting for race and gender, theorists found black men were likelier to be stopped than white men, and black women were likelier to be stopped than white women (local and state police).[100]

Peculiarly, research shows Hispanic men and women as less likely than white men and women to be stopped by police.[101] In such instances, it is possible that "unaccounted for" interactional effects may be at play, working to decrease the likelihood of Hispanic stops compared to white stops. For example, culture could play a role here, especially as Hispanic women may drive less than black and white women. Additionally, it is possible that Hispanics are likelier to car pool or ride in groups, decreasing the number of Hispanic drivers on the road compared to black and white. However, in instances where Hispanic citizens were stopped, like black motorists, they were least likely to feel their stops were legitimate and most likely to believe officers behaved improperly compared to whites. When accounting for gender, men in general were least likely to believe that their stops were legitimate compared to women.[102]

Like police reporting, self-reported data has also been met with criticisms in that citizens may underreport when questioned about particular kinds of information. However, the benefits of self-reporting surveys outweigh the negatives. They provide insight into instances where police behaviors and encounters, particularly among people of color, further negative experiences and attitudes. Moreover, although citizen-reported surveys do not account for the totality of citizen experiences with the police, there is a wealth of data that does. In the next section we gain greater insight into (1) the cumulative experiences of blacks, captured and chronicled through previous ethnographic research (largely in the form of community studies); and (2) factors that contributed to the differential experiences of black citizens and the effects of those factors as they shaped citizens' attitudes toward the police (ATP).

While racial-profiling data gained from police ride-alongs, police-stop forms, and citizen surveys provide insight into black citizen–police interactions, it has been limited in accounting for citizens' full experiences. Its benefits stop short of being able to translate the significance of statistics/percentages to the detailed everyday occurrences as faced, understood, and shared by blacks. In this light, ethnographic and qualitative interview methodology is particularly well suited to eliciting the stories of minorities, whose experiences are often ignored or lost in the larger social debate over citizen-police relations. Consequently, many projects have used interview research to address the interactive relationship between race, place, and policing from various angles. For example, Michelle Fine and colleagues used interview research to gain greater insight into how youth perceived the police and other authority figures as agents of surveillance in public places.[103]

Michelle Fine and colleagues found that youth experience "microaggressions," in which they are likely to be disrespected/suspected by police and others in stores, schools, and on the streets; youth are likely to have a distrust of adults; youth are likelier to be open and receptive to adult views, but believe they are not open to theirs; and black youth are least likely to believe that something could be done to provoke social change with authority.[104] Additionally, the project extends citizen-police dialogue, especially as "belief that adults stereotype because of appearance" emerged as a recurring theme.[105]

Ronald Weitzer, on the other hand, used in-depth interview research to focus on the significance of community context and perceptions of racialized policing.[106] For example, Weitzer sought to gain greater insight into the perceptions of black versus white residents and whether they believed policing behaviors varied depending on the communities they lived in. After conducting interviews with 169 residents from three communities (white middle class, black middle class, black lower class), he found that the majority of the residents believed that *race* made a difference in how people were treated by the police (82 percent Spartanburg, 65 percent Merrifield, 71 percent Cloverdale).[107] Regarding the significance of community context, this study also found that both black and white residents believed their *neighborhoods* to have an influence on how the police treated them.[108] Interestingly, as the black professionals living in the affluent crime-free neighborhood believed the police viewed and regarded their community in the same fashion as the white, middle-class neighborhood, their white counterparts rejected this characterization and instead likened police treatment in their community to that of "any" black community.[109] This leaves to question whether discrimination lies in class disparity, as argued by William Julius Wilson, or in racial disparity.[110] History suggests interactional effects between race and class, rather than one over the other.

Similarly, Elijah Anderson's *Streetwise: Race, Class, and Change in an Urban Community* provided insight into the experiences and perceptions of residents from a black disadvantaged neighborhood as well as those from a white affluent one.[111] This study ethnographically chronicles fourteen years of shared experiences of racially diverse residents in separate places with overlapping spaces.[112] Though Anderson's primary focus is on the black residents of Northton, as they are the more disadvantaged and most destitute of the two neighborhoods, he elicited stories that relayed clear messages about the way the two neighborhoods interacted. Through the residents' narratives, we know and better understand how and why black men are feared in a predominantly white affluent neighborhood, and more specifically, how they come to be viewed as suspicious by both the white residents and the police. This ethnographic research furthers our understanding of how stereotypes have a tremendous effect on the experiences of minorities. Even regarding the way they are dressed, blacks, especially men, face being marked for surveillance and experiencing differential and discriminative behaviors by white affluent residents and by police.

Anderson's *Code of the Street* also provides accounts of disadvantaged urban life as lived and understood by black residents and furthers our understanding of the interactive relationship between race and place, the emergence of black-on-black violence, and other distinct sets of behaviors constantly being negotiated between poor, black urban residents.[113] Anderson analyzes how, when, and where such behaviors manifest and the ways in which they are perceived and understood as the "code of the street."[114] Thus, *Code of the Street* provides readers with a better understanding of the overlapping, everyday difficulties/oppressions as faced and voiced by disadvantaged, inner-city blacks. Also, it gives significant attention to race, place, and policing dialogue, especially as it is in poor black communities that "the influence of the police ends and personal responsibility for one's safety is felt to begin."[115]

Research by Neil Websdale also relied on ethnographic research for analyzing citizen-police relations.[116] He conducted several police ride-alongs and interviewed officers and citizens residing in Nashville's predominantly black housing projects, one of which is the site for a community-policing project. Differing from Elijah Anderson, this study called attention to the experiences of blacks as they exist alongside community policing.[117] Websdale discussed and interpreted the residents' experiences by situating them in historical and community context. More specifically, Websdale called attention to the history of policing in those particular housing projects, where residents spoke openly about incidents of police aggression and brutality.[118] So, while there is community policing in the projects as well as in other disadvantaged places, this study found that most residents did not recognize their presence as making a difference in the community. Moreover, it was concluded that community policing was more about increased surveillance and control of the poor. The program seemed to have been strategically placed in poor, black communities in an effort to target and implement harsher penalties on crack cocaine versus powder.[119]

Work by Rod Brunson and Jody Miller is also significant in the advancement of race, place, and policing dialogue.[120] Considerably influenced by its framework and target location, it served as a template for this project, making this study a natural progression to the overall black citizen-police platform. Brunson and Miller's studies are situated in the City of St. Louis, and they account for black citizen-police interactions in disadvantaged, urban communities. These communities can be characterized as predominantly black-populated, with high rates of poverty, unemployment, and female-headed households.[121] They are segregated, isolated, and drug-and-violence infested, similar to the disadvantaged black communities described by Neil Websdale and Elijah Anderson.[122]

Brunson and Miller began data collection with a survey, followed by in-depth interviews with young men and women ($N = 75$) from targeted neighborhoods.[123] They provide a comparative analysis for how young black men and women experience policing. They found that most of the youth knew someone who had been harassed or mistreated by the police (67/75); very few youth, male or female, believed the police were easy to talk to (10/75); few youth thought the police were polite to those in the neighborhood (6/75); a significant number of youth said "the police often harass or mistreat people in the neighborhood" (47/75); and young men were likelier to be "harassed or mistreated" (33/40) compared to young women (16/35).

Gendered experiences with the police were most visible in the harassment or mistreatment faced by young men compared to young women. These notable differences were acknowledged and discussed by the respondents, particularly the females. Though the young women discussed being harassed by the police, they believed the treatment they received from the police to be somewhat minor compared to the young men.[124]

The police usually focused on truancy and curfew violations with the young women and were likely to approach them at night. The young men were viewed and treated as criminals and typically approached during the daytime. Even when approached, the young women spoke of the police as mostly just talking poorly to them; whereas, for the young men, the young ladies recalled witnessing incidents of aggression/excessive use of force (e.g., stops and searches, slamming heads into the car) and arrests.[125] When young men were approached in the presence of women, officers were noted as being less aggressive.

The young black men in Brunson and Miller's study faced proactive policing strategies and involuntary contacts with the police.[126] These men reported officers suspecting them of being drug dealers, resulting in frequent stops and pat downs. This is harassment, a proactive policing strategy experienced by most of the young men in the sample (83 percent), regardless of actual delinquency.[127]

When accounting for other experiences and perceptions of young black men toward the police, researchers also found that most young men knew someone who had been harassed or mistreated by the police (93 percent); many believed the police to do a good job enforcing the law, *sometimes* (42 percent); many believed the police to *almost never* respond quickly to calls (46 percent); the police were believed to work hard at solving neighborhood crimes, *sometimes* (42 percent); most felt the police were *almost never* easy to talk to (66 percent); many believed they were *almost never* polite to people in the neighborhood (49 percent); and many believed that they *almost never* did a good job preventing crime (49 percent).[128] Brunson and Miller's studies paid considerable attention to the "accumulative experiences" of blacks.[129] After all, it is through such experiences, positive or negative, that attitudes are formed toward law enforcement, regardless of race, gender, age, and so on. Rod Brunson states:

> Most studies regarding black citizens' perceptions of police have relied on survey research or official data on citizen complaints and have typically focused on discrete, one-time experiences rather than on cumulative measures of police contacts. And although these examinations have highlighted the importance of race and age differences, they have not elicited the kind of information that would allow researchers to acquire deeper understandings. . . . In-depth

interview techniques provide a unique opportunity to examine the interplay of direct and indirect contacts to better understand the range of experiences that may influence attitudes toward police.[130]

ATTITUDES TOWARD POLICE (ATP)

As race and place interactively produce negative policing experiences for black citizens, such interactions lead to negative ATP. Citizens often express their attitude toward negative police interactions through protests and platforms. However, ATP have also been studied more formally, to identify both the attitudes themselves as well as the factors that determine those attitudes. ATP analyses have focused on individual-level variables (age, race, gender, class) and contextual variables (political alienation, police presence, expectations of police, frequency/nature of police contacts, victimization/fear of crime, community conditions, space, and place).

Individual Variables

Individual-level or demographic factors that have been studied have included age, sex, race/ethnicity, education, and income. Beginning with age, youth populations are likelier to have negative ATP than adults.[131] Youth view themselves as targets for police harassment, surveillance, and restriction.[132] Youth resent surveillance, as they are generally more concerned with freedom and independence than with safety and protection. In general, youth ATP often correlate with attitudes toward other authority figures, such as parents and teachers.[133]

In terms of gender, boys/men are likelier than girls/women to have negative ATP.[134] Boys/men are likelier to come in contact with the police under suspicion and as assailants than are girls/women. Consequently, male ATP is generally defensive and apprehensive, while female ATP tends to be more credulous and composed.

Negative ATP vary and may be further exacerbated when factors are combined, such as age with socioeconomic status (SES) or gender with race/ethnicity.[135] Studies show an increase of police surveillance, harassment, and other aggressive tactics in minority neighborhoods, particularly among disadvantaged males.[136] The criminal justice system, local and otherwise, has a long-standing history of positing young black men as the likeliest perpetrators of crime. While such stereotypes work to create hostile police practices directly and indirectly, an attitude of hostility is then reciprocated by young black males.[137]

Additionally, at the intersection of gender, race, and class, black women in disadvantaged neighborhoods tend to have negative ATP.[138] While their ATP may not equally reflect the threats as often perceived and felt by black men, they are still pertinent in that black women view the police as personal threats to their loved ones. While such experiences and perceptions are common among disadvantaged black populations, they tend to be least experienced or felt among white men and even more so among white women.[139]

As race and socioeconomic status (SES) are intractably intertwined, it is virtually impossible to measure ATP solely on the basis of one or the other; so it is not surprising that many studies analyze the effects of SES and disadvantaged communities alongside those of race.[140] ATP among low-income, disadvantaged white and minority populations tend to be less favorable compared to those of middle-class populations.[141] More specifically, disadvantaged minority (i.e., black) populations are likely to have less favorable ATP compared to predominantly white middle-class populations.[142] Black middle- and upper-class populations are equally likely to have less favorable ATP compared to their white middle- or upper-class counterparts.[143] And since communities reflect the income status of its residents, these trends tend to remain the same when accounting for community context.

Contextual Variables

Contextual variables, such as political alienation, police presence, expectations of police, the nature and frequency of police contact, victimization and the fear of crime, community conditions, and space and place, are crucial to analyses of ATP. Theorists have either relied on individual variables, relied on a combination of individual and contextual variables, or neglected contextual variables altogether. In short, many researchers have focused their efforts on controlling for sociodemographic factors such as age, gender, and race, while failing to consider or control for nondemographic factors such as social/political alienation, contact with police, and community context.

Type of police contact is important in shaping ATP. Studies suggest that blacks are "more likely to leave an encounter with the police upset or angry."[144] Consequently, it is essential to take into full account the circumstances through which they become acquainted.

Direct, personal contact is often the vehicle through which, historically, black populations have faced public discrimination. Examples of such discrimination may include personal experience(s) of racial profiling and excessive use of force. Indirect or "vicarious" contact is knowledge gained through police contacts as friends, family, or others have experienced them.[145] This is frequently the case among blacks, who often share stories with one another, detailing their experiences and the experiences of others with the police. Like in the case of Rodney King, some individuals come to internalize the experiences of others.[146]

Research treats "voluntary and involuntary" as additional forms of police contact.[147] While both forms are generally understood and discussed as direct (personal) contacts, they differ in that voluntary contact is initiated by the citizen and involuntary contact is initiated by the police. Who prompted the encounter may differently affect citizens' experiences and attitudes. While voluntary contacts may prove favorable in certain situations, both voluntary and involuntary contacts can lead to unfavorable ATP.[148]

Voluntary police contact is likely to have been prompted by an emergency situation and/or precipitated by fear—perhaps fear of crime or an actual occurrence of crime.[149] Under such circumstances, citizen ATP may be favorable in that they look to police for protection; on the other hand, negative ATP can also occur if citizens hold the police responsible for the occurrence of crime. Citizens may perceive the police as inadequate or incompetent, and lack confidence in them and their ability to protect them.[150] Negative ATP may also come from voluntary contacts in which citizens believe the police perform poorly and offer low-quality service.[151] Studies show that black citizens more than others often experience delayed responses, no responses, unjust resolutions, or no resolutions.[152] Involuntary contact, by its very nature, typically results in negative experiences and attitudes.[153] Blacks are likely than whites to have more involuntary encounters with the police, such as surveillance and harassment.[154]

Social and political alienation has also been significant in understanding ATP. Minority populations tend to be systematically and discriminatively isolated, leaving minorities feeling as though they do not have a stake in the everyday functioning of the larger society. Consequently, black ATP may reflect their attitudes regarding overall social/political structures.[155] Minorities have a tendency to perceive social/political institutions and its agents (e.g., police) as sources of prejudice and inequality, a perception fueled by the disproportionate incarceration of blacks, unjustifiable acts of aggression and violence toward black citizens in disadvantaged communities,[156] and the ability of involved officers to escape prosecution and conviction.[157] Furthermore, they often see them as culturally and racially/ethnically insensitive, dictating and restricting values, behaviors, and lifestyle. Police are often viewed by blacks as restrictive and discriminative enforcers and protectors of the dominant way of life.

Community context significantly influences ATP. It is within communities that citizens and police alike define and interpret one another's positions, expectations, and experiences.[158] The culture and experiences in a disadvantaged, urban setting differ from those in a middle- and upper-class setting.[159] Low-income communities tend to be disproportionately populated by blacks, isolated, found in structurally unstable locations, lacking in resources, and conducive to crime. Linqun Cao and colleagues call attention to such community conditions as a significant factor in citizens' confidence in the police or lack thereof.[160] When accounting for *community disorder* such as littering, noise, loitering, teen rowdiness, and deteriorating property, they found that the effect of race became insignificant. In other words, regardless of race, citizens lacked confidence in the police in places where there was social and physical disorder. This confirms the importance of accounting for both race *and* place in analyzing black-citizen relationships with the police.

CONCLUSION

All of the research discussed so far suggests that black experiences with the police are worse when situated away from black places and closer to or in predominantly white places. Researchers argue that the threat level among whites significantly increases as blacks move closer to white communities. This prompts more aggressive police tactics, especially as the very nature of police work is to serve and protect the interests of the dominant populations.

Many studies have accounted for individual variables, such as race or gender, or contextual variables, such as neighborhood/community context, as influencing negative or positive ATP, rather than as interacting factors that contribute to particular experiences. However, addressing individual variables or contextual variables alone does not adequately account for the effects of overlapping variables as they appear in everyday interactions.

This book's focus on black-citizen police attitudes in the predominantly black Meacham Park, adjacent to the predominantly white, upper-middle-class

Kirkwood, adds to the race, place, and policing dialogue in the following ways: (1) it brings to life intimate black experiences, as lived, understood, and shared by them in poor segregated neighborhoods; (2) it challenges the presumption of place and the totality, and thus, quality of black experiences in *diverse* spaces (3) it explains black experiences with regard to exclusion, fear, and policing by situating them in historical and community context; (4) it calls into question the history, justification, and benefits (or the lack thereof) of policing communities; and (5) it illustrates the effects of aggressive policing within the context of black residential integration into white, affluent suburban locations.

Historical contextualizing of the emergence of race- and place-based policing are crucial in understanding relations between Meacham Park residents and the police. It is through awareness of codes and laws, the regulation and segregation of towns, racial profiling and attitudinal factors that differential patterns and trends will reemerge in my account (in chapter 2) of the history of Meacham Park, specifically this community's devolution from an unincorporated black enclave thriving with black-owned businesses to a mostly demolished and segregated neighborhood annexed to the predominantly white, affluent City of Kirkwood.

"You're nothing but trash over here..."

BLACK FACES IN WHITE PLACES

Any society, any nation, is judged on the basis of how it treats its
weakest members: the last, the least, the littlest.[1]

CARDINAL ROGER MAHONY

ROUGHLY FIFTEEN TO TWENTY MILES west of the Mississippi River
and St. Louis's downtown district lies an affluent, white, historic St. Louis
suburb. This suburb, the City of Kirkwood, or Kirkwood for short, happens
to be St. Louis's first planned suburban community west of the Gateway
Arch. It is a predominantly white, quaint community lined with beautiful
trees, picturesque homes and neighborhoods, its own city hall, and a vibrant
downtown district of small charming shops, restaurants, a farmers' market,
and frequent festivals. It is surrounded by museums, parks, and recreational
centers, with a passenger train station at its hub (see figs. 1–5).

By contrast, Meacham Park is a poor black neighborhood situated
between Kirkwood and two St. Louis metropolitan arteries: Interstates 44
(east-west) and 270 (south-north). It is part of the City of Kirkwood and has
been described as the uncharacteristic portion of the suburb: the predominantly black, disadvantaged, annexed part—isolated and invisible to most—
where sidewalks, street lights, and a sewer system reflect recent but minimal
community development. Meacham Park shows signs of wear and tear. Most
homes are rented—a few of which are shabby, boarded up, or condemned
with unmanaged yards and sitting next to vacant lots. It is a one-way-in, one-
way-out neighborhood. Vibrant black-owned businesses that once reflected
the pulse of the neighborhood are all gone; one-third of its original acreage
has been leveled, forcing hundreds of black families to relocate. Hence, the
rich history and community pride that once existed in this neighborhood has
been reduced to black street names, an annual homecoming celebration, a
neighborhood association, a remodeled elementary school inaccessible to the

FIGURE 1. Neighborhood in affluent Kirkwood. Photo by author.

FIGURE 2. Another neighborhood in affluent Kirkwood. This and the previous figure display the predominantly white side of Kirkwood, "lined with beautiful trees, picturesque homes and neighborhoods." Photo by author.

FIGURE 3. Kirkwood's downtown district consists of "small charming shops" and restaurants. This photo displays a few restaurants with outdoor eating directly across from Kirkwood City Hall. Photo by author.

FIGURE 4. Kirkwood's farmers' market is also located in its downtown district. It too is a nice gathering place, where residents have their pick of fresh fruits and vegetables to local events and activities to attend. Photo by author.

FIGURE 5. The Amtrak station in Kirkwood provides a midtown connection for St. Louisans looking to travel. Often St. Louis suburban residents rely on the Kirkwood station, as it closer than the downtown St. Louis location. Photo by author.

neighborhood, an exaggerated reputation of crime and lawlessness, and years of distrust and racial contention with its local government (see figs. 6 and 7).

A dichotomous relationship exists between Meacham Park and Kirkwood. In theory, the neighborhood of Meacham Park is just as much a part of the City of Kirkwood as the numerous white affluent neighborhoods are. However, in practice, they are socially disconnected in ways that have proven disadvantageous to both. Francis, sixty, described their relationship as she sees it, particularly following annexation:

> The best description of it [the relationship] in my understanding is when Kirkwood annexed the community [Meacham Park], it was in what you considered deplorable condition. However, that does not equalize the fact of the haves and have-nots, those who had taken from those that had not. They [Kirkwood] identified and characterized this area [Meacham Park] as an area that didn't have . . . it was like a big fish in a little pond, so when the developers [hired by Kirkwood] came to Meacham Park they were the big fish, we were the little pond. So what did they do? They overruled and made a landslide profit.

Francis, a local school district retiree, has lived in Meacham Park all of her life and has been an avid opponent of what she believes to be years of discriminative tactics used by the City of Kirkwood. She believes Kirkwood seeks to advance its economic and political agendas at the expense of the poor, uneducated black residents of Meacham Park.

Similar beliefs are held by Dorothy, fifty-seven, who has spent much of her life in Kirkwood. Dorothy lived in Crestwood, a neighboring suburb, for much of her childhood but spent her adolescent and adult years in Meacham Park. She too was candid about her perceptions of inequitable dealings with the blacks in Meacham Park, and thus, characterizes the relationship between Meacham Park and Kirkwood as divisive and contradicting:

> I don't see Kirkwood opening up like that to embrace the African-American community [Meacham Park], to make it a true part of this city as far as having all the full rights and privileges and respect that we deserve . . . it's just always this wall, us and them.

This chapter delves into the history of Meacham Park and Kirkwood and residents' interpretation of the controversial annexation that gave way to one community (Kirkwood) assuming ownership of the other (Meacham Park). In doing so, it explores past stereotypical ideas and practices surrounding black threat, the segregation and preservation of place, and differential policing

FIGURE 6. Meacham Park entrance sign. This sign sits at the intersection, where "Kirkwood Proper" ends and Meacham Park begins. This is also the same intersection where participants describe various interactions with the police. Photo by author.

FIGURE 7. Vacant home in Meacham Park. While there are nice homes with managed yards located in Meacham Park, this photo displays one of many homes and apartment dwellings there that gives way to lower property values for others and "ghetto" characterizations. Photo by author.

coinciding with those of the present. The overlapping experiences and interactions of poor suburban blacks and affluent whites reveal social progress or the lack thereof in Meacham Park / Kirkwood, and more broadly, throughout the nation. The ways the local government, and more specifically, the police delegate and regulate at the crossroads of race and place set the stage for examining dominant agendas—step by step—as they are often cloaked in progressive rhetoric, while resulting in dated consequences.

IN THE BEGINNING

The history of Meacham Park has at least two versions. Some black residents contend that the community is named after John Berry Meachum, a freed slave known for his significant contributions to black education in the St. Louis region.[2] However, documents traced the original landowner to a white man named John McLaughlin in 1878, who later sold the acreage to co-owners Chas A. Baker and Henry B. Seammel. On July 8, 1892, Baker and Seammel sold the 158-acre community for $33,308 to white real-estate broker Elzey E. Meacham of Memphis, Tennessee.[3] It is from Mr. Meacham of Memphis that the unincorporated community ultimately acquired its name as well as became known for its unusually small, subdivided parcels of land (twenty-five-foot lots) that in some instances sold for as little as ten dollars a lot.[4] Because its lots were inexpensive, Meacham Park from its inception was mostly composed of blacks and few whites. It became one of eleven original black settlements in the Kirkwood region, and to date, the last of two to remain. The other is a black-only burial site known as Quinette Cemetery (see fig. 8).

Prior to World War II, Meacham Park could be characterized as rural, with an initial population of roughly thirty-five hundred, and then thirteen hundred to two thousand residents following the war. The community was once self-sufficient and largely made up of dirt roads and farms. Its black residents had been known to garden and raise hunting dogs, mules, hogs, and chickens, and they were hired for various tasks by Kirkwood residents.[5] Many of its original street names—Attucks, Sarotoga, Aldridge, Chicago, Handy, Spears—several of which no longer exist, are believed to have been named after blacks. A number of Meacham Park residents associate aspects such as its street and affordable lots with their belief in the community as having been originally owned by a freed slave (John Berry Meachum) rather than white man Elzey Meacham. As Jeremy, twenty-four years old, says:

FIGURE 8. Along with Meacham Park, Quinette Cemetery represents one of the last black settlements in the City of Kirkwood and is a historic landmark. It is the oldest African-American cemetery west of the Mississippi, dating back to 1866. Photo by author.

There's history behind Meacham Park. A lot of people don't know about it. But before my grandma died, we used to have a lot of talks, you know. Meacham Park was awarded to a slave and they named it after him and for them to destroy something like this hurts me personally. It's sad . . . this ain't no regular neighborhood.

EDUCATING MEACHAM

Like most U.S. communities during the late nineteenth and early to mid-twentieth centuries, the Meacham Park–Kirkwood schools were segregated. Though separate communities, the residents of Meacham Park relied on Kirkwood schools to educate its children.

After parents from Meacham Park petitioned their wishes, the City of Kirkwood established Meacham Park's first school in 1908, but it was accessible only to the white children in the community.[6] In 1911, Kirkwood established the first school for black children in Meacham Park, but this school would be short-lived. The Meacham Park School—later named the James Milton Turner School, after a Missouri slave turned Union soldier—opened its doors in 1924. Even then, the affairs of both Meacham Park and Kirkwood were significantly intertwined and complicated. Not only was there a divide of black children from white within the area, but also an added separation among black students—those from Kirkwood and those from Meacham Park. Furthering the complexity between the two communities and their residents, lifelong relationships developed between children and their families that extended themselves across racial and economic lines, and residents inescapably found themselves challenged with a continuously evolving contentious social climate.

Pete, fifty-nine, who was born and raised in Meacham Park, still owns his parents' home there. When asked if he felt he is part of Kirkwood, he answered yes, and began recalling both his school years and those of his brother-in-law, who was six years older.:

> Well, here's the thing. Everybody that grew up in Meacham Park especially during the time with me and before me, I can say this because I believe my brother-in-law who is now sixty-five or so, his first class was in the Kirkwood schools and we've always gone to school in Kirkwood. We walked to get to those schools, so Kirkwood was a part of our community. I don't think we felt separated in that sense from Kirkwood cause we've always been a part of, not only the school system, but our parents worked for folks in Kirkwood or

FIGURE 9. James Milton Turner School is also a historic landmark. It is named after a Missouri slave turned Union soldier. While it once served to educate black children in the Meacham Park community and had been proposed as a location for a recreational center, it is currently home to several white-owned businesses. Photo by author.

alongside of them. There are some friendships of Kirkwood and Meacham Park people that go some seventy, eighty years or longer.

Today, the James Milton Turner School is most accredited for educating the blacks in Meacham Park. Though now a remodeled office building housing white owned businesses only, it is listed on the National Register of Historic Places and remains a permanent fixture in the neighborhood (see fig. 9). Hence, as the governance of the Meacham Park community and the City of Kirkwood has always overlapped, there has always been a deep racial and economic divide. In lieu of relationships developed between the two communities, Kirkwood has historically been the lead, "parent" city and Meacham Park its dependent benefactor.

AT THE CORE

Following the Great Depression and World War II, Meacham Park lagged in community development. It was a community with outdoor plumbing, no sewer system, and substandard housing (see figs. 10 and 11).[7] Additionally, its racial composition was significantly changing. As it faced black migration and white flight, its residents encountered increased resistance and racism from Kirkwood's white population. Bill Jones, a black resident of Meacham

Park since 1945 and once editor of its only black newspaper, *In Our Opinion*, recalled the following in the *Webster-Kirkwood Times* online edition:

> I remember later, in the 1950s, white people used to drive their cars through the Meacham area on Sunday afternoons and they'd point their fingers at the run-down houses and the outhouses—and they'd be telling their friends, "This is our colored section here." That used to make me angry. It was upsetting for all of us who lived here.[8]

Nevertheless, the history of Meacham Park had already begun to flourish. As early as 1930, Meacham Park had organized its own volunteer fire department and police department—which consisted of two constables—and a traveling exhibition baseball team.[9] By the 1950s, its residents were tied to organizations such as the Legionnaires and the Republican Club; it had begun its own Women's Community Club, as well as established a black-owned and -operated business district, consisting of "five grocery stores, five beauty shops, two service stations, a cleaners, an auto repair service, a radio and TV shop, and a trash disposal service."[10] There were numerous churches throughout the community, in addition to a widespread sense of pride, tenacity, and neighborhood cohesion that would be lasting.

Dwayne, fifty-four, who owns a commercial real-estate company, is one of many residents who credits his achievements to the legacy of blacks in Meacham Park:

> Some of the things that I've accomplished, that, um, wherewithal, I get from growing up right here in this community, seeing the people that raised me survive. We had businesses out here, with no sewers. We had businesses, thriving cleaners, bars, stores, construction companies ... ever since I can remember, I use to say, "I wanna have my own business one day." I didn't want to have to work for somebody else all my life. I wanted to be the man at MY company in MY neighborhood in MY circle.

Dwayne's sentiment is a testament to the resolve of blacks in Meacham Park in spite of its deplorable community infrastructure. As Terrance, thirty-eight, puts it: "They [black residents in Meacham Park] spent their lives trying to keep small businesses out here." Like other participants, Dwayne and Terrance attribute the success of Meacham's black entrepreneurs to "survival," resourcefulness, and black ingenuity. On the one hand, the community lacked basic amenities necessary "for a welcome living and lifestyle in a community for anyone, no matter what the color of their skin might be"

(Francis). On the other hand, its earlier residents left an invaluable legacy, one with lessons of ownership and relationships, where the significance of culture in its entirety were conveyed for succeeding generations. Take a look at Pete's family:

> This is the third generation. My grandparents built a home in Meacham Park. My mother and her family, aunts and uncles, grew up in that particular home, added on to it and so on. We've been here for many years. I believe the house was built in 1914. I may be mistaken, I have to grab the deed on that but I believe it was around that time frame. That's one piece but there are other properties in Meacham Park we currently own too. My mother set up a plan for my sister's family and my family to where their kids—and even their kids—have lived in that house and what she did was she [his mom] kept a portion of the rent and you could stay there for two years and you'd get portions of the money back to buy your own . . . and that's worked for my sister's children, which one of them is now fifty, have lived there and then their sons have lived there, along with other family people.

Pete, fifty-nine, still owns seven parcels of land in Meacham Park, not including the one his family home sits on. His story, like countless others, captures how social forces that work to separate and denigrate people, directly or indirectly, only become sculpting tools for the resiliency of those most vulnerable to it. The residents of Meacham Park experienced loss and gain reciprocally.

> A different piece, a different transition, but Meacham Park will always be here, I believe . . . I believe there's a core.

"DIRT ROAD PIMPING": THE ROAD TO ANNEXATION

> I was born out here with a house, with an outhouse. That was only forty years ago and most of the people that dug these streets—my daddy's daddy [grandfather] is gone . . . there was no running water and half of the reason they [the blacks in Meacham Park] annexed to Kirkwood was for fire and police protection. Those were the reasons why we as a people voted for the annexation to Kirkwood, we'd have fire and water protection. So you [Meacham Park residents] were for it in terms of fire protection . . . and no, I'm not saying "I" was for it, I'm just saying most of the people that voted for it, voted for fire protection . . . general common courtesy is what they [Kirkwood] sold us on for annexation.
>
> TERRANCE

FIGURE 10. Homes in Meacham Park, 1965. Photos by Paul Schaefer. Courtesy of the Kirkwood Historical Society.

In the 1970s, in the wake of a 1966 deadly house fire killing five children due to a failed fire engine, efforts began to annex Meacham Park to the City of Kirkwood. Given that the community continued to face a dilapidated infrastructure and lacked basic amenities, such as a modern water-and-sewer system, streetlights, and fire and police services, to name a few, for some, it seemed befitting to adjoin the community to another so that its residents

FIGURE 11. More homes in Meacham Park, 1965. These photos and the ones shown as figure 10 were taken when Meacham Park was composed of dirty roads, outdoor plumbing, and substandard housing. Photos by Paul Schaefer. Courtesy of the Kirkwood Historical Society.

could benefit from a broad range of services reflective of progressive times. As depicted by a local journalist, "Two men walked on the moon before Meacham Park had paved roads and modern sewers."[11] The City of Kirkwood was the obvious choice to annex Meacham Park, especially as the two communities had a preexisting history of Meacham relying on Kirkwood for educating their children, among other things.

The transition to annexation was not an easy one. For many Meacham Park residents, the idea of attaching their community to another meant the loss of identity, a loss of culture that reflected who *they* were, what *they* were aspiring to be, and what *they* believed they needed. This was about negotiating a delicate balance as *they* saw fit: one in which the residents of Meacham could improve their living conditions without compromising their own efforts and integrity at the expense of white dependency and control. After all, the community had previously experienced a loss of its original acreage to eminent domain resulting from the 1968 construction of Interstate 44. The residents of Meacham were not too keen on the possibility of losing more. For them, independence was on the chopping block, and consistent with the spatial-assimilation model, annexation meant acculturation. Their decision to adjoin Kirkwood came down to their ability, or perhaps their willingness, to assimilate to the predominantly white, affluent City of Kirkwood.

After years of deliberation and despite black reservation, annexation of Meacham Park by the City of Kirkwood passed with an 83 percent vote of approval from the residents of Meacham Park and a 72 percent vote of approval from residents in Kirkwood. Many Meacham Park residents conceded to the annexation because they believed they had no alternatives. A sizable number of them were aged, uneducated, and more importantly, thought they could improve their living conditions with a modern infrastructure and better access to human services. Denise, sixty, was one of them. Like Terrance, she explained the deplorable conditions of the community that influenced the decision to annex:

> Before annexation, this [Meacham Park] was an unincorporated county area. It was just not getting the kind of services that modern communities have. If we annexed the community, then we would get funds to fix up the neighborhood . . . and there were those of us FOR getting the neighborhood fixed up because we had lived here for years in a redlined district. No one would allow us to get loans, NO ONE. None of the banks would loan the money. People owned their homes for years and they had no improvements to their properties. I saw the bathrooms and kitchens and the shotgun houses that had nothing . . . people that didn't have furnaces, they had old stoves and would order their oil at the beginning of the winter . . . and you thought they had a basement [*shaking her head*], rocks and dirt floors in the basement of houses . . . in this day and time, people living in these kinds of conditions . . . every time it rained, there was water in my basement and it wasn't water from the sewers. It was spring water. There was a stream that ran all the way through Meacham Park and anytime the water got to be a certain level, everybody's basement would flood.

What Denise describes is a dilemma faced by many blacks in disadvantaged communities. The residents in Meacham Park were economically shut out, living in horrific conditions with no available resources with which to pull themselves up and out. Hence, the Meacham Park vote for annexation came out of residents being institutionally pigeon-holed in deprivation and desperately looking for a way out.

The 1991 annexation of Meacham Park meant that it was no longer an unincorporated community, independent of others; it now belonged to the City of Kirkwood. It was official: Kirkwood was now the parent community and Meacham Park, its colony. Despite promises that Meacham Park was synonymous with Kirkwood's original neighborhoods or subdivisions and would be treated as such, to many these pledges seemed to be empty rhetoric. In fact, many of the participants depicted the annexation as having turned from a "negative means to a positive end" approach to neighborhood improvements to what they perceived as nothing more than a "land-grab" as Francis called it—shrouded in manipulation and broken promises. Francis stated:

> I can best describe the annexation as an effort for Kirkwood to come and take the land. The initial plan and the annexation was to come and to bring amenities to this community. Well, once the annexation passed, the city came and they had another plan. The City of Kirkwood came and spoke with a fork tongue, asked for twelve acres of land to do a strip mall but they took fifty-two.

Francis is speaking of a multimillion dollar contract that took two-thirds of Meacham Park's land for commercial development shortly after the annexation. The loss of the community feared by many of its residents had happened. Addendums had been made to the original agreement offered by the City of Kirkwood, which translated to the loss of more acreage, homes, and businesses in the Meacham Park neighborhood.

With Meacham now annexed to the City of Kirkwood and thus at the mercy of a new government, the land acquisition was inevitable. A small shopping center was in the works, they were told, and the resulting tax increment financing (TIF) or tax dollars would be used to improve the community's infrastructure. However, the small shopping center became a large shopping plaza, filled with big-box stores such as Wal-Mart, Lowes, Target, and more, at the expense of leveling two hundred homes that had fallen prey to new Kirkwood ordinances, uncertainty over obtaining second and third mortgages, ignorance surrounding buyouts/payouts, and inevitably eminent domain for a second time (see fig. 12). Hence, feeling disempowered, duped, and unable to fully comprehend what they signed up for versus what they actually got with the annexation and redevelopment plan, the racial divide widened between the two communities in immeasurable ways. Terrance characterized the dealings of Kirkwood to Meacham Park as being like a pimp to a prostitute. He stated:

> For the most part, Meacham Park has always been the lower end of the tracks, where white people come to kick their heels up and ain't nuthin' changed but the year. [To Kirkwood] Meacham Park just still back roads, dirt roads ... and dirt road pimpin' ain't changed. It [the annexation] was more about money, a tax bracket, and Kirkwood Commons ... to me, that's all it was ever about.

House for a House, the Buyout, and Eminent Domain: The Untold Stories of the Deals Made

Meacham Park homeowners within the redevelopment zones were entangled in a series of offers regarding their property: (1) they could accept the buyout, initial compensation offered for their properties, and then relocate; (2) they could accept the "house for a house" deal, agreeing to have a home built to replace the one they lost; or (3) they could be forced to sell through eminent domain, a process whereby land is legally seized by the government for public or private use.

Participants shared stories, detailing their decision-making processes when they were given these choices. They described intense and often dubious exchanges from contractors to attorneys as they weighed their options in the face of a multimillion-dollar redevelopment project, what was to become Kirkwood Commons. Dwayne's parents decided to accept the "house for a house" deal. He recounted the exchange between contractors and his parents as they bargained for a new home:

Can you tell me what you recall about the annexation process?
   What I recall about that process is that a lot of people were offered a home for a home. I'm a little disappointed that a lot of people didn't take 'em [the developers] up on that offer. But then again a lot of people took the money and ran. My parents built a home here in Meacham Park from the ground up ... but when they [developers and Kirkwood] were building these homes, it was a great thing that these people were getting them. But on the other hand, some of these people got taken advantage of.

FIGURE 12. This picture is a reminder of Meacham Park's secluded status. It is a wall that separates the community from Kirkwood Commons, once Meacham Park land but now a strip mall. In this picture, you can also see the back of several big box stores. Photo by author.

How so?

Well, there was an instance where they told my parents to settle up.

And who are they?

The developers I think. [*Quoting the developers:*] "You know, we'll build you a house three, four bedroom house for sixty thousand, seventy thousand dollars, whatever the price is on your house right now IF you got the money." Well, you know, they were talking to them [his parents] like, "Hey, you guys are dirt poor so yea if you got the money, we'll build it like that" ... [the developers] not knowing that YOU know there are financial institutions that have to be involved ... so by the time you get through paying on that sixty thousand dollars it's really gone cost you about a hundred grand or whatever. So my dad said okay, whatever. [*Quoting his dad:*] "So if I got some property right here and I give you [the developer] sixty thousand dollars you'll build me a house to my wife's specification, a three bedroom?" [The developer:] "Oh yeah, Mr., IF you have sixty thousand, we'll build you that house." My dad said OK. So my mom and dad sought counsel from their lawyer and he introduced them to a real-estate lawyer. Well, you know, my parents were retired at that time and they had the kind of money to do that. My dad told my mom that he wanted to build her a new house before he died and it was a good opportunity to do it, he had some property down here. So my dad spoke with his attorney and he told him to get the offer in writing. [Dad to developers:] "Well, sure. I want you to build me a house for sixty thousand dollars to my wife's specification." Well, you know by the time he got done [agreeing to the deal] ... the developers said, "Well, you know you gotta go to the bank, you gotta go do this, you gotta do that." [His dad:] "No, I'll write you a check ... I'll write you a check right now and let's sign the contract, I want that house built on my property down here, four months, five months," because the developers specifically told them [my parents] that they'd do that. But they [the developers] didn't think they had sixty thousand just sitting around ... But they didn't understand that some people like my parents, all they did was went to work ... they saved a little money sending me and my sisters to college but mostly we got scholarships. They saved and after retirement, all they did was went to church and went to the store. Some of these people out here, they're not all alcoholics, drug addicts; they're not all welfare recipients. Some of these people do have a little bit of money out here. But if you tell me you'll build me a three-bedroom house for sixty thousand and I got sixty thousand, then I want you to build me that three bedroom house. So the meetings ... I went to with my parents and those were some of the things that I paid attention to.

In your opinion, was the annexation beneficial or harmful or a little bit of both?

I don't think it was so much harmful because the people made the decision they wanted to make and that's what this country is about.

What people?

The people of this neighborhood, they made the decision on it. They wanted it. They didn't fight against it, they took the money and relocated. They had their choice and that's the choice they made and you got to respect it. And with that being said, yes it's a nicer community. There are fewer rundown homes out here that I see. No shacks out here that I see compared to when we were growing up. When we were growing up, there were shacks out here. We didn't have paved streets and a lot of homes didn't have indoor plumbing, you know. So, um, I like this community and always have. I liked it when we didn't have paved streets. I like Meacham Park. I take a little bit of Meacham Park with me everywhere I go, inside me.

Dwayne's parents were among only a few residents that accepted the "house for a house" offer. It was a program designed for displaced homeowners as follows:

To receive a $40,000 premium plus the St. Louis County appraised value of the house . . . owners of some new homes also obtained second and third mortgages at extremely low interest rates to help them buy a new house. The second mortgage was at o percent, and the third mortgage was at 1 percent. The homebuyer made nominal monthly payments of $25 on the second mortgage and $21.67 on the third.[12]

In the *St. Louis Beacon,* William Freivogel also stated:

The second mortgages were a source of misunderstanding in the community. Some residents thought Kirkwood was taking control of their houses; some said they felt as though these mortgages were being held over their heads and that they could lose their home if they said something that angered city officials.[13]

Denise also explained the distrust of residents in accepting the "house for a house" deal. She explained:

They [the developers and Kirkwood] had come up with a plan, a house for a house for those wanting to stay in Meacham Park and DESCO [the developers] would have to build them a house so they could stay here, and instead, they just gave up their houses and property. Only eight people out of almost two-hundred-something folks, two hundred homeowners accepted that and all of them were aware of the offer. They were so suspicious and so untrusting and so ignorant that they didn't understand the deal, a new house for their old house.

Denise accepted the offer. She thought it was a good program and was disappointed that others did not take advantage of it. However, Francis understood the plight of residents that did not and she explained the disadvantages of the program:

> Because they [the developers and Kirkwood] knew that the people would not be able to afford the houses for a long length of time and that the taxes alone would be a deterrent for them. This was an older community; it was dying . . . so if you do your numbers, when you got a sixty-year-old person purchasing a house with a ninety-year-old mortgage, it won't be long, you'll [the developers and Kirkwood] have the house back. Fixed income, elderly people . . . that's a destabilization characteristic that would benefit commercial. It doesn't benefit residential.

Already socioeconomically disadvantaged, many homeowners could not pay the difference on a new home like Dwayne's parents. This meant some would have to agree to second and third mortgages that they could not sustain. In such cases, the "house for a house" plan seemed more disadvantageous than the alternative: accepting the buyout and relocating.

Mark, however, opposed both options. He did not participate in the "house for a house" program and refused the buyout; as a result, he was forced out through eminent domain. Mark wanted fair compensation for his properties and believes he was singled out for not cooperating. His story is characterized by perceivably inequitable practices and what he believes to be attempts by developers and Kirkwood to bully him into compliance:

> I disliked the annexation, not just for myself, but how people in general were treated in the Meacham Park area when it came time for the buyout. I believe we were separated and divided from the people that they [the developers] wanted to deal with first. We weren't willing to sell at the prices that they wanted us to and I was put into a category to where developers were, like, "Don't be like him, he didn't settle with us or he didn't deal with us the first time so we're going to put him through eminent domain." I was asked by Cookie [Charles "Cookie" Thornton] to come in and let the developers talk to me. He [Cookie] was very influential in that [the annexation and commercial development] and suggested that I at least speak with the developers. But after reading the fine print [on the offer], I wasn't really sure that we were going to be treated fair and we weren't . . . they [the developers] told me that I should've owned my property longer than what I did. I had my property free and clear. As a matter of fact, I had six of them that were free and clear at the time and they told me they couldn't give me the same as my neighbors because I hadn't owned them long enough. So I showed them the door and then the

eminent-domain process started right after that. We went to Kirkwood with groups of people that owned property to try and get Kirkwood to help us negotiate with the developers ... to be treated fairly ... our land was taken, they [the developers] basically knocked down trees, poked holes in roofs ... I remember, they [the developers] walked us through the area to get appraisals of our property and it looked like a war zone. Our property was taken for residential when they [the developers and Kirkwood] had the intent to do commercial. You don't have to be that educated to know that you're not being treated fair when they're only offering you two dollars a square foot.

What do you mean when you say "our property was taken for residential"?

They [the developers] tried to pay us residential prices because it wasn't commercial at the time ... and even though we tried to use Turner School to encompass the wood company and the guitar shop and showed them that Meacham Park had a viable barber shop and was basically holding its own, it just seemed that the appraisers they used, all seemed to be working together against the value of our property.

So just to be clear, did you support the annexation?

No.

And as of this date, or at any point, did you ever?

Well, if I would have seen something positive from Kirkwood ... It just seemed like there was basically a plot to make things go wrong, I mean how they brought in HUD homes and the green space went away. As you could say, it began to be like the city to us out here in the county [the suburbs], to where there were several instances of people on top of each other. We used to have nice basketball games. You could count on people being able to pitch horse shoes, you know, just have good home style fun for the age group that would respond to that and we mentored each other. But things changed after a while. When you go back before the annexation you got Meacham Park, those were positive things. The negative things came in after the development.

But did your support for annexation ever change or has it always been no?

It hasn't always been no. They put the sewers in and, um, the streetlights, improvements to the street. Those were positive things. But some of the negative things were they [Kirkwood] spent more money on the park, than helping people maintain a standard of living ... and in some cases, *we* bettered *ourselves* in the community. But in other cases, when you look at how they [Kirkwood] used their own developers, their own contractors, you couldn't pick who YOU wanted ... and to change subjects, there was a time when I know they were able to steal people's property, make them move out of this area. They [the developers and Kirkwood] just promised to do a lot for you and once you let them into your home, in some cases, they would condemn it and then there goes another property. Kirkwood stated they were going to help them [homeowners] fix them, and in turn, they condemned them.

So, off the top of your head, how many families do you think that happened to?

This happened to probably about two or three families that I can think of off the top of my head [thinking]. They got some property for as little as five hundred dollars per buildable lot. It was just that I had never seen so many black people duped at the same time and think that the amount of money that they [the developers] offered them was okay . . . and a lot of people, once the contracts got signed weren't supposed to tell one another about it. That to me was just a really unfair process used by DESCO [the developers] and the Kirkwood city officials. After they got the amount of people they needed, they pushed eminent domain and the rest of us got run over. As a matter of fact, one of the lots that I owned was taken, I've had one stolen from me.

When you say stolen, what do you mean?

I consider it stolen, because I had all of the paperwork, paid all of the taxes, and it took ten thousand dollars to get it back. I was eventually compensated but I wasn't able to sue the county.

How did they [Kirkwood and developers] steal it from you?

They sold it on the courthouse steps.

How did they manage to do that? Are you talking about eminent domain?

No, this was a separate deal after eminent domain. As a matter of fact, I was never sent a letter stating that someone may be purchasing the property. This is a case that I won, but you know, they basically did everything that they could to keep me out of money, to keep me quiet and to keep me working because I was boisterous at the time and I did try to assemble people, either the Meacham Park Association or just stopping and talking to the older ones [residents] trying to let them know the value of their property, you know. After I got my property back, there was no suing [Kirkwood] for selling it.

How did they [the developers] purchase property that was already owned by you?

Exactly. They just took it. I was told to stay off my land for at least two years. The only way I found out about it was because I had a trailer parked there and one of my relatives went down there to get the trailer and a white man tried to scare him off, which could've been another bad situation. But that's how I found out about it.

But doesn't the city keep records?

Yes. Yes, they do. As a matter of fact, they knew of it and prior to me having the property, the city [Kirkwood] had me go to St. Louis County [Meacham Park's government before annexation] and they told me about all of this, the laws, and tried to scare me. This is one of the houses that was taken when the city went in and said they were going to help the family, and in return, the owner said I would rather sell it to you than to have to let it go to the city. So I purchased the property and as a matter of fact, I had another person do the tear-down [level the house on it], and Cookie did my hauling. Cookie also did the contractor's lien for the hauling and Kirkwood wrote me two nasty letters after I had it torn down. But I went to St. Louis County and paid for the asbestos test. One of the guys had gone on vacation and I had already paid for it. So when he did come back and I got the letter, I tore it [the house] down the same day and it was gone in, like, four hours. So they [Kirkwood] been kind of after me since. So you know, it's really hard to swallow the things that I've had to endure over the years. One by one, they picked them [properties] off. I was the last one to go through the eminent domain process in court. I've had to change lawyers two or three times, and at the end, I had a prominent lawyer and he was sick at the time I was due in court, the judge told me, "You've been here two or three times and you just keep prolonging this situation." He said, "You're going to go home and you're going to come back tomorrow with or without a lawyer to represent yourself."

Did the people of Meacham Park have any representation throughout the process?

There was a lawyer that a lot of people used when they wanted to buy out; they thought they were getting a good deal.

I'm assuming people had to first sign off on their properties right?

Yes, and that's another issue. I know a property right now in our family that has been taken and they built homes on it. Plus, I got a cousin . . . a developer actually hit his house with a bobcat and if it would've been us [blacks], on the opposite end of town, we would've been put in jail. But the City of Kirkwood told us that it was a civil issue, and they couldn't do anything about it. There were so many different issues.

[Interrupts.] Is this all after annexation?

This was all after annexation, after the stores had been built and they [the developers] were filling in [building] homes. I'm kind of jumping around. But you know this, it's really hard to tell the story after fifteen years and fit everybody in, but we in the community [Meacham Park] had been really treated unfairly. We went to Kirkwood about this and I went with a group of people, different ones that were in the Meacham Park Neighborhood Association. And with that group, the things that I wanted to discuss with them, the unfair treatment . . . Kirkwood only wanted to talk to me by myself. They wanted to single me out, they wanted me to come up there [Kirkwood City Hall] but I refused to go and take any underground payments or be patted on the back or have them tell me to be quiet. This is why I'm doing the interview today. I feel the truth should be told on the processes that they used. It was unfair, inhumane, and to have to live through it, to me, is like living through slavery all over again. If they [whites] don't get what they want, then we [blacks] can't get nothing. Like I said, there were so many discrepancies on how they actually moved [gained] the properties.

When asked if she supported the annexation and how she felt about the outcome, Lola, fifty-nine, answered:

> Yes and no. There were good points and then bad points. But we had pictured it was going to be so much better for the residents. More services and everything, it'd be one big happy community, but it didn't turn out that way.

The annexation and redevelopment affected the residents of Meacham Park in several ways. One, it left the remaining residents of Meacham Park angered, bitter, and at odds with each other; and two, it caused them to be even more distant and distrustful of their white, affluent Kirkwood counterparts. Not only did they blame the City of Kirkwood for the loss of property and what many perceived to be dishonest tactics to gain it, but they also blamed them for failed promises, for assurances made to the community at the onset of annexation that had yet to materialize. As a result, division and distrust became the mantra of relationships between some of the residents of Meacham Park, and even more so, between their neighborhood and the larger part of Kirkwood.

Disharmony between some of the original residents of Meacham resulted between those who settled and left the community versus those who fought and stayed, as well as between those who supported the annexation versus those who did not. Denise is a prime example: she describes feeling trapped, caught in the middle, and backed into a corner by the annexation, a plan that seemed inevitable. Here is how she explained the dissension among the remaining residents of the Meacham Park neighborhood,—the backlash, as she understood it, in the aftermath:

> When people's homes were taken, they took advantage of moving out rather than staying and trying to help change the whole situation. So people whose homes weren't affected were up in arms because they saw the breakdown of their community and with Kirkwood also saying, "It's gonna improve, it's gonna improve." People may not have really believed them [Kirkwood] because Kirkwood had not been a trusted friend to Meacham Park and so it was white folks against the black folks. White folks had money, power, and the plan to destroy Meacham Park and black folks that weren't apart of the process saw those of us that were part of the process as sellouts. "You're working with them, you're trying to destroy our neighborhood." But we [blacks] needed to have a voice in the plans that were taking place, so there could

be compromises to the plans. There were lots of things that if we [blacks involved] had just sat back and let unfold, the whole community would have been gone.

Denise's statement is very telling. It clearly illustrates blacks' distrust of whites, particularly as she, an ardent supporter of the annexation, worked from the inside in an attempt to minimize what she thought could result in a total loss for the community. Interestingly, Denise's situation also highlights an all-too-common quandary faced by blacks. Historically, blacks have found themselves torn and divided on a broad range of social issues, while advocating for one another in ways that often proved problematic for each other. It is in such predicaments that activism presents an impasse: the idea of feeling forced to do something without knowing what, and the notion of having to choose sides, voluntarily or involuntarily, while not knowing if a greater difference will be made working from the inside or from the outside. Inside is where the opponents' moves can be observed and perhaps influenced; outside is where the opposition can be aggressive, unpredictable, and inevitably uncomfortable.

Like Denise, Mark also talked about a divide, an "A" and "B" divide among the blacks in Meacham Park created by commercial developers:

Meacham Park used to be a community where we knew each other and everybody stuck together, basically hung out and had fun. You know I used to own a lot out here to where, once the project started, they called it the A area. They separated it back then and there was the A area and the B area. What that means is when the project started, OPUS [the first developers] came in and they did their studies on who and what, and they made a map of the areas that they wanted to purchase. The A area meant that the people in that area were going to be bought out and the B area, those were the people that may be displaced or get a government home. But they basically divided us back then, by A or B.

As Meacham Park worked to adjust to the changing climate of its newly annexed community, its relationship worsened with the larger Kirkwood. Residents were continuously assessing and working to make sense of the annexation process—what they lost versus what they gained, promises kept versus those not kept. Many participants voiced discontentment with the City of Kirkwood. For starters, they believed Kirkwood faltered on their agreement to provide the community with job opportunities. Since Kirkwood Commons now sat on what used to be two-thirds of their community—a neighborhood where many of its residents were no-income or low-income—it seemed only right that the city would pay it forward by making employment opportunities available to the people most affected. However, this is not what happened. Listen to what Marsha, fifty-nine, had to say regarding her attempt to land a job:

> They actually took half, gutted our community . . . and listen, when they had all the job listings, the possible positions to be filled or what have you, it was up here at the American Legion. And so they had all these tables, you [me] gone love this, they had all these tables on jobs and everything and I kinda looked through their [job listings] and . . . I said, "Who's in charge of this"? And they took me to the person and I said, "Well, I am a resident of Meacham and I'd like to know if there are any management positions available here," and they said no . . . and I said [*in a raised voice*], "So you mean to tell me that you've taken half of my community and the only job you're offering is janitorial, stock, and other frivolous jobs, is that what you're telling me?" And they said, "Well, no, we're bringing people from other stores because we do need people that know how to run the store that knows the chain's way." I said, "Isn't that what training is going to be about?" You said you were going to build or open this brand-new store up here and you're not having any mass training? So they looked and they said, "We only have one management position." I said, "What is it"? They said, "It's in automotive." I was the only black department manager in October 2000 when they opened that store. The only one and they said, "You mean to tell me you gone take it?" and I said, "Uh huh [yes]." [*Laughs.*] Then they sent me all the way to Festus for six weeks to train. Yes, ma'am, that in fact happened because I was just irritated and kind of raised my voice a little and I said, "You mean to tell me you just took half of my community and there's not one management position available . . . So are you saying there's no one qualified to run a department or anything like that?" I said, "Is that what you're saying to me?" I can just go on and on cause it's deep.

Marsha was fortunate. She managed to get a job that was not posted, leading her to believe that stores had reserved the better jobs for nonresidents and left only menial jobs, if any, for the Meacham Park residents. Her persistence as well as previous work experience paid off. She landed a management position, while others in Meacham Park remained underemployed or unemployed as the new shopping plaza hired hundreds within feet from the rejected applicants' homes.

Like Marsha, many participants felt insulted by the employment process. The manner in which they were treated made them feel demeaned, as if they were less than, different, underserving. All the while, the City of Kirkwood insisted—verbally, at least—otherwise. However, for the residents of Meacham, actions spoke louder than words. In fact, such acts—which happened one after another—are what they came to believe were symptomatic of Kirkwood's lack of consideration for them.

Along with concerns about employment opportunities, there were other areas where participants believed Kirkwood failed to make good on things most important to them. Take Jasmine, forty-two, for instance, who expressed frustration over the lack of accommodations for neighborhood youth:

> Turner School [for example], they said they were going to have a recreational center for the kids to go to, but the kids just still hang around on the corners.

Jasmine's concern has far-reaching implications. The absence of a recreational center or structured programs for the youth in this neighborhood has proven detrimental. In fact, it has often been with youth, aimlessly wandering around, that many tense police-citizen exchanges emerged in Meacham Park. Consequently, having a place where teens can go similarly to teens in the other parts of Kirkwood could have gone a long way with improving community interactions inside and outside of Meacham Park. After all, as we see in chapter 4, Kevin Johnson, a Meacham Park teen, is now (as of 2014) awaiting execution for the murder of a Kirkwood police sergeant.

As participants expressed frustration with what they believed to be Kirkwood's failure to keep promises, they discussed Kirkwood as mishandling the finances involved. For example, along with her horrible employment experience, Marsha also complained about contractors hired by the City of Kirkwood who provided shoddy home improvements to the residents in Meacham. She stated:

> We ended up with shoddy work and shoddy contractors, underbidding and half-ass doing the job and what have you. So we [she and other residents] fought a lot for the people with that and when they [the contractors and their work] flooded our house, we [she and husband] were beyond angry. But I said, "You know what, we are the right ones for this to happen to cause they know we're not going to go away and we gone carry the rest of them [other residents] on our back." And so I went to City Hall and I showed them pictures. Pictures don't lie because people had been complaining about the shoddy work and the misappropriation of funds, you know, how they put railings out there [in front of her house] and then they [City of Kirkwood] turned around and less than two years later and said the railings weren't high

enough. So you're tearing down two thousand dollars worth of railings to put another three thousand dollars worth of railings? Then it went from three feet high to five feet high. You know what I'm saying? Just shoddy, just shoddy workmanship.

Tiffany, thirty-six, also irritated by what she believed to be a constant waste of money, described several instances where she equated Kirkwood's disservice to the neighborhood with a misuse of funds:

Right up the street from my house, I'm not exactly sure how much, but they built a concrete wall. For about two blocks, it was just a big ol' long concrete wall and they spent all that money putting it up. Well, they didn't like the kids sitting on it, and because they didn't want the kids to be sitting on it, they paid to tear it down. Well, a lot of the homeowners were saying that it was TIF [tax-increment financing] money and that they were supposed to use that money to put back into the community toward other things, but it was like they used the money on stupid stuff. Why would you put a wall up? I don't think it was even a month or two when they tore the wall back down. It wasn't even up that long and now the kids still stand up there on the corner. Now they're sitting on the grass or the lil' hill part. But it's kind of, like, what was the point? Plus, before they [Kirkwood] took over, we had four parks in this community and now we only have one park that they spent so much money on. But they made it to where it's just for people with young kids and there's not that many people out here with young kids to go to the park. So the park has been turned into [become] teenagers just sitting there [see fig. 13].

Likewise, Dorothy, fifty-seven, took exception to Kirkwood's mishandling of funds:

Kirkwood, this shopping center, they've been doing very well from day one They're making money hand over fists up there, but I felt like job programs and job training should've been implemented cause we asked. We asked that Turner School be turned into a community center for this area because the need was so dire, you know what I'm saying . . . and health, they closed down the health center. I felt they should've taken all this into consideration, but instead they just wanted to displace people.

Interestingly, Turner School, the place repeatedly proposed for a recreational center and the only remaining black landmark in the neighborhood, has been mostly inaccessible to the community. There were a few Meacham Park Neighborhood Improvement Association meetings held there, but the once "black-only" school functions solely as an office building, housing multiple white businesses that serve no benefit to the neighborhood. Here's what Travis, forty-five, had to say about this following a neighborhood meeting:

> I just really detest and hate racism, and I see it, hear it, and feel it all the time, like here in this building [Turner School]. You have all different facades of companies here in the building and of all the companies in the building, no one has hired African-Americans. And you have over [*counting offices in the building*] ... one, two, three, four, five ... You have over ten owners in the building that have their own businesses and none of them employ African-Americans, not a one and you have Meacham Park with all African-Americans, but yet and still, none of them are employed in this building. Figure that one out!

As Dorothy extended her concerns to employment issues and the loss of the neighborhood health center, like other residents, she too was bothered by the fact that teenagers in their neighborhoods had nothing to do. Rather than making Turner School a recreational center for youth, which would have been consistent with its legacy and the requests of the local residents, it is reserved for businesses, which happen to be white. The only remnant of the school's history is the glass display case of graduates' pictures on the main floor (see fig. 14).

Residents venting about a broad range of problems called attention to the larger issue: a persisting disjuncture between what the residents of Meacham Park needed versus what the City of Kirkwood provided them. This is the temperament of their relationship, and more broadly, the nature of colonialism whereby the dominant territory takes ownership of a subordinate territory and deciphers what it thinks is best for its inhabitants. The nature of the relationship suggests that the oppressed group was discovered uncivilized, inept, and unable to know what is good for them or to express it intelligibly.

These are the power dynamics of Meacham Park and Kirkwood; there is an intense rift between the two areas. Participants constantly expressed distaste with Kirkwood acting as if it knew what was best for them, and thus, erroneously making decisions on behalf of them that generally worked to their disadvantage while simultaneously working to the larger Kirkwood's advantage. What many of the participants took issue with is the fact that Kirkwood promised to funnel tax money accrued from Kirkwood Commons back into improving their neighborhood. But rather than doing so, Kirkwood mismanaged what were technically "Meacham Park" funds, in some ways exacerbating their situation rather than improving it. In either case, one

FIGURE 13. This park is located in the heart of Meacham Park and has been one of many sources of conflict between the community and local government, ranging from overspending on its construction to teens hanging out there, leading to negative interactions with officers. Photo by author.

FIGURE 14. A display case on the main floor of the James Milton Turner School, filled with class pictures of black children, is a lasting reminder of the school's historic significance. Though now filled with white-owned businesses, the school is often the meeting place for the Meacham Park Neighorhood Improvement Association. Photo by author.

thing is for sure: the residents of Meacham Park wanted improvements for their community and though they got them, they tended to be minimal, sporadic, and unreliable. As Dorothy put it:

> Well, I just wish it could've been different, you know. I just wish that the African-American community [Meacham Park] of this City of Kirkwood had been embraced and respected and assisted in the improvement of their lives and their well-being rather than being used, mistreated and disregarded. It could've been a great thing because when the people in Meacham Park annexed, voted to have this area annexed, it was never their [the residents]

intent to be manipulated into a situation where they would not gain and Kirkwood would, at their expense.

"All These Rules"

> The City of Kirkwood can never be safe, healthy, or economically strong as long as the conditions in Meacham Park are allowed to exist.... Potential criminals, raised in an atmosphere devoid of police protection, are not respecters of municipal boundary lines.... Incidents of civil disorders which have emanated from similar deprived areas in other communities stimulate our concern.... Because Meacham Park is in the R-7 School District, the general high standards of our educational system are threatened because of a relatively large group of children coming from a deprived area.[14]

While the Meacham Park vote for annexation was won mostly in search of community improvement, the white, affluent Kirkwood vote was achieved through fear, that is, the notion that "by saving them (Meacham Park), we save ourselves (Kirkwood) from them." In this sense, "saving them" is really synonymous to "controlling them." It is about taking command and implementing rule in ways that will lessen the threat of a nearby disadvantaged, black population. Hence, the City of Kirkwood—the white, affluent portion referred to by the participants as "Kirkwood Proper"—tightened its reign on Meacham Park in the following ways: one, it was no longer a community with multiple entrances/exits, but rather a one-way-in, one-way-out neighborhood; two, there were strict new ordinances; and three, there was an increased presence of a now different police department to regulate and enforce the first two.

The community of Meacham had changed. As Herb Jones, the former mayor of Kirkwood put it, "That was a city ghetto sitting in a suburban community. Now it looks like a normal neighborhood."[15] However, amid progress with its community development, other things remained the same or worsened. Dorothy stated:

> They did do some things, you know. They gave out some grants and they built some homes that were supposed to be affordable for some of the people who could qualify for a loan and they made a lot of improvements as far as the infrastructure and the cosmetic appearance, you know curbside appeal but I still don't feel like I'm a welcomed citizen in Kirkwood, I really don't and that's just my opinion, how I feel personally. I never shop in Kirkwood.

When I go out to eat, I don't go to Kirkwood, you know what I'm saying? I do go to some of the stores in the shopping mall up here, that's because it's so close. But as far as Kirkwood, the downtown Kirkwood, I never go up there.

Like others, Dorothy acknowledged improvements with the neighborhood's infrastructure, but she also emphasizes the persisting suburban divide, since Kirkwood had not done enough to mend what many perceived as manipulative and discriminative treatment down through the years.

Well it goes way back, you know, when I was a kid. I remember my dad and I taking my grandmother to the grocery store in Kirkwood. It was called A & P then and this is just one incident among several others but we were just grocery shopping, and I remember this [white] lady just looking at us like were trash or like we were animals and it just left a scare, it really did. I just never felt like Kirkwood was a place I wanted to be. So this is another incident that stands out in my mind. After I had gotten married and started a family, I just remember going in some of the smaller shops [downtown Kirkwood] and I was treated the same way as when I was a kid, like, "Why are you here, what do you want, this really isn't for you," you know what I'm saying? and it left a bitter taste in my mouth and until this day, when I go shopping or I have to go to a store or whatever to do business, I do not go to Kirkwood.

The annexation did not erase the racialized experiences that Meacham Park blacks faced with some Kirkwood whites. Through the actions of some white residents, and at times, even their words, they perceived whites as thinking, "You're nothing but trash over here" (Kim, sixty-two). Much of what Kirkwood did or did not do in the best interest of the neighborhood in the years prior to and immediately following the annexation did not work to the betterment of the racial divide but instead made it more transparent. So, most still refer to the black and white sections of the suburb as if they are still separate; the poor black neighborhood is "Meacham Park" and the rich affluent white portion is Kirkwood or "Kirkwood Proper."

As many things remained the same, Meacham Park continued to be a neighborhood plagued by low educational attainment and high rates of unemployment. Neighborhood improvements were not enough to make it characteristic of Kirkwood Proper. It was still different, racially and economically, and residents were constantly reminded of this by the actions of their new local government.

Prior to annexation, numerous streets led in and out of Meacham Park. However, after annexation, those streets had been reduced to one. Some default to a driveway that cuts across the back parking lot of Kirkwood Commons to get out, taking them from behind the stores to the front— where they have to drive the duration of the shopping center's parking lot before reaching actual streets. Otherwise, this neighborhood had been officially cut off and separated from everyone outside of it. Here is what Francis had to say.

> There's only one in and one way out. To go up and out, underneath, to exit this community by way of the shopping mall is really not an acceptable exit and at any given time, it can no longer be accessible to the community because Kirkwood Common owns it [the driveway–parking lot]. We should have a legal entrance and exit and more than one and we asked that that be included but the city said no.

With the back of Kirkwood Commons on one side, Interstate 44 on another, and a gated apartment complex on a third side, Meacham Park had become noticeably boxed in (fig. 15). This had become a hot issue, causing some residents to theorize about why their local government had made such a bold move. As Pete put it:

> Now there's a built-in piece that happened in Meacham Park as far as police . . . but it's an urban design piece. I'm familiar with it and I have to tolerate it . . . it really cut us off and then you bind us in with one-way-in, one-way-out kind of thing. But that's being done all over, in urban communities and it's really to keep the bad guys from trying to get away.

Given that no other neighborhood was enclosed as such in the City of Kirkwood, the fact that the black neighborhood was once again contradicted Kirkwood Proper's declaration of inclusion. Meacham Park's isolation from the remainder of the suburb became so apparent that participants in this study perceived the new infrastructure to be nothing more than a strategic move to restrict their movement. Pete, for instance, compares the design of his community to "urban design" in the City of St. Louis, where flowerpot barricades are used to direct traffic. Such barriers are placed at the ends of streets, preventing through-traffic in an effort to reduce crime, as well as to increase awareness and vigilance.[16] But even this tactic has proven controversial, as residents complain about the streets' inaccessibility to them and to emergency vehicles which need to reach segments of their blocks.[17] Interestingly, while officials in Kirkwood Proper are well aware of the residents' feelings, the residents of Meacham Park continue to live boxed in, for

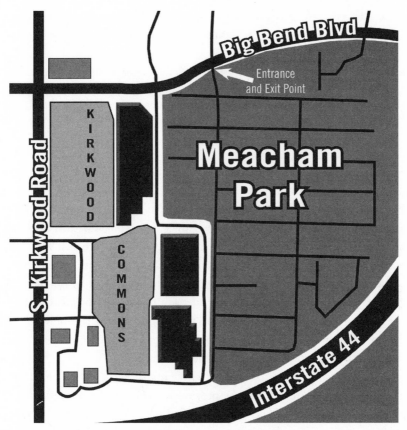

FIGURE 15. This line map displays Meacham Park following the 1991 annexation. It is a boxed-in community, with Kirkwood Commons and parking lots to its west, Interstate 44 to its south, and Kirkwood Proper to its north—where people enter or exit Meacham Park, while simultaneously entering or exiting the larger part of Kirkwood. Photo courtesy of Lennon Mueller, graphic artist at Lindenwood University—Belleville.

better policing of "undesirables" entering and leaving their neighborhood. Again, this is a very distinct model for the City of Kirkwood, particularly since no other neighborhood in the suburb can be found with similar arrangements. The black neighborhood becomes the exception.

As Kirkwood Proper strengthened its control, policing the community of Meacham to enforce new ordinances and codes became a priority. This means that residents were now subjected to "new rules," restrictions they did not have when they were unincorporated. New ordinances and the consequences for not following them did not always make for great transitioning.

Rather, this became another dot to connect in a long list of acts that did not mesh well with some residents in Meacham. Rodney, fifty-five, stated:

> They [Kirkwood] are trying to *really* take over . . . you got all these rules . . . back then [pre-annexation] there weren't too many rules and you had more old folks out here. Now it's flipped, you got more young folks out here . . . plus, before that mall was here, it was like everybody was happy . . . Now everybody tense.

Meacham Park had traditionally been under the jurisdiction of the St. Louis County Police Department or what many St. Louisans refer to as "County Brown"—so named because, one, they policed unincorporated suburban areas or places unable to finance their own department within St. Louis County, and, two, their officers wore distinctly brown uniforms. They were now transitioning into a suburban neighborhood with its own policing agency, and therefore, the annexation not only situated them under a new government, but it also placed them under a different policing jurisdiction—the Kirkwood Police Department. This meant that the residents of Meacham Park needed to become acclimated to a different kind of enforcement, along with adhering to a new government and ordinances.

Unlike the single entrance/exit of the neighborhood, the city's ordinances applied to the entire suburb. As previously explained, some residents of Meacham Park accepted and readily adopted them, while others in the community did not. Since some were extremely distrusting of Kirkwood Proper, they believed the city and the police applied and enforced the ordinances inconsistently. For example, some residents complained about youth being ticketed for walking in the street. Tiffany explained:

> They were a couple of our kids that got tickets for walking in the street. We never had sidewalks around here until they annexed, so a lot of people, especially the older people, never walked on sidewalks. So that took a minute to adjust to but officers were giving people tickets for walking in the street, not just warnings, but they were giving them tickets.
>
> *So did the police say what the charge was or the reason?*
> I think it was loitering. I don't know and I was trying to tell some of the kids and they just didn't understand and then I had to explain to them that there are laws that are really stupid that people don't know nothing about like jay-walking, stuff like that. So it would seem like laws that the police [in general] would never enforce was the ones that they would out here [in Meacham Park] in order to mess with people.

Interestingly, the residents of Meacham Park desired better policing for their neighborhood. Some participants expressed dissatisfaction with County Brown and believed they would be better served if they were under the jurisdiction of the Kirkwood Police Department. After all, Meacham Park did have its share of crime. Like other communities, particularly those characterized by disadvantage and isolation, there were periodic incidents that often left residents fearful and concerned about safety. Therefore, desiring improved police services was one of the most salient factors in winning the vote to annex. Here, Marsha describes a break-in in the neighborhood just days before the vote:

> Eighty-one percent of the homeowners were at least seventy-six years old, with the maximum of seventh-grade education, and they wanted the annexation with the promise of police protection. I, as a matter of fact, stood right down here in this church on this corner [*pointing*] and said, "We do not have to sell our land, we do not have to sell out in order to get police protection." Now, I have a theory because Ms. Smith, ninety-six years old, okay ... this man broke into Ms. Smith's house on Friday, the vote for the annexation was on Monday. Now, I cannot prove my theory but I will go to my grave saying it was just a little bit too coincidental for me, okay, and not only that, the police, the County [County Brown], arrested a guy. The neighbor across the street looked out his window and saw this man breaking into Ms. Smith's side door and when the guy turned to come out of there, he [the burglar] come out to the barrel of a double barrel shot gun. The neighbor, who I know his name, held the man there [at gun point] until the police got there and they arrested the neighbor and not the man. Now that is my personal opinion.

Marsha has a theory for what she believed secured the Meacham Park vote of approval. She wasn't alone. City Councilman Scheidegger was quoted in the newspaper as stating: "There are many people in Kirkwood who don't understand what's involved, and they're against it until they find out what it would do for both parties. It would help with the crime problem; it would help with housing standards and code; it would help with sales taxes. It would be a good thing for everybody."[18] The notion of crime, potentially left unaddressed, is a common tactic used to elicit political support for seemingly unpopular issues. It would not be strange if a break-in occurring days before the vote swayed or guaranteed the vote of a vulnerable Meacham Park, especially as many residents were aged and defenseless. Consider what Ricky, fifty-six, said:

> Ninety to ninety-five percent of Meacham voted for that annexation because they wanted better police protection. I don't remember the name of the lady,

but it was a lady in this community that had been raped and that was part of the reasoning for how this annexation started, how it came about in the first place.

Despite differing details, it is likely that this may be the same incident that Marsha spoke about. What is certain is that something happened and word spread throughout the neighborhood, thus prompting concerns and warranting an increased need for better police services that would provide a more rapid response and perhaps better solutions than County Brown over the years. As Jackie, thirty-four, said:

> St. Louis County [County Brown] wasn't really doing their job. If you gave the police a call, it took hours for them to come out here or if they do come out here, it's nothing they'd really do about the problem.

Although County Brown had been identified by some participants as ineffective in policing, following annexation other participants expressed a preference for them. Post-annexation, they were situated where they could compare the two—County Brown versus Kirkwood Police Department. Nevertheless, most commonly agreed that it took County Brown longer to arrive, if needed, because of their required drive time, and consequently, they had fewer encounters with County Brown compared to Kirkwood Police Department. By contrast, Kirkwood Police Department was within closer proximity and had officers now assigned to frequently patrol their neighborhood.

In either case, two things deserve considerable attention, especially as they shape the contexts of the chapters to come. One, the residents of Meacham Park had always wanted effective police services, as evidenced by their vote to annex. So, while ideals about criminality and police contention in poor black communities often lead people to perceive blacks as inherently criminal or protectors of criminals, nothing could be further from the truth. In fact, it is quite the contrary. Crime in disadvantaged black communities involves the indiscretions of a few but is used discriminatively to stereotype and denigrate many. Hence, poor black communities are not heavily populated with offenders, but rather with nonoffenders who fall prey to them. Consequently, like whites, they too want police protection and to feel safe in their neighborhoods. Their often negative attitudes toward the police have nothing to do with whether they *want* to be policed, but everything to do with *how* they are policed.

This takes me to the second point. The residents of Meacham Park wanted a particular kind of policing: fair and impartial law enforcement that would judiciously address neighborhood crime and issues regarding public safety. Unfortunately, like other things they blindly bargained for in the annexation, they did not fully realize the riders that attach to changing police agencies. Most of all, they wanted to be safe, and for some, that trumped the fact that Kirkwood police had always been known to harass residents of Meacham Park. After all, the only time they encountered each other was once residents crossed out of Meacham Park into Kirkwood Proper. Otherwise, contact was minimal, especially as Kirkwood police could not enter the community prior to annexation. It was outside of their jurisdiction. However, what some residents did not consider was the magnitude at which police would enforce its new regulations and ordinances; they also did not account for perceived threat among both the criminal and noncriminal residents of Meacham Park.

The residents were still trying to come to grips with the loss of their community. During most interviews, no matter the topic, participants regularly compared their pre- and post-annexation experiences. This time was no different. I could not help but think about senior citizens who find themselves in situations where they have to relinquish their independence to their children. Nothing could be worse than being someone who had always managed his or her own affairs, now suddenly having to hand this independence over to another. In such cases, they often lessen their grip a little bit at a time, especially as some things are easier to turn over than others. However, this negotiation rarely happens without a fight or some form of defiance. It is not because the person finds solace in rebellion, but rather because in that place he or she takes what might be a last stance. Such people use insolence to make it known that they are not easy kills; they demand respect while making clear that they are not so weakened until they are moved by someone's new sense of authority or need to exert it. For these reasons, we should understand the difficulty some residents of Meacham were experiencing with complying or answering to a new local government, especially one that had established an unreliable track record.

CONCLUSION

Escalating tensions between the residents of Meacham Park and City Hall had the issue of policing at their core. What began as a hope for improved crime control and police protection in a socioeconomically depressed community, for many Meacham Park residents, turned into years of unwelcomed interactions with their local law enforcement. Where policing efforts should have empowered residents—making them feel safe in their neighborhood— they in fact made them more vulnerable: more susceptible to neighborhood crime, to police suspicion, or to both, regardless of criminality.

This is the nature of race, place, and policing. It is a socially constructed intersection, where the lines of fairness become skewed based on stereotypical ideas of race and place. Consequently, some citizens are automatically afforded courtesy and sensitivity by their local police, while others are not. In the case of Meacham Park, many residents experienced the latter.

The next chapter presents the everyday experiences of Meacham Park residents with local law enforcement. In these encounters we witness persistent differential treatment—historically and structurally. I argue that this differential treatment is the most salient reason for how and why blacks, especially poor blacks, come to have tense interactions with the police, and inevitably negative perceptions of them.

THREE

There's a New Sheriff in Town

THE POLICE MAKING CONTACT

You have to understand the tenor of the times. There were riots over police brutality in America's major cities and assassinations of civil rights leaders like Martin Luther King. I went to Meacham Park over a period of years to speak about our concerns, and I will admit that on occasions I was scared. Emotions ran high . . . I saw anger and fire in the eyes of some of the young people there when I talked about police protection. They shouted back incidents of harassment and some of their concerns were justified. At one heated meeting some kid set a cherry bomb off and I thought I was a goner.

ROBERT G. REIM, FORMER MAYOR OF KIRKWOOD[1]

BLACK CITIZEN–POLICE RELATIONSHIPS OFTEN prove tumultuous nationwide. Though at different junctures, such exchanges do not occur in isolation of one another; instead, they are symptomatic of broader crises. Former Mayor Reim said it best: "You have to understand the tenor of the times."[2] In other words, we must first consider the existing conditions from which black citizen–police relationships emerge. It is in this context that we must situate the policing experiences of black citizens in Meacham Park. They are encounters formed out of overlapping national and local conditions marred by racial prejudices and the persistent differential treatment of blacks.

With limited education, poverty, several land grabs, a loss of communal identity, and segregation and isolation as a backdrop, crime and structural detachment is virtually inescapable in communities like Meacham Park. The very nature of segregation and isolation in and of itself is reflective of a broader social reality that often benefits the dominant group. In the case of Meacham Park and Kirkwood, the dominant, most empowered citizens are the white, affluent residents of Kirkwood Proper. Decisions made by the local government have often benefited them while hurting or obstructing progress for the poor black residents of Meacham Park. Former Mayor Reims described this relationship and its effects as follows, calling attention to the role of local structures and institutional practices that not only gave way to Meacham Park's demise but solidified it and then used it as justification to maintain separation from it:

> The City of Kirkwood has been equally guilty with the surrounding cities and St. Louis County in creating a ghetto-like effect in existence in Meacham Park through neglect, discrimination, and annexation over the years which have included valuable commercial and industrial areas, but which avoided the Meacham Park area.[3]

Meacham Park community leader William (Bill) Jones reiterated this role of local structures in his community's demise. He cited a study wherein student Edmund Bailey examined the relationship of the two communities:

> The press is playing up Kirkwood as the "great white father" who, at the last minute, is stepping in to snatch Meacham from the jaws of a horrible fate. The truth is, as is readily admitted by Kirkwood leaders . . . Kirkwood must share the blame, with other communities surrounding Meacham, for the [poor] conditions. . . . Early Negro settlers who desired homes in the Kirkwood area found themselves shunted to Meacham by white realtors in this area who controlled and/or owned much of Meacham.[4]

In essence, the City of Kirkwood—Meacham Park's local government—bears culpability for Meacham Park's deplorable condition. It helped create an environment conducive to social inadequacy, separation, and indifference. Under the circumstances, Meacham Park residents and others like them are least likely to be satisfied with their local governments and law enforcement agencies. In general, they perceive the police and their tactics as only representing more of the same—an agenda that works to protect the interests of the dominant at the expense of those most vulnerable. After all, the police are enforcers, and thus, they ensure adherence to the all-too-often-biased policies and practices of the local government. Indeed, officers enter police academies and departments with their own biases. Everyone has them; however, who, where, and how they play out is often determined by the institutions with which we are most associated. So, while changing to a new jurisdiction should have made the residents of Meacham Park feel safer and more inclusive, for some, it only made them more vulnerable and cognizant of *who* they were (race) and *where* they were (place): poor blacks living an intersection away from affluent whites. Consequently, stereotypical ideas about black criminality fueled concerns that crime and insolence might spill over to the white affluent community.

This chapter examines police contacts: the manner in which some Meacham Park residents encountered the police; what their interactions were with the police; and in the end, how they came to perceive the police as a result of their experiences. More specifically, the chapter will explore involuntary police contacts: what they are; the circumstances through which they occur; and the effects that they have on black citizen–police relationships. With more than two-thirds of participants reporting such encounters—unwelcomed, uninvited advancements from their local police—residents' discomfort with them became pervasive. The participants in this project described officers as intrusive and believed their actions to be the result of persisting suspicion towards them. Therefore, some of them directly referenced their encounters with the police as harassment and misconduct and then provided accounts accordingly. Others simply discussed how they felt about the police and why, also describing interactions consistent with harassment or misconduct. As we turn our attention to crime in Meacham Park. It is important to note the residents' perceptions of crime in their neighborhood—how they feel about it and manage it in relation to the perceptions of others.

CRIME IN MEACHAM: THE ORIGINALS AND THE IMPLANTS VERSUS THE PRESS AND THE POLICE

Every community has its share of improprieties, but structurally weakened neighborhoods like Meacham Park are most susceptible to them. Consistent with theories of ecology and social disorganization,[5] disadvantaged black neighborhoods disproportionately experience higher rates of unemployment, family instability, substandard resources and services, social isolation, and so forth—all the makings for crime and other desperate acts committed in survival mode. While social disorganization and ecological explanations of crime often apply to urban communities, so too do they become applicable here, given that the structural and socioeconomic characteristics that exist in Meacham Park as a suburban neighborhood are very much the same as those in the inner city. As this community experienced *concentration effects,*[6] or overwhelming social deprivation and "macro-social patterns of residential inequality," crime became inevitable in its neighborhood.[7]

Like many poor black urban communities, Meacham Park consists of two factions—its law-abiding residents and then a few troubled ones. The law-abiding residents, often referred to as the "originals," can be characterized as persons or families who own their homes, have been in the community for generations and/or are older persons, those whose everyday lives are governed by an etiquette of respect in and out of the community. They value conventional norms and the sanctity and preservation of their neighborhood, and they hold true to *old-school*, transgenerational black cultural ideas about *making it:* hunkering down and confronting with integrity often overlapping, persisting challenges relating to family, finances, community, and spirituality.

The "troubled" residents, on the other hand, or what some originals refer to as "implants," are often described as government-subsidized renters planted in Meacham Park by the Housing Authority, who have little or no regard for the neighborhood and live very *hard lives,* meaning they endure everyday hardships by relying on seemingly easy, impromptu, desperate, quick-fix street solutions that inevitably make life's circumstances even more difficult. In other words, while their ingenuity may provide immediate relief, they generally exacerbate their problems in that (1) they are temporary fixes, (2) they are unconventional, and thus, often characterized as deviant, and (3) they tend to be criminal or lend themselves to the suspicion of such.

While both groups (originals and implants) share the plight of blackness, they approach it differently. The originals blame the implants for behaving in ways that not only contribute to the demise of the neighborhood, but also further stereotypical ideas about the inability or unwillingness of blacks to abide by rules and laws, thus imposing added, unsolicited pressure on the community. As an example, Denise, sixty, explained how public housing and the behaviors of the implants increased police presence in their neighborhood:

> This area, Stonecrest was St. Louis Housing Authority projects also known to the Meacham Park residents [originals], as Chocolate City. Chocolate City was a whole community of people who were implanted here because they [the apartments] were low-income houses ... and most of the people who lived there was no-income as well as low-income. So in our community, there was a whole section of folks that weren't a part of Meacham but was a part of us because their day-to-day activities constantly kept the community with police running in. Out-of-control kids, domestic disputes, and Chocolate City fights, if the people in the city wanted to have an apartment or house

for their family and their name came up on the list, they could not choose what area they got to live in. They [housing authority] would say, "There's a house in Meacham Park that you can live in," and so we had a separation in the community, people who were here and wanted to be and people who were here that didn't. This is crazy. I think this is a very divisive kind of system.

Jackie, thirty-four, expressed similar feelings:

I feel like a lot of families, you know, [the] majority of these people were raised out here [Meacham Park]. They have been out here all their lives. But whenever public housing got their programs started and people started to move here from the city, it's like it got worse.

What Denise and Jackie described are the sentiments of the originals about having additional poor people, from the entire St. Louis metropolitan area, placed in their neighborhood. Similarly, the implants expressed dissatisfaction. Listen to what Lisa, thirty-four, had to say about her placement:

I was put in this neighborhood. I didn't choose to come to this neighborhood ... you don't get to go pick your house. They [the government] tell you your address and they give you three or four days to give them the deposit. It's HUD [Housing Urban Development]. I was put in this neighborhood, so don't treat me like I've been in this neighborhood for forty, fifty, sixty years.

In Lisa's comments and others that are similar, we find implants blaming the originals for making things worse *for them*. After all, they are new, unaware of and uninvolved with the years of feuding between Meacham Park and the City of Kirkwood. They see themselves as even more vulnerable than before relocation, particularly as they have been relegated to a place with preexisting contention and expectations imposed by the two warring factions: the originals and the local government.

These dynamics only compounded the preexisting difficulties of the community, and consequently, the originals—particularly as they are mostly owners—argued such actions were divisive and disadvantageous to their neighborhood. However, like other attempts by residents to evoke what they believed to be best for the community, their efforts had little effect. While annexation did lend itself to the demolition of the old housing project (Chocolate City) in Meacham Park, it is in the same sense that it gave way to a new one (Stonecrest). Hence, the problems of the community continued, and unfortunately the local government had no tangible solutions either. Rather, increased policing for all Meacham Park residents—old or new—

became the solvent in a place where black sensitivities were already heightened as a result of social struggle. So, irrespective of their different neighborhood statuses and approaches in dealing with hardship, it is through like encounters with the police that the originals and the implants came to be unified.

As the Kirkwood policing agenda for Meacham Park mirrors the policies and practices of its local government, officers frequently patrol the neighborhood addressing issues from teenagers loitering to drugs. Albeit, some of these problems are not much different from those in the surrounding affluent neighborhoods, except in how they are addressed and the backlash. Meacham Park residents are policed aggressively and proactively. While the neighboring white communities have crime as well, they typically manage to escape stigmatization. Contrarily, every incident experienced in the Meacham Park neighborhood is perceived by some residents as overexaggerated, as further depicting and stereotyping their neighborhood as inherently criminal. Tiffany, thirty-six, expressed frustration with local crime reporting. She not only reported previously feeling safe in her community; but apart from a few incidents, she suggested that she was often unaware of rampant crime. She stated:

> I was born and raised out here, so it's like if I went to the city, I wouldn't feel safe. I guess it's about where you were born or where you at . . . so yes, I feel safe. Kirkwood-Webster have a newspaper that they send out every week and they have a section where they list all the crime that happened in Kirkwood, Glendale, Shrewsbury, Webster—all the surrounding suburbs—and I read it every week now. I was really surprised because you see all the crime happening and you be like, "That happened over there? That happened in that part of the county?" They have more crime happening in their area [the white, affluent suburbs] than we do in ours. I think that it's just that when something happens out here [Meacham Park], they publicize it so badly that it seems like we have all the crime in our community when that's really not the case. When the police comes up to the meetings [neighborhood association meetings] every month and give the crime report and stuff, a lot of us be sitting there like, "What, *when* did that happen, *where* did that happen?" We don't have a clue [about crime here] until you read it or somebody tells you about it.

Similarly, Rodney, fifty-five, described what he perceived to be differential crime reporting and its effects on Meacham Park compared to the surrounding affluent, white communities. He explained:

> Take for instance, we get a Kirkwood-Webster Times paper every Friday. I read it every Friday. Kirkwood, Rockhill, Webster Groves, Shrewsbury,

Sunset Hills, it lists all the crimes they have. I might be exaggerating but I read that thing, four Fridays in a month, for like two months straight, and there was nothing in there about Meacham Park. All crimes occurred across Big Bend [a major street]. See Big Bend separates what we call Kirkwood and Meacham Park, so you cross over there [Kirkwood Proper and the surrounding areas], you got break-ins, you got kidnappings and folks molesting people [e.g., Sean Hornbeck], folks getting busted with meth but you don't hear all that. But as soon as something happens, an incident out here [Meacham Park], it's all wrote up in the paper—this, that, and the other. That's just the way they do things.

Tiffany and Rodney are aggravated by how Meacham Park is portrayed, and their comments call attention to several issues: one, the differential ways in which crimes are reported for their community versus the white; and two, how such information distorts the public's perceptions of what is real versus not.

Tiffany and Rodney downplayed crime in their neighborhood. While they communicated some awareness of problems, they were mostly puzzled and resistant to suggestions that their neighborhood was crime-ridden. Likewise, 90 percent of this study's participants thought Meacham Park was safe, and therefore believed periodic incidents to be insignificant. Like the police, they too mostly thought about neighborhood crime in relation to place; that is, they compared their knowledge of crime in their community to that of others, local, urban, and national. Locally, over half of the participants believed that they experienced less crime than the surrounding affluent, white communities, less crime than the inner city, and an average amount of crime nationally. In fact, when asked to name a crime problem in the neighborhood of Meacham Park, Kim, sixty-two, answered, "I guess drugs, but then you go two blocks down from the White House and you got the same problem there."

Context matters. It makes a significant difference in how we see the world, as well as our place in it. Furthermore, it is the psychological space wherein we situate a totality of experiences and then rely on them to make sense of our environment, as well as our social expectations and everyday interactions within it. Context mattered in Kim's admission to drugs being in the neighborhood of Meacham Park; it was a cautious admission, so as not to defame her community. Instead, she normalized it. She put neighborhood crime in perspective, and indirectly called for me to do the same—to recognize it as a broader social problem rather than a *poor, black, Meacham Park* one. Likewise, Tiffany and Rodney also acknowledged and contextualized their neighborhood crime problem. As a result, they were able to manage their responses in less disparaging ways. Unlike the media, some of their affluent, white counterparts, and police, they relied on the power of place—the whole of society—to lessen the stigma of race. They believed others deferred to biases about blackness and criminality to polarize place, and consequently, treat it and them as its inhabitants accordingly.

Crime of Place or Race of Place?

Difference of place leads to differential, racialized policing; it results in an interactively circular policing approach. In other words, race and place are inseparable; their effects are intertwined. Therefore, policing one (i.e., place) means inevitably policing the other (i.e., race) or vice versa, especially in racially segregated neighborhoods. So even when policing is shaped by crime mapping or the frequency of crimes in particular places, as in hotspot policing or stop-question-frisk policing, it is not independent of race. Rather, such practices bear racial undertones in that their intent and the effects thereof, advantageous or disadvantageous, are felt by the race (people) of a place, irrespective of criminality. Likewise, in situations where policing appears to be shaped by race, as in racial profiling, such approaches are predisposed to place.

Amid the above-described social interchanges policing reaches an impasse—crime drives police to pay attention to certain locations and increases their "racialization of place." So, in the case of thirty-year-old Haitian Abner Louima, was it "crime of place" or "race of place" that led to his brutal beating and sexual assault while in NYPD custody?[8] Officers were responding to a brawl when they initially came into contact with Louima. Interestingly, this was an altercation that occurred outside of Club Rendez-vous, a nightclub popular among members of New York's Haitian community. Hence, it could be reasonably concluded that both—the knowledge of crime that led officers to the scene, as well as the race of the patrons at the scene—spurred unprecedented aggression by NYPD officers. With claims of officers hurling racial epithets, nothing wreaked of racial denigration more than Louima being repeatedly beaten and sodomized with a broom handle in the restroom of a police station.

As four white officers faced a slew of charges, resulting in two convictions (Justin Volpe and Charles Schwarz) and two overturned convictions (Michael Collins and Thomas Bruder), what is important to note is the nature in which these officers policed Louima.[9] The reason they were called to the scene was lost as a result of violating his civil rights.[10] The most salient of messages became not one of maintaining law and order or fighting crime, but the frequency and comfortableness with which respect and human decency for people of color are compromised by officers through everyday interactions. Efforts to decrease crime and victimization, particularly in vulnerable communities, become indistinguishable when the trade-off is police aggression arbitrarily applied. Entire communities face criminal indictment—aside from criminality—and consequently, become predisposed to maltreatment from their local law enforcement officers. At the crux of this social and political gridlock, some residents of Meacham Park perceivably succumb to undue police suspicion, leading to adverse interactions with and negative attitudes toward them.

Police Suspicion: Hunches or Bias?

> Because some of these boys have dreads, they're sagging, they're young, smoking cigarettes. They (police) stereotype them, instead of letting them do wrong first before they judge them. In Kirkwood (Kirkwood Proper), they (police) trust their residents more. But they think we always into something, so they spend more time out here (in Meacham Park). It's like they're just waiting on us to do something.
>
> PAM, TWENTY-ONE

What Pam described is how easily she believes black citizens, particularly young men, come to be targeted by police suspicion in Meacham Park, and consequently, are policed differently. Similar to Trayvon Martin's hoodie, clothing and other extralegal characteristics such as hair styles, sagging pants and so forth are often associated with deviance. As such characteristics multiply, so does police suspicion. They are unconventional visuals, and the more there are, the greater the social distance appears to be between those persons and the dominant society. In short, appearance becomes a kaleidoscope of social irregularities. It is under those circumstances that preexisting racial and spatial stereotypes become exacerbated, thus, giving way to unfavorable black citizen–police encounters.

Seventy-three percent of the participants in this study believed the police to have been suspicious of them on at least one occasion (table 1). As a result, they found themselves surveilled, stopped, questioned, frisked, or arrested by Kirkwood police. More specifically, twenty-two (twelve men, ten women) out of thirty participants were scrutinized by the police for reasons ranging from loitering to suspicion by association. Appearance and location gave way to police scrutiny: that is, the idea that someone "looks suspicious." Travis, forty-five, described an incident in another predominantly white suburb—an even more affluent community than Kirkwood—where a culmination of visuals made him vulnerable:

> I was stopped in front of a friend's house actually while in Chesterfield [Missouri]. I was sitting in front of his house, waiting on him to pull up when the police pulled up and we got into it pretty good.
>
> *So what did the officer say when he pulled up?*
> "What are you doing?" And I asked him, "What are you doing?" We both laughed. He just proceeded, he questioned me and I questioned him, you know. He said "Well, um, you look suspicious." I told him, "You look suspicious too." So we went at it. By the time we finished doing that, my buddy pulled up and he [the police officer] just called me a smart ass and went on his way.

While Travis's encounter with the police occurred in another suburb, it is still relevant. It is an example of how *misplaced* race—black faces in white places—along with other visuals can easily give way to presumptions of deviance. Police suspicion is subjective, and even when well intended, can lend itself to invasive, uncomfortable exchanges between blacks and the police. Interestingly, in discussing the young men in his Meacham Park neighborhood, Travis also based his perceptions of people on appearance and social location. He explained:

> If you're a twenty-year-old, educated kid, you're not subject to wearing your pants low . . . you won't try to fit in with the homies in the hood or the criteria of being cool with sagging pants. If you're eighteen to twenty-five and you're not so informed and educated, then you'll fall into that "I can sag and look like a knuckle head, so what" category.

Travis is careful to not criminalize the young people in his community. His initial perception hinged on youthful folly. He suspected them of nothing more than trying to be cool and failing to understand the ramifications of doing so.

Similarly, Dwayne, fifty-four, also addressed the appearance of young men in his community. He directly linked appearance to police suspicion:

> You draw attention to yourself with your pants hanging down off your ass, mouth full of gold teeth, dreadlocks, tattoos . . . the only people that's going to be interested in you are maybe these little girls and the police.

TABLE I Involuntary Police Contacts: Perception of Suspicion

	No. (N=30)	%
Believed the police to be suspicious of them, on at least one occasion, resulting in uninvited contacts	22	73
Did not believe the police to be suspicious of them, resulting in *no* uninvited contacts	8	27

Dwayne's comment is from a series of conversations he has had with the young men in his neighborhood. Like Travis, Dwayne perceives them to be ignorant, and he reported frustratingly talking with them occasionally about not doing things to solicit police attention. He wants to inform them, to help them avoid police scrutiny. After all, he too has perceivably come to be suspected by the police, and similarly to Travis, recognizes the vulnerabilities of black men in relation to the criminal justice system.

There is much to be said regarding police suspicion—hunches, biases, or where the two may become skewed or conflated. On the one hand, hunches could turn up "hits" or actual crimes/criminals, benefiting citizens and justifying proactive aggressive policing. On the other hand, biases or hunches skewed or conflated by officers' prejudices can make criminal conjectures unavoidable for all, especially blacks.[11] Case in point: if Travis and Dwayne—both well-respected men in their community—are not exempt from police suspicion, where then does that leave those who are not as well respected? In Tiffany's opinion, it leaves them misread and presumed deviant.

> A lot of these boys that just be standing around are the sweetest boys IF you knew them personally . . . they have never ever been in trouble. They just don't have anything to do. So basically, they're just standing around out there [outside] talking. But in the police's eyes, it's like they're trying to stir up trouble.

Interestingly, a few participants—two women and three men—attributed officers' continued suspicion of them to their knowledge of past criminal activity. They believed the police to be suspicious of them even when they were staying out of trouble. Consequently, this group had the most frequent contacts and the most extensive interactions with the police, ranging from being stopped and questioned to being subjected to force. Participants' troubled pasts ranged from pedestrian and vehicular stops to police kicking in their doors during drug raids.

TABLE 2 Involuntary Police Contacts: Harassment and Misconduct

	No. (N=22)*	%
Reported what they perceived to be a form of police harassment, on at least one occasion	15	68
Reported what they perceived to be a form of police harassment, escalating to misconduct	7	32

* Twenty-two out of thirty respondents that reported involuntary police contact.

TABLE 3 Involuntary Police Contacts: Perception of Harassment

	No. (N=22)	%
Reported what they perceived to be a form of police harassment, on at least one occasion—with a criminal past	5	23
Reported what they perceived to be a form of police harassment, on at least one occasion—without a criminal past	17	77

Seventeen of the twenty-two participants had no previous history with the police. Yet, in some ways, they experienced treatment similar to those who did. They too experienced direct police contact, though mostly through pedestrian and vehicular stops. Those stops were then followed up by questions, reinforcing participants' perceptions that officers thought most of them to be criminal, particularly since they were black, disadvantaged, and lived in Meacham Park. Theorists refer to this as "unilateral suspicion," suspicion of citizens regardless of their criminal histories.[12] Black men in the community were likeliest to come under unilateral suspicion, which then precipitated involuntary police–black citizen contacts. Such involuntary police contacts are often experienced as harassment and misconduct (see tables 2 and 3).

INVOLUNTARY POLICE CONTACTS: HARASSMENT AND MISCONDUCT

Involuntary contact is imposed police contact for legal or extralegal reasons. Legal reasons may be malfunctioning headlights or taillights, speeding, and so forth. Police encounters occurring as a result of an actual problem is consistent with *crime of place*. Extralegal factors, similar to *race of place*, are contacts influenced by characteristics such as gender, race, ethnicity, place, and other personal effects such as hair styles, clothing, and tattoos. In such cases, the motivation for contact often stems from suspicion based on stereotypes or particular persons being in certain places. Under both circumstances, legal or extralegal, citizens may be stopped, questioned, frisked, or arrested by the police.

Since black citizens experience police contacts at a greater frequency than whites, they are more likely to question procedural justice, meaning blacks are likelier to believe they were contacted by police for illegitimate reasons.[13] Subsequently, they are likelier to leave such encounters with negative impressions of the police, labeling their actions as harassment and misconduct.[14]

While all participants had some experience with their local police, again 73 percent of them (twenty-two out of thirty) reported it was involuntary or uninvited. Men were likelier than women and younger participants were more likely than older ones to experience such encounters through surveillance, stops, questions, frisks/searches, and arrests. Sixty-eight percent of the participants who involuntarily experienced the police characterized their encounters as police harassment, while 32 percent described theirs as police misconduct (table 2). On at least one occasion, most of them believed, they had been unjustifiably targeted for suspicion and scrutinized, disrespected, or mistreated while interacting with the police (table 3). As participants described police harassment and misconduct, they often did so with suspicions of their own. They believed the police stereotyped them, a belief that pervaded their accounts of how the police treated them and their perceptions of officers' attitudes toward them. How some poor blacks in Meacham Park perceivably faced police harassment, singularly or collectively, becomes clear through examination of the following: surveillance and stops, questioning and frisks. Such encounters gave rise to arrests and other improprieties, such as police-citizen disrespect.

Harassment through Surveillance

Police surveillance—indirect, involuntary police contact—has been associated with differential treatment as historically experienced in black communities. Many participants described being harassed by the police, often in the form of officers slowing down, watching them, or tailing them. Surveillance is a proactive policing tactic aggressively applied in black communities.[15] In this study, men, youth, and participants with a history of run-ins with the police were likeliest to experience surveillance. Consistent with the literature, young black men were likeliest to be surveilled by police while hanging out in groups and walking or driving in and out of the community. Surveillance then increased for them and others who had previous negative encounters with the police.

Hanging Out. Over half the participants, mostly young men, reported being watched by the police while hanging out—that is, standing in groups in public places. Indeed, studies show that young men hanging out in groups can lead to police suspicion.[16] Rodney described youth hanging out, particularly late at night, as attracting police attention:

> After eleven, it's the bewitching hour cause you got that night squad coming in geared up and ready for whatever. I call them "the harassers," cause that's when you get harassed late at night. In the summer, everybody out: kids don't go home, trying to find something to do, hanging out in the park.

This account describes hanging out in a particular context, late at night. The participants that experienced surveillance realized that it increased for them depending on the circumstances in which officers found them. Felecia, thirty-seven, also recalled being surveilled by the police:

> It could be us sitting out. [Police] keep on riding past, slowing down, and we ain't doing nothing wrong, sitting on our front. So what's all the riding around and slowing down? We don't having any loud music. We just sitting out ... Like an incident we had recently, [*laughs*], [me and] my friend, we'd been taking groceries out the car and the police at the time was coming around and he was looking so hard, you could see his face like pressed up against the window. Instead of him driving, he watching us. And he [the friend] kinda like, "What are you [police] looking at?" But that's to me harassment.

As the number of involuntary police contacts increases, so does participants' discontent with the police. Thus, frequent surveillance becomes part of the collective memory of the community. While the police did not make direct contact with Felecia and her friends, there was still contact in that they were in their space, watching them as if they were anticipating criminal behavior.

Another woman, Pam, shared accounts of police surveillance as experienced by young black men while hanging out. While Pam's accounts are based on observations rather than personal experience, they are still important:

They [police] try to pick at them [the younger generations]. Like if it's a gang of young boys at the park and they're just sitting under the pavilion, it's like they'll [police] just like keep riding past just to see what the boys are doing . . . Or if they're walking down the street or you know, they'll just keep riding past looking.

Pam attributed police surveillance of the young men to officers "picking at them." In other words, she too believed officers to be excessively watching and checking to see what the young men were doing. Pam's observations are consistent with previous studies regarding police surveillance of youth. Michelle Fine and colleagues found that when accounting for age, youth are likeliest to come under police suspicion.[17]

Being Tailed. Men also reported being followed or tailed by the police when they were walking and driving in and out of the community. Ed, fifty-five, recalled coming under police suspicion in his younger years as he and his friends, young black men, exited Meacham Park and entered Kirkwood Proper:

> Yeah, it was like a "You don't belong here" attitude. Yeah, that's how we grew up. It was like we weren't supposed to come out of Meacham Park, not even going to school. I always got the impression we were being watched. The police would go up [*pointing up the street*] and turn around or they'd go up ahead of us and watch as we're coming, you know . . . [*police impersonation*] ". . . just seeing where these guys are going, what these guys are doing." I just got the impression that they [police] were told we were going to commit a crime.

As Meacham Park is a segregated enclave, "Kirkwood Proper" is a label commonly used by Meacham Park residents when referring to the white, wealthier part(s) of Kirkwood. Ed sensed through officers' surveillance that he and his friends did not belong. The fact that officers did not openly communicate with the young men directly did not mean communication between them did not take place. The young men felt unwelcomed and sensed it when walking out of Meacham Park.

Other men echoed similar experiences when driving out of Meacham Park. Steve, twenty-two, leaves early in the morning for work; he described being tailed by the police:

> I know they used to follow me to the highway a lot. I left here one night, they followed me all the way to the highway. They didn't pull me over or nothing. [I would be] leaving out of here [Meacham Park] at like three o'clock. Strange thing about it, he stopped at a green light, waited until the light changed and

then followed behind. I don't know, I didn't feel right. I felt like he was picking on me. But he didn't stop me so I really can't say he was picking on me. But he did stop at a green light, kinda puzzled me. When he saw me coming out of Meacham Park, I was making a right onto Big Bend. He slowed down real fast at the green light. He probably ran my plates, but everything was right on my car so he didn't bother me.

The suspicious behavior of the police led Steve to believe he was being tailed. As he pulled up to the intersection, he observed the officer immediately break speed, stopping at a green light. While he could not state unequivocally that the officer "was picking" on him, he perceived that he was. For the police, this is routine, proactive policing. However, in black communities, particularly for young black men, this is aggressive, differential policing. It is perceived as harassment. Terrance, thirty-eight, also recalled being tailed by the police as he exited Meacham Park:

> I used to take my cousin to work . . . I did it for like three months and even she noticed. One day she told me to pull over, six o'clock in the morning. She realized one day, cause what they do is they follow me and one of them will then turn off and then another one would take a block or so and then another one, and this was going on for like four or five days where now we realize, and she [the cousin] made me pull over. We pulled over and she got out the car and they pulled up. She asked: "Why ya'll following him?" [The police officer said,] "We ain't following him." Every day they sit up here . . . you can listen to the police scanner and somebody's getting pulled over, right here where you come in and come out.

Terrance and his cousin believed the officers' behaviors to be an obvious pattern and eventually confronted them, creating a potentially hostile situation. Again, while surveillance is generally experienced by men, this is an example where a woman also experienced the close surveillance of police. Ed's, Steve's, and Terrance's experiences reflect the race-and-place effect in that police suspicion of them increased as they exited their predominantly black community and entered a predominantly white one.[18]

A Ripple Effect: Stopped, Questioned, and Frisked

As participants spoke extensively about being harassed by the police in Meacham Park, twenty-two of them reported actually being stopped, questioned, or frisked (or property searched) by the police at least once. Twelve were men and ten were women. Of those stops, six were pedestrian, seven were vehicular, and nine occurred while individuals were at home, sitting on porches, in parks, or in other public settings. Over half of these participants reported being stopped and questioned by the police more than once. Again, the participants with the most stops were mostly men and participants with criminal records.

For many, police harassment produced a ripple effect: it began with one proactive aggressive police act that inevitably triggered others. By design, participants who were stopped by the police were also, at minimum, questioned by them. Consequently, as stop, question, and frisk policies are exercised, they routinely lead to uncomfortably escalating interactions between disadvantaged people of color and the police. The state of police relationships with communities of color remains tenuous, and consequently, exposure to more police aggression bears risk of intensifying them.

National debates have intensified over whether such policies violate the Fourth Amendment, citizens' constitutional right to privacy over government intrusion. Proponents of "stop, question, and frisk" often argue its legitimacy on the basis of "reasonable suspicion" and decreases in crime. However, in doing so, they fail to account for its drawbacks: increased distrust, alienation, and a lack of cooperation from communities of color. After all, citizens' willingness to comply or assist with crime-fighting efforts has been linked to their confidence in the police—the belief that officers are doing the right things, the right way.[19] It is with these sentiments in mind that Georgetown University law professor and former U.S. prosecutor Paul Butler stated:

> If a citizen thinks of the police as the rough men who humiliated her grandson by throwing him against a wall when all he was doing was walking home from school, she is not going to be eager to help them.[20]

Police legitimacy becomes compromised when citizens question officers' actions or when the idea of "reasonable suspicion" in and of itself warrants suspicion. This tends to be the case when the reason(s) for stops are unclear to that citizen or, as theorists would suggest, it "is vague even to the officer making the stop."[21] Principally, if citizens perceive officers' suspicions of them or their stops to be subjective and questionable, they will scrutinize the procedures that follow: "it is, therefore, not just *what* police do that is important but, also, *how* they do it."[22]

One of the goals of this project is to redirect the discourse. Dialogue should not be shaped by those unlikely to face proactive aggressive policing; rather, significant attention should be yielded to those who are—as *they* live and report it. Otherwise, successful crime fighting becomes impossible, particularly in communities like Meacham Park. Stop, question, and frisk applied haphazardly and irrespectively of its effects on people of color only stands to widen the black citizen–police divide rather than close it. As police aggression mounts, tense exchanges between black residents and their local police become visibly endemic.

Stopped and Questioned. Several participants experienced pedestrian stops. Rodney was one of them. Take note of how the police stopped and questioned him one night and the exchange that ensued:

> I'm walking late at night, they [police] wanna slow down and stop you, like "Where you going? Can I see some ID?" Like I told them before, "If I haven't done anything, I don't have to tell you who I am. [Police] just coming up to me and saying, "Can I see some ID." First, you gotta tell me what I've done, why you stopping me, before I give you all this information. As a matter of fact, who are YOU? I don't know if YOU are the police or not.

In this scenario, Rodney experienced proactive policing, what officers often refer to as a routine stop. Like other participants, mostly men, Rodney has a history of negative incidents with the police, including a history of routine stops. He resisted the officers' questions, refusing to subject himself to what he believed to be unwarranted police scrutiny. While Rodney admitted to negative behaviors in the past, he associated many of those incidents with his younger days. Frustrated by stigmas from past indiscretions and now 55, Rodney attempted to empower himself in the situation by responding to officers with questions of his own. It was an opportunity to express his suspicion of them in the same fashion he believed them to be suspicious of him.

Likewise, Ed recalled being stopped by the police and questioned while walking and driving. Unlike Rodney, he had no criminal history. When I asked if he had ever been stopped by the police and if so, how many times, he responded, "Three or four" and proceeded to describe both pedestrian and car stops:

> *What were those stops for?*
> I'm not sure. There was never a reason given to why we [several young black men] were being stopped or questioned.
>
> *Were you on foot or in a car?*
> Both, but we weren't given any reasons for why we were being asked questions, you know.

So what did those incidents look like?
  I would have to say "hassled."

What would they [the police] stop you and say?
  Where are you fellas going? What are you fellas doing? Where have you fellas been?

Again, with no criminal history, Ed's experiences seem to be aligned with Geoffrey Alpert and colleagues' findings that in instances where there were no suspicious behaviors, black men still became targets of suspicion.[23]

This was also the case for Mark, fifty, as a motorist. He referred to officers' suspicion of black men as "subtle." He was also stopped and questioned, despite having no criminal record. He described his experience as follows:

One time I was driving a new truck that I had bought. One of the cops stopped and asked me whose truck I was driving and I pointed to the sign on the side of the truck and said, "That's my name."

Was there any other reason given for your stop?
  No, just whose truck is this?

Mark is retired and had purchased a truck for hauling equipment. After twenty-eight years spent working at one of the most lucrative plants in the St. Louis region, he now provides a broad range of services from plowing to landscaping. Nevertheless, having his name and his business posted on the side of his truck did not deter officers' suspicion of him. Driving a brand new truck as a black man, traveling away from Meacham Park toward Kirkwood Proper, made him vulnerable. Consistent with previous studies, the police's decision to stop and question him likely began with him first as a motorist—particularly as motorists are likeliest to be stopped—and then intensified based on characteristics such as his vehicle (new), his race (black), and community context (traveling at the border of poor black and rich white neighborhoods).[24] Likewise, Andrew Gelman and colleagues' stop-and-frisk data reveals race and place to be significant factors with pedestrian stops.[25] In any event, whether pedestrian or motorist, cases like Rodney's, Ed's, and Mark's are common and suggest blacks—particularly men—are subject to police aggression no matter the circumstances. Having no criminal history did not safeguard Ed and Mark from being stopped and questioned. Drawing from such experiences, it is likely that police suspicion of them was more about them being black men and associated with a troubled community than about criminality.

Interestingly, Mark no longer lived in Meacham Park at the time of his stop. He was raised and continues to own property there, is an active member of the neighborhood's historic Crown Royal Motorcycle Club, and has family and friends there whom he visits regularly, but he now lives in Kirkwood Proper or what he refers to as "the other side of the tracks." Nevertheless, he continues to defer to Meacham Park as part of his master status and perceives the police and other members of the local government as doing the same. In essence, it is as if he has never left the neighborhood.

Frisked or Searched: Gendered Police Aggression. This section examines the gendered circumstances of police frisks and searches among blacks in disadvantaged places. The way men and women enter into tense police exchanges and how those encounters play out affirms the significance of personal attributes—beyond race and place—over criminality. As Dorothy, fifty-seven, stated:

> See, they were trying to run this place like a Gestapo camp at one point. You had to be checked to come in and checked to go out. They had, at any given point, a police car up there at the entrance, because you know there's only one real entrance in and out of here [Meacham Park]. But that's their mentality. If you were male and you were driving they would use anything to pull you over. It was so bad that my children were afraid to come and visit me and they still have scars about that. I just talked to my son today and he was supposed to come out here and take me to lunch and he said, "Momma, you know I don't like to come out there to Kirkwood, they pull you over." They [police] search you, search your car . . . Nobody likes to be pulled over, cause if they pull you over, they gone run your plates. God forbid you have a taillight out, just any little thing. It was crazy, they stopped everybody. You could be a black female and look disenfranchised, you gone get pulled over.

What Dorothy describes is the susceptibility of both men and women to police stops and searches (or frisks) upon entering the neighborhood of Meacham Park and the long-lasting effects they have on its visitors and residents. Pam, also described her experience with being stopped, questioned, and searched by the police:

> They searched my car one time, for what reason I don't know.
>
> *They didn't tell you?*
> No.

Well, what did they say? How did it happen?

They asked me for my license, asked me where I was going, where I was coming from, and then was like "I need you to step out of the car," and they searched the car. This was like when I was sixteen. I was, like, "What did I do, you didn't tell me what I did, you didn't tell me why you stopped me." I asked the officer why he pulled me over and he just got an attitude like he didn't want to tell me.

Was that incident in Meacham Park?

Yes.

So did he eventually tell you?

No. I didn't get an answer until he put it on the ticket. So basically, I found out on the ticket, right before I pulled off, [it was] my plates.

Though typically less often subject to suspicion and stops, questions, and frisks compared to men, on occasion, women did face police aggression. Many of their encounters hinged on personal relationships. Dorothy's experiences with police searches extended from problems her children had, while Pam perceived hers to have occurred due to the people in her car. Pam continued, "They only wrote a ticket for me one time out of four . . . the other times, they gave me a warning." Interestingly, the times where she received warnings, she was driving alone and stopped due to speeding. However, she reported that it was only in the instance where she had young men as passengers that her stop escalated to the point of an unexplained search.

Of the twenty-two participants who experienced involuntary contacts, eleven—five men, six women—reported being frisked or searched by the police (table 4). Though both men and women reported being frisked or searched, there was a key difference. All five men experienced having their bodies searched, while the six women experienced searches of their possessions—their homes, car, and a purse. Black men are targeted more for suspicion as they are likelier to be perceived as perpetrators compared to black women. Overall, the women in this project were less likely to experience pedestrian and/or vehicular stops than men. This translated to women also being less likely to be frisked. Instead, woman faced searches that generally took place in private locales rather than public. However, even in instances where they were stopped in public, they were unlikely to have their stops extended to frisks or car searches. Pam's vehicular stop was the one exception in this study.

Four women reported searches of their homes. In two cases, their homes were searched while police were in pursuit of young men. For the other two, searches were in the context of drug raids. One woman was a homeowner while the other was a resident at the home who, coincidentally, was also the young woman (Pam) who had previously experienced the vehicular search. Therefore, Pam faced two police searches, one as a sixteen-year-old motorist and years later as a resident caught in a drug raid. Even in this instance, it is likely that the raid was associated with officers' interests in the homeowner's boyfriend. Meanwhile, the fifth woman had her purse searched as a result of a shoplifting incident and the sixth had her belongings searched in lieu of being sent to a juvenile facility.

As for the men, two frisks occurred during pedestrian stops and two occurred during vehicular stops. In one pedestrian stop, police found drugs and the participant was arrested. He claimed that officers "free-cased" him, or planted drugs on him during the pat-down. In one of the vehicular stops, the frisk was extended to include a vehicular search, resulting in the participant being maced, physically roughed up, and arrested. I revisit these incidents with greater detail in my discussion of police misconduct.

Meanwhile, a third male respondent recalled being pulled over, frisked, and searched while out with his brother. In this study, black men were likelier than black women to have multiple experiences in each stop. Those stops became public spectacles, open displays in which multiple young black men are out of their cars, often lined up side by side, being questioned, frisked, and having their vehicle searched by the police. Steve described such an experience:

> I had an older model car. Me and my brother got stopped, twice. I was coming home. They [the police] pulled us out the car and searched, everything checked out. One time they said the vehicle was loud and then the other time, they say they couldn't see the sticker because my license plates were dirty. That's what they say.

> *And so how did both of those incidents turn out?*
> Fine, they let us go. They didn't give us tickets or anything.

While Steve does not have a criminal record, again, these incidents are among several he has had with the police. Interestingly, in instances in which Steve was driving alone, he reported only being tailed. Consistent with the literature, police suspicion becomes heightened and even more salient when young black men are in groups.

Jasmine, forty-two, described an incident where she was both questioned and searched by the police. Her home was raided by drug enforcement and her vehicle searched by officers in Meacham Park. Of the nine women who reported involuntary police contacts, Jasmine has had the most extensive history, ranging from stops to use of force. She is one of two women in this study who have personally experienced police use of force, and the only one to have interacted with the police under the most aggressive circumstances. One was a drug raid at her home and the other was an arrest during which she was maced by the police. In both instances, her boyfriend was involved. He too was targeted for suspicion in the drug raid, and was also responsible for the call that led to even more police aggression for Jackie—the aforementioned incident, where she was arrested and maced.

In no way does the involvement of Jasmine's boyfriend excuse her actions. However, her involvement in both incidents lends itself to discussions of black female criminality to the extent that women's involvements in crimes are often "grounded in exploitation ... sexual exploitation, abuse, poverty, and structural inequality."[26] More specifically, given what we know about women's roles in the drug market, they are often powerless and dependent on men in the industry. Consequently, when they are involved in drugs, it is generally at the lower levels of the industry, while negotiating volatile relationships.[27]

With this in mind, let us take a closer look at Jasmine's story, especially as she experienced having her home and vehicle searched simultaneously. Apparently, the police had been tailing her boyfriend prior to the raid, and then proceeded to do the same with her. Jasmine recalled:

> I look up and I see the police behind me and he does like this [*she imitates him signaling her over*]. So I think he's telling me to get out of his way, so I swerve to the other lane and he swerves behind me. So I pulled over and he kept asking where my boyfriend was and I'm, like, "I don't know, he left" ... it was like he was stalling because he kept being like, "Um, um, um" and I'm like, "Why did you pull me over?" and finally, he said, "We're kicking your house in." I said, "Well, you don't have to kick my house in, I'll be glad to let you in." So he tells me, "Just step out of the car, let me search the car, and I'll call ahead and see if we can just let you open the door for us." I'm believing him the whole time, that he's going to call ahead and he's stalling. [*Continues as if talking to the officer.*] "[He] got me standing around while you search the car, and the whole time, you're not calling anybody." So he's searching my car and they're kicking my house in and so he finally says, "We're going to let you go." I went back home, went across the street to my friend's house and sat on the porch. I was never given a search warrant and all they could tell me is that they were searching for drugs. They let the dog in my house,

which actually didn't go any further than the front door, tore all of my food up out of my refrigerator and had everything all over the kitchen. So I crossed the street and I'm like, "I guess you're feeling funny now because you didn't find anything." That's when they told me to put my hands behind my back and I said, "For what?" and they were like, "Because we found drugs." They came out with a Ziploc bag which they said was an ounce of cocaine, soft and hard, and I kept telling them, "No, you planted it," and everybody [the police] started laughing. So they took me to the police station. They already had my boyfriend there because they pulled him over on the highway.

Jasmine's interrogation mostly involved questions pertaining to her boyfriend. Jasmine was adamant about her innocence and believed she was unfairly and erroneously targeted for a raid. She described being interrogated by officers as if already charged and convicted of dealing drugs:

They argued me down saying I was cooking dope and I was supplying dope dealers out here and this is what they're telling me the word was on the street. And at the time, my gas was cut off and I asked them, "If I'm doing all this, how can my utilities get cut off, my gas get cut off?"

She believed the officers' questions to be illogical; if she was really the drug supplier as they accused her of being, at the very least, she should be able to pay her gas bill. Jasmine continued to vehemently deny having any involvement in drugs:

They kept trying to interrogate me about the money, then one detective said, "Oh don't bullshit a bullshitter, you are a girl of the neighborhood, you know everybody." [They] kept asking me where the money was and how could I afford the food that was in my freezer and why did I have all the baking soda I had in my refrigerator.

Like Rodney, Jasmine confronted officers with questions of her own. Mimicking their approach, she relied on what she believed to be evidence in her home (disconnected utilities) to support her innocence in the same way officers relied on what they believed to be evidence in her home to confirm her guilt. While the participant's innocence or guilt and the officers' motives cannot be unequivocally determined in this situation, it is important to note that the participant, a definite target of suspicion along with her home and vehicle, was subjected to a particular line of questions, statements, and behaviors consistent with aggressive policing. In the end, she was released and he was held.

After also having her home searched by the police, Dorothy stated,

They [police] don't think rationally when it comes to black people. Well, they didn't with me.

She too was furious following her experience with the police. Dorothy, who had no criminal record, came under suspicion as a result of her son's actions. Police suspicion of him resulted not only in her home being searched, but also in an officer pulling his gun while in her home, in front of her other children. She described her experience:

Officer came to my door and asked me was he [her son] here and I said, "No, he's not," and they said, "Well, can we search the house." I said "No problem." And they went up the steps, that's when all of my kids were still at home, and my other boys said that when they got up there, they had their guns drawn. And I let them in my house in good faith. But my kids are not murderers and killers. Yes, he [my son] got into a little scrap [fight] but that [pulling guns] was uncalled for because they didn't have a search warrant or nothing. I didn't like that. I volunteered to let them search my house. I mean, I welcomed them in my home, and you know, I tried to be as cordial as I could. But if I was trying to hide my son, I wouldn't let them come in my house without a search warrant. I'm not stupid. But you're going to pull out a gun when you get up the steps and put it back in before you get back down, so I can't see it?!?

Dorothy experienced involuntary direct police contact through no fault of her own. When asked about her son's whereabouts, she cooperated with the police by answering their questions. At that point, Dorothy perceived she too became a target of suspicion. Officers asked to search her home, despite not having a warrant and being told that her son was not there. Such actions were perceived by Dorothy as officers' distrust of her. She stated,

I felt when they came to my home okay, but when they pulled guns on my kids looking for my son, I felt violated.

Again, this exemplifies aggressive policing, even when participants were cooperative.

When asked about how the police handled crime in the community, Tiffany answered, "Very, very, very excessive." Tiffany's comment derived from having had her home searched following a police chase. She described the incident:

You know how teenage kids are. Well, come to find out, there had been some guys down in the basement with my son and daughter and one of the guys had left. Well, supposedly, he had sold [drugs] to an undercover police officer.

The police chased him and he ran in my back door, ran into my son's room and hid. Well, I was getting ready to get in the shower and I heard the police banging on the door. It was a big commotion. So I put some shorts and a top on. I didn't even have on shoes. When I opened the door, the officers were yelling, "Where he at, where he at?" And I didn't know what they were talking about, so I kept asking, "Where who at?" And they just started looking around and telling me that if I didn't tell them where he was, I was going to be arrested. I had just gotten home and didn't know what was going on. So we're arguing back and forth, them saying I'm lying and me asking what's going on. They [police] looking all through my house, up under beds and everything.

Moments before Tiffany's arrival home from work, a young man had run into Tiffany's house attempting to hide from the police. He knew the back door was unlocked since he was friends with her teenage children and had been there earlier that day. Despite not knowing any of this, Tiffany recalled being met with police suspicion right away. Officers questioned her as if she was eluding them in an effort to help hide him. As with Dorothy, Tiffany had no criminal history, but faced scrutiny as if she did. Tiffany was upset and very vocal. Like other participants when met with what they perceived to be unfair treatment by the police, she became defensive and openly refuted police accusations. In the end, officers perceived Tiffany as defiant, accused her of interfering with a police investigation, and arrested her, along with the young man. She described feeling humiliated as officers took her to the county lockup in skimpy shorts, a tank top, and no shoes. Tiffany is one of several participants who detests and completely distrusts the police as a result of experiences like this.

Arrests. Of the eleven participants frisked and/or searched, each of them reported being arrested on at least one occasion (table 4). Six were men and five were women. Like frisks and searches, the arrests occurred along gender lines. The men were all arrested for public violations, ranging from drug offenses to traffic incidents. The women's arrests were mostly connected to relationship altercations. For example, four women were arrested following a disagreement between friends, with a boyfriend, and in Tiffany's case above, the arrest came in the context of a police search for a teenager. The fifth woman arrested was a result of a traffic ticket. But even then, the arrest occurred in court versus on the street. Women in general were least likely to experience incidents with the police in public compared to men.

TABLE 4 Involuntary Police Contacts: Stopped, Questioned, Frisked/Searched

Experience reported	No. (N=22)	%
Being stopped by the police, on at least one occasion	22	100
Being stopped and then questioned, on at least one occasion	22	100
Being stopped, questioned, and then frisked (or having property searched) by the police, on at least one occasion	11	50
Being stopped, questioned, frisked/searched, and then arrested by the police, on at least one occasion	11	50

PWA: Police with Attitudes

> It's just the way they [the police] talk to you. They come out here with an attitude. That's the main thing. They come out here with an attitude and I know it. Cut a brother a break or something.
>
> RODNEY

"Police with attitudes" was a common theme among participants. Those who experienced involuntary, direct contact with the police through stops, questions, frisks/searches, and arrests also reported the police as being rude and bad-mannered. More specifically, they described instances where they believed the police disrespected them, yet expected and demanded respect from them. After having a police officer scold her surrounding an incident with her children, Jackie's take on disrespect was that:

> It's not what you say to a person, but how you say it. Sometimes, they [police] just talk to you like you are beneath the earth."

Jeremy, twenty-nine, who has had several incidents with the police, also reported having experienced disrespect. He added,

> It's known out here that they [police] don't respect us and if they disrespect us, then why should we respect them?

In other words, he believes respect is earned and police officers are not the exception.

The participants in this study did not respond well to what they perceived to be officers' mistreatment of them. In fact, in two instances, participants' (one man, one woman) responses to police with perceivably bad attitudes or disrespect led to their arrests. In incidents with involuntary, direct contact with the police, participants complained of being disrespected by the police in the following ways: through their initial approach, name calling and cursing, being given the finger, and being threatened. These interactions further negative perceptions of the police.

The Initial Approach.

> I won't allow that [disrespect]. I won't allow that by anyone. When I've been pulled over before by a police officer, when he approaches my car, it depends on how he addresses himself to me. If he's respectful, then we'll have a pretty intelligent conversation. If he's disrespectful, I pretty much let him have it.
>
> TRAVIS

Travis has had direct experiences with the police through numerous stops. As a result, he expressed strong feelings about police disrespect. While he does not give a specific example of disrespect, his statements provide insight into a particular mindset. Travis considers himself to be intelligent, and thus he sees disrespect in officers' approaching him condescendingly.

Other participants also expressed dissatisfaction with the way officers talked to them. In fact, several reported incidents where the police cursed and called them names. This happened mostly during routine stops, though in Rodney's case, it was neighborhood patrol. Rodney recalled an incident when an officer out patrolling pulled up to his residence and immediately began interrogating him. He perceived the officer to be disrespectful and his questioning to be unwarranted. Consequently, Rodney refused to answer his questions and instead followed up with questions of his own. The way officers approach citizens is crucial. It sets the tone for what takes place during police-citizen contacts. More directly, for blacks in disadvantaged communities like Meacham Park, it sets precedence for persistently negative police-citizen interactions. With that in mind, Rodney's situation quickly escalated. According to him, what began as a relatively calm day with his nephew and cousin sitting in front of his house quickly erupted into a heated exchange with a local officer.

> My nephew and cousin was sitting on my property, just sitting there talking . . . and there were two of them [officers] and one knocked on my door. He said, "Who's that over there?" [pointing]. I looked over there and said, "My nephew and cousin, why you worried about who's on my property?"
>
> *They just rode up, knocked, and asked you this out of nowhere?*
> Yeah. They just rode down because the kids were sitting out there. Like I told them, "That's the street [pointing], and I don't have nothing to do with that, but

this here is my property. If somebody's sitting on my property, it's somebody in my family." So I said, "Man, get on, you know who that is and you know this my property." So [walking away] he called me a bitch and I said, "You a bitch too," you know what I'm saying. He talking to me like I'm a punk. So then he told me to shut the fuck up. I said, "You shut the fuck up, bitch ass punk, now get off my property." So when I said get off my property, he got in the car and he stuck his finger out like this [*gives the middle finger*]. So I said "Fuck you too, big motherfucker," you know, and start walking in the house. And when I got ready to walk in the house, he jumped out the car, "Come here, you under arrest." I just shut the door on him and looked at my old lady and said, "He said I'm under arrest, Goddamn, now he gone get me for resisting arrest because I came in the house." So I went back outside, just turned around [to be cuffed]. We get to the station and he still talking crazy to me. He arrested me for resisting arrest and disorderly conduct. It seem like to me, I was baited in.

While this was an extremely tense exchange between Rodney and the police, it was just one in a long string of negative incidents Rodney has had with the local police. He perceived the police actions to be nothing short of harassment, a blatant disregard for him, his family, and his property. So when the officer cursed at Rodney and gave him the middle finger, he responded with name calling and cursing. Such responses are consistent with the literature's findings that when citizens, particularly black males, are met with degrading police behaviors, they tend to respond similarly.[28] As a result, Rodney was arrested, and interestingly, under the same set of circumstances described by Jeremy. Jeremy, who also has a history of negative encounters with the police, explained:

Meacham Park is small, you know, and they [police] know everybody's name and so they want to jump out on you so you can get smart and then they can hit you with resisting arrest, which they shouldn't be able to get you on because of how they went about it. But they don't care. They just want to get you off the streets for a little while.

Jeremy's explanation implicates the police as setting up citizens, as purposefully saying and doing things to agitate them, and in turn, using their responses to incriminate them. Both Jeremy and Rodney interpreted the officers' actions as efforts to provoke them. It is under these circumstances that black citizens continue to perceive the police negatively. Their everyday experiences have conditioned them to believe that when police engage in inappropriate behaviors with citizens, there are no consequences, but when citizens respond accordingly, they are punished.

Mark also discussed disrespectful behaviors he had seen and heard about:

> There were instances that I heard about and seen where the police, after things had happened with one of the shootings out here, they would call them [youth] out of their names, give them the finger, flash lights in their face, you know. These days, the youth don't too much respond well to those types of treatments.

Along with being likeliest to experience police stops, questioning, and frisks, young black men are likeliest to be subject to police disrespect. The fact that they are often stopped in public, mostly in groups, allows this police disrespect to be observed by others. These are negative contacts with young men that take place on corners, in the park, and other places throughout the community. Participants reported paying close attention to police behavior when there were police-citizen stops in the neighborhood for them to observe.

Felecia also reported disrespect by the police as a problem in the community. She explained:

> The problem is respect. They [police] want us to respect them, but why they don't show us respect?

> *OK, and how do they not show you respect?*
> When they're cursing us out, looking at you or just get out, asking us what we were doing . . . you know what I'm saying? We ain't bothering nobody, so why question us? Why talk to us nasty?

Again, participants that experienced random or routine stops and questioning were likeliest to report police disrespect. Felecia's accounts are based on her experience with being stopped, questioned, and disrespected by the police. Additionally, she has been in groups with young men when they were stopped and questioned without cause. Those who experience such exchanges perceive them as harassment and the officers involved as rude, offensive, and disrespectful.

Finally, participants also reported being threatened by the police. Jasmine recalled threats made by officers following the drug raid at her home:

> I heard one of the detectives tell him [her boyfriend], "Well, we'll see you in ninety years." Then I heard them put him in the cell and the detective came to me and threatened me, telling me I was looking at thirty years, I better tell him the truth. One was telling me that I was looking at thirty years and he wanted me to give names of who was actually selling and they threw names at me and I was like, "I don't know."

Jasmine reported feeling powerless and bullied. Following her interrogation, she was released without having been charged.

Felecia recalled a situation where she learned of police threats to someone else:

> A guy that used to live out here, he don't live out here anymore. They [police] knew him by his name. They just, you know, try to pump him for information and he had a warrant so, if he doesn't tell them what they want to hear, then they'll take him in. But if he tells them what they want to hear, they won't take him in. Now, I have seen some cops do that.

These aggressive tactics may seem warranted to police as a way to obtain information, but they fuel distrust among citizens. Many participants believe that the police are "scandalous," and that they engage in disrespectful, threatening behaviors because they have the authority to do so. Barbara, fifty-three, stated:

> They'll [police] keep on stopping you. It's legal for them to do it. So how can you say "they're picking on me" if they're doing it legally? So, it's kind of hard to prove. They [police] can find anything. You can't really fight against them. That's just normal with the police.

While she has not personally experienced mistreatment by the police, her son has. Barbara is really speaking of discretionary power—commissioned power to stop someone at will—and the fact that officers have been known to extend that power in inappropriate ways. Through personal and vicarious experiences, Barbara and others understand that they can be subjected to legally justified mistreatment by the police at any time.

Police Misconduct

> They might jump down on you, but if they're really not tripping off of you, then they'll just take what you got, I don't care what it is: a gun, some drugs, whatever it is and whoever they don't like and they catch, that'll be THEIR case.
>
> JEREMY

Jeremy spoke freely about his run-ins with the police, his stint with the Missouri Department of Corrections. Given his history of negative encounters with the criminal justice system—especially the police—he believes himself to be knowledgeable and credible in reporting their behaviors. He

Experience reported	No. (N=22)	%
TABLE 5		
Direct police misconduct	7	32
Being slammed, shoved, roughed up, or maced	4	18
Having false police reports used against them	2	9
Having evidence planted on them	1	4.5

TABLE 5 Involuntary Police Contacts: Police Misconduct

has had his fair share of experiences with what he believes to be good as well as bad officers. Despite his past, he feels his accounts of what he perceives to be police lawlessness should be no less valued than their reports of his.

Seven of the twenty-two participants who reported involuntary police contacts recalled incidents of perceived police misconduct, ranging in behaviors from physical brutality to the planting of evidence. Four participants (two men, two women) experienced violent incidents with the police. Those incidents included being slammed, shoved, roughed up, or maced by the police. Two other participants reported false claims made against them by officers (two men), and one reported being "free-cased" (said that officers had planted evidence on him) (man). In sum, participants spoke candidly about police unlawfully extending their authority in ways detrimental to them. Subsequent sections explore how bad policing led some residents of Meacham Park to face factions of the criminal justice system they may not have otherwise (see table 5).

Physical Brutality. Physical brutality in Meacham Park consisted of various forms of unjustifiably violent police behaviors such as unnecessary force, macing, and slamming and shoving citizens against squad cars. Two participants—Rodney and Jasmine—reported being maced. Both have had extensive histories with the police, and thus faced escalating police aggression in multiple ways. In Rodney's recollection of being maced—and Jasmine's later—pay especially close attention to why it was perceived as police brutality. Rodney stated:

> I've been handcuffed and maced. I've been maced twice. One time the police pulled me over; I had a warrant. I knew I had a warrant so I got out the car. He [the officer] called me by my nickname. So he get out the car, I got out the car. He says, "You got a warrant, man?" I said, "Yeah, I know damn, shit." So I put my hands [up]. He turned me around, then he maced me, strung me in the car.

So were you cooperating?

Yeah, because I knew I had a warrant. If I wasn't cooperating, I would've ran, you know, I would've ran. But you know, what's the sense of running? I'm right here. I don't have time to be playing those games, them looking for me, me looking out the window and all that. If I got a warrant, I'll just turn myself in or whatever, you know what I'm saying.

And so he maced you?

Yeah, I got maced twice, just on GP [general principle]. I didn't even curse him, fight or resist him or nothing. Because I thought you get maced when you resist or you're fighting or something, you know. It's just, police out here [Meacham Park], they're kind of . . . [*thinking*] they're young, they're scared, they wanna be tough. They're scared.

Note that Rodney claimed that he was maced while restrained. He says that he cooperated and did so understanding the consequences if he did not. In other words, Rodney cooperated trying to avoid what he says happened: unnecessary aggression by the police. He told a story of what he believed to have been unjustifiable force used against him due to officers' inexperience, fear, and the need to prove themselves in the community.

Jasmine also spoke of being maced while handcuffed. Her incident occurred during a pedestrian stop. While walking, Jasmine was approached by the police. She had been drinking and been involved in an altercation with her boyfriend when he called the police. When officers first attempted to make contact with Jasmine, she was driving, and she ignored officers and instead drove home, went in the house, and fell asleep. Later, while walking through the neighborhood, she ran into officers a second time. Jasmine described her encounter:

She [the police officer] asked me to put my hands behind my back and she was handcuffing me and then the male officer maced me in my face, after I was already handcuffed.

Were you saying anything?

Nope, not at all.

This is after you were cuffed?

This is after I was cuffed. One of my cousins live right across the street. She was sitting on her porch at the time. So she ended up calling my parents to let my parents know exactly what happened. So they [police] took me in and I had to be bonded out and the charge was for disorderly conduct. It [mace] burned so bad. I couldn't tell you what was said. All I know is that I ended up in the backseat of the car. And the female officer had me in her car. She put me in her car and transported me to the Kirkwood police station and all I remember was my eyes burning, my skin burning, and my body was getting hot. So when I got there, she finally took the handcuffs off me and told me to go over to the sink and put my head up under the water.

Again, Jasmine has a history of negative experiences with the police. While the other experiences left her with negative perceptions of law enforcement, being maced trumped them all. As Jasmine recalled the incident, she seemed accepting of the fact that she was stopped by police and clearly understood why she had been stopped. However, what she found problematic was what ensued during the stop.

While only two participants reported personally being maced in this study, Felecia reportedly witnessed a young black man in the neighborhood being maced and beaten up by police:

Well, you see it a lot. I saw a boy there on the corner [*pointing*]. He was watching the police arrest somebody else. He was just standing there, they [police] maced him.

How did that happen? Tell me how that went down.
We all were standing out. He [the young man] was standing on the corner. They [police] were messing with some other people on the corner and the police was telling him to get off the corner. I'm like, "for what?" [*thinking to herself*]. He's just standing here. He's not doing anything. That cop just wanted him off the corner, but he wasn't doing anything. So they had got kinda aggressive with him. They maced him and everything.

Even as an observation, it is equally significant. The participants in this project internalize what they see and hear regarding the police, especially those with negative contacts of their own. They are more inclined to take notice, particularly since they understand firsthand the negative turn police-citizen interactions can take. Additionally, they do not trust the police to be fair, as many of them feel they have not been treated fairly. Hence, whether directly or indirectly involved, cooperative or uncooperative, participants reported police using force excessively. In this project, this occurred with those who had extensive histories with the police.

Three participants—Rodney, Jeremy, and Crystal, nineteen—reported other forms of physical brutality. Jeremy has had multiple incidents with the police. He described what he refers to as a "jump down":

This is how it goes. They'll [police] jump down on you, beat you up, lock you up, then just hold you for twenty-four hours for no reason. And then they'll put it in a report as if you did something to make them react like that … they're always jumping on somebody. They pull you over, put you against the car, put you in cuffs, search your cars without permission and when they can't find nothing in the car, the average person is going to speak up on it. And when you speak up on it, now they want to hit you with resisting arrest or jump on you, when you haven't had any type of physical aggression. Yeah, they bruise you up real good.

Jeremy has a history of negative encounters resulting in negative perceptions of the police; likewise, the police perceive him negatively. Jeremy has been "beaten up" by the police and he knows other disadvantaged black men that have been beaten up by the police. He views both himself and them as defenseless targets that are preyed on, beaten on, and then lied about by the police.

Crystal shared an account where she claimed to have been mishandled by the police following an incident between her and her mom:

I walked out the back door and I hadn't even made it halfway up the street and the police officer, he came out of nowhere and just like slammed me on the car. I was jerking away from him like you know, get your hands off of me. I was already mad. But he didn't have to do it [approach her] like how he did it. I kept jerking away from him, just the way he kept grabbing my arms. You [police] know I'm already mad and I was real young then and it was just how he did it. He didn't have to do all that.

Angered from an altercation with her mom, Crystal left her home walking. She did so while the police were there investigating, and consequently, she was followed and reported being violently accosted by one of the responding officers. This is the second account from a female of excessive use of force, one through macing and one physical mishandling. Crystal's complaint, "he didn't have to do all that," suggests that it was not the stop in itself that she had a problem with but rather the actions that accompanied the stop. She perceived it as unnecessary and excessive.

Research shows a growing number of black women being subject to police violence, as Jasmine's and Crystal's cases show.[29] Women often do not recount direct police aggression or brutality, or at least not enough incidents have been accounted for in police-citizen research to warrant such discussion. It may be that such experiences are exclusive to men, in very public ways. In fact, Rod Brunson and Jody Miller found that officers acted less aggressively when women were present during police interactions with men.[30]

Black women are often single parents or "heads of household" working to negotiate a myriad of relationships and hardships in disadvantaged neighborhoods, and they are often victims of male violence and of intersecting social stratum (race, class, gender, sexuality). Negative police-citizen encounters and brutality among black women becomes an extension of male victimization and an additional tract for exposing blacks to the criminal justice system.[31] In effect, disadvantaged communities become even more destitute, as does the hope for mending bridges between them and their local law enforcement.

Jasmine and Crystal felt violated and as though they were being treated "like men"; after all, these were behaviors they observed happening to men. Pam also witnessed a police-citizen encounter in which violence ensued. Pam described two young men being chased, and one being caught and roughed up:

> They [police] tried to take the front of the car and pin them up to the fences up there by those apartments. Instead of getting out and chasing them [on foot], they chased them in the car. They're too rough-like and since they couldn't catch one of them, they just tried to run him into the gate. I guess he was trying to hop the gate so they tried to pin him to it with the car, but they were going too fast. But then when they chased the other boy and finally caught him, they had their knees in his chest, just yanking on him to get up off the ground. They have too many officers for one person.

Pam found the number of engaged officers to be excessive. Like other eyewitness accounts, the physical aspect of the encounter itself creates concern. In this situation, Pam perceived the officers as bullies: too many, too involved, and too amped to digress from a perceivably increasingly out-of-control situation.

Meanwhile, Barbara spoke of an incident where a young man was slammed to the ground by police. She is a friend of the young man's father, from whom she learned of the incident. She described the police using unnecessary, excessive force against him and the police being reprimanded for having done so:

> They [police] accused him [the man] of doing something and the police slammed him to the ground, said a lot of different things, and locked him up. The chief came back and reviewed the tape and reprimanded the officer, apologized to the family, and everything else.

Again, Barbara did not personally witness this event. However, when asked about policing behaviors and misconduct in the community, she found this incident important to discuss. Her experiences with the police have been positive, but because she knew and had heard of incidents in the community that suggest otherwise, she did not want to discount bad policing behaviors.

Falsified Reports. Ricky, fifty-six, and Jasmine, both of whom had previous negative contacts with police, complained about the police lying. They reported incidents where they personally encountered the police falsifying reports. Ricky, who generally had favorable views of the police, recalled an instance where he was mistreated by them. He believed an officer engaged in misconduct by deliberately falsifying his accident report:

> We were sitting here one night, we were playing cards. I drunk one beer, got up, took a bath, and she [wife] wanted a pizza so I was going to get a pizza and the guy next door was coming home. So when I got to the stop sign, I stopped and he short-cornered me. Well, he runs into my car but he says I ran into his. To make a long story short, I said, "Don't move your car." So he moves his car anyway . . . one officer came to the scene and then another officer came to the scene. She smelled my beer, "You're drunk and you're under arrest." Took me to the police department, made me blow, it blew zero, they had to let me go. When she wrote up the police report, she wrote it up entirely wrong. She wouldn't even take the witnesses' accounts. The white guy across the street saw the whole accident. She wouldn't even put his name on the report. So we went up there one night. I said, "I don't want anybody to make me right or wrong but I want an accurate report and I want my witnesses on it." When I got the accident report, I read it and I told my wife, "This lady [police] is terrible. She's just not telling the truth here" and she even had on it that I was drunk falling out the car when she got on the scene. And that's what she told me and my wife in front of her supervisor. So I told him, I said sir, "Your officer is lying, and first of all she was not the first officer on the scene and you can question the other officer." And I said, "You can also ask the other people that were there." So to make a long story short, they went and did an investigation, found out that I was totally correct. So they made her tear up that report and rewrite it the way it should've been with the witnesses and everything. I think it was misconduct what she did to me.

While Ricky has come into contact with the police involuntarily, he reported that more of his contacts occurred through service calls. In these instances he was pleased with their service. However, with this incident, Ricky was angered by the officer's actions. After reporting this to the officer's superior, the original report was thrown out and a new, corrected report was drawn up in its place. Despite the problem(s) being fixed, Ricky believed he was mistreated. He believed the officer's behavior to be nothing short of police misconduct.

In a similar incident, Jasmine described her son as being erroneously ticketed for failure to show proof of insurance. She explained:

> My son had left my house and got pulled over in my car. I had gotten everything registered, the insurance, the plates were right. He [police] asked him for his insurance, my son showed him his insurance and he gave him a ticket anyway. Somebody saw that my son was pulled over and gave me a call. One of my girlfriends took me to where they was at and my son was telling me that he gave him a ticket anyway and I asked him [police], "If he showed you proof of insurance, why did you give him a ticket anyway?" So the officer told me, "Well, we can't block traffic here, let's go down to Quick Trip." And I'm like OK and I got in the backseat of my car and we [she and her son] rode down to Quick Trip. We were right behind the officer. Instead of the officer pulling over at Quick Trip, he turned like he was going to Quick Trip but he kept going. We pulled on Quick Trip lot, we sat there thinking he may turn around and come back. He never did come back. So the next day, I called the Kirkwood police station to ask for his sergeant, to talk to his sergeant. The sergeant told me, "Yeah, he told me about it," and for me to come and bring the ticket up to him. And when we got there, he took the ticket and tore it up in front of me.

As young black disadvantaged men are disproportionately targeted for surveillance, they are often met with harassment and other aggressive tactics used by the police toward them.[32] Had the young man in this case challenged or questioned the officer's actions, he could have easily been perceived as resistant or possibly combative. While the situation clearly did not escalate to that point, it is still serious in that a stop occurred and a false ticket was issued, both of which, according to Jasmine, seemingly went unexplained.

Planting Evidence

The final type of misconduct is planting evidence. Terrance reported direct experience with having an officer plant drugs on him in the community.

> We're standing outside of one of my friend's houses and they [police] just pulled up on a general search. [They] just pulled up, got out and started patting people down, it was two police officers. But the original [first] police officer patted me down. I remember I had on some gray sweat pants and some

red shorts. I had some red shorts on and I didn't have nothing in my pockets. My sweatpants, [I] didn't have anything in those pockets. They searched me. The first cop that pulled up searched me, searched me and sat me on the car, then searched my two friends and then Moore [an officer] pulled up and I'm sitting on the front of the car already searched and Moore walked up to me and said, "Let me search you again." He patted me down and I'm sitting on the bumper, the parking bumper, you know what I'm saying . . . goes down, he pats me, and comes back up with an ounce of marijuana. Gave me a ticket, but took my boy to jail. That was a bad day. Where the marijuana came from, I don't know, that's just straight up square business. He patted me down and came up and just pulled out an ounce of weed and said, "This is yours." I said, "No, it's not." [Terrance talking to officer] I didn't even fight it.

Terrance's account is another example of police suspicion, particularly in instances where young men are visibly congregating and hanging out in the community. As the police are leery of them, they then approach them and question them (stop, question, frisk), which may inevitably lead to pat-downs, or in Terrance's instance, "free-casings"—the planting of drugs or other evidence.

Jeremy has been beaten up by the police and also claimed officers planted drugs on him. While his experience occurred in a different community, it is still important to note. Similar to others, it is part of his collective experiences with the police. Black citizens' distrust of the police is typically the result of "accumulative experiences."[33] They occur in increments across time and place. Jeremy does not trust the police, and believes that running from them is a way to avoid evidence planting. He explained,

See here's the thing, when they [police] jump on you, you better run because if you ain't got nothing on you, you will.

Jeremy's statement provides a plausible explanation for why many young men run from the police. Running for him is not about belligerence but rather about avoidance. As a result of previous encounters, Jeremy believes that the consequences resulting from running are better than those of not running. Not running could mean being "free-cased" and possibly beaten up.

Crystal also witnessed a police pursuit and possible free-casing in the community. She described the scene as she and others in the community looked on:

They [police] kept telling people to stay back and it was just like five or six police officers down there on him and he was yelling, "Somebody help me, they're trying to put something in my pocket." He just kept yelling, "They're trying to put something in my pocket!"

While Crystal could not prove whether officers actually planted drugs on the gentleman in custody, she seemed inclined to believe him. Due to her negative experiences with the police, she is distrustful of officers and believes that the man being subdued would not have been yelling for citizen intervention unless he was genuinely concerned with being "free-cased."

CONCLUSION

Accounts of involuntary police contact were shared by participants and referenced as reasons for why they distrust law enforcement. While they do not prove guilt or innocence for either the citizens or the officers involved, they are significant accounts and worthy of discussion. They reflect the nature of black citizen–police interactions in the wake of a new police department. Such stories provide insight into the real-life perceptions of Meacham Park citizens as they persistently faced mounting stereotypes and disadvantage in their neighborhood. The social drawbacks, for them, have been tantamount to and are the effects of foregoing race and class injustices exacerbated by communal isolation and police aggression.

As a consequence to social disenfranchisement—a strategically orchestrated commitment to avoid and failure to attend to the sensitivities of its most vulnerable residents—insolence emerged that could not be denied. Meanwhile, unbeknownst to everyone, the motives of the murderous acts of Kevin Johnson and Charles "Cookie" Thornton were taking shape. In this study, they represent the breaking points of social constraint—instances where people and life's circumstances (black/white, lack/surplus, exclusion/inclusion) finally give way to friction, igniting inconceivable tragedies. This was certainly the case for the City of Kirkwood, a continuously evolving suburban community where its residents coexist separately. They share suburban status, while simultaneously representing the two ends of the social spectrum—poor blacks and affluent whites. In the next chapter, the stories of Kevin and Cookie, both black men from Meacham Park, illustrate how social quandaries left unaddressed became life altering and catastrophic for all.

FOUR

"It's the same song . . ."

THE TRAGEDIES OF KEVIN JOHNSON AND CHARLES "COOKIE" THORNTON

They got me trapped, can barely walk the city streets
Without a cop harassing me, searching me
Then asking my identity
Hands up, throw me up against the wall
Didn't do a thing at all . . .

. . . . .

Bang, bang, count another casualty
But it's a cop who's shot in brutality
Who do you blame? It's a shame because the man's slain
He got caught in the chains of his own game
How can I feel guilty after all the things they did to me?
Sweated me, hunted me
Trapped in my own community
One day I'm gonna bust
Blow up on this society
Why did ya lie to me?
I couldn't find a trace of equality . . .

. . . . .

Trapped in a corner, dark and I couldn't see the light
Thoughts in my mind was the nine and a better life.

"TRAPPED," TUPAC SHAKUR[1]

TERRANCE'S ASSERTION—"IT'S THE SAME SONG . . ."—could not seem truer. Thousands of miles apart, at different ages and life phases, and even through death, we find ourselves examining the narratives of blacks in disadvantaged communities as they face police aggression and inequality. While their circumstances may differ, their plights are constant. Poor black citizens experience extreme social isolation (racial, economical, political) and face further disenfranchisement when their pleas are met with perceivably blatant disregard, avoidance, and irreconcilable backlashes. Hence, they feel "trapped," abandoned by a system that has historically been insensitive and inattentive to the needs of the poor, people of color, and women. This was certainly the case in the City of Kirkwood, and what follows were the circumstances that inevitably gave way to its misfortune.

Years of differential treatment for poor blacks in Meacham Park—reportedly met with denial, negligence, and in some instances revenge by its affluent, white government officials—were coming to a head. As some blacks vocalized concerns about the racial divide and persisting tensions between themselves, city officials, and the police, Lola, fifty-nine, recalled feeling like they had reached a stalemate:

> Separate but not equal, we have the Meacham Park Neighborhood Association. We have meetings and we get with Kirkwood and we just don't see eye to eye. Kirkwood feels that we don't have a problem, everybody's equal. They say we have no racial problems here.

Kirkwood made no substantive moves to eradicate the racial tension. Despite long-standing racial tension, pre- and post-annexation, no awareness was raised or changes made to lessen the distrust and alienation of blacks in Meacham Park. So while it appeared to be business as usual—poor blacks and affluent whites coexisting amid steady differential treatment—the effects of isolation took an unprecedented turn for the worse. Neighborhood estrangement became lethal, giving way to black-on-white violence rather than the typical black-on-black. Ironically, as Kirkwood annexed Meacham Park to presumably curtail, control, and contain poor black crime and insolence from its affluent, white neighborhoods, it created an atmosphere conducive for it. Hence, detachment became the mode of operation in this suburban community. Kirkwood officials seemingly remained inattentive and aloof regarding the quality of life for its disadvantaged black citizens, and reciprocally, some of those citizens became detached in preserving life for its affluent, white ones.

Therefore, in two separate shootings, one in July 2005 and one in August 2008, all citizens of Kirkwood—poor black, affluent white, family, friends, and coworkers alike—were left to contend with eight fatalities. No one could have anticipated these incidents, though in hindsight, the signs were visibly intensifying. In either case, murder is never the solution. Violence should not be the only way to elicit attention, address conflict, or provoke social change. However, this is the state of our society, and more directly, the downside to inherently inflexible social structures unwilling to review, revise, and correct its policies and practices, even amid crises.

This space of rigidity and obstinacy is where we find ourselves as survivors, wounded and perplexed, fervently working to make sense of countless tragedies. It is with this bewilderment in mind that I write this chapter. My goal in recalling the stories of Kevin and Cookie is in no way to condone their acts of violence or champion them as murderers. In the same sense, neither is my goal to further condemn them. Rather, I aim to provide a broader picture for how escalating social inadequacies, left unaddressed, lead to callousness. Like those they preyed upon, the shooters undeniably also felt targeted. Through varying circumstances, they were first ambushed by what they believed to be injustice.

Replacing emotions with objectivity, this chapter examines the experiences and perceptions of both shooters through the accounts of their neighbors in Meacham Park. All but two of the study's thirty participants came into information through the stories of others in their neighborhood: two of them reported actually being on the scene—one at the home where the search for Kevin initially took place and the other around the corner at the scene of McEntee's shooting.

As we turn attention to the stories of the shooters, let us reserve judgment, especially as our personal impressions of them and their actions prove ineffective in prompting social change. Instead, focus on the shooters' beliefs, *their* frame of minds—as nonsensical as they may appear to be—as communicated and understood through witness accounts. I believe that this is where we may find answers, and thus inform ourselves in ways that may work to offset future incidents, honoring the lives of the fallen.

"AN EYE FOR AN EYE": THE MURDER
OF SERGEANT MCENTEE

Kim's account is one of many chronicling the events leading up to and following the murder of Sgt. McEntee:

> They [officers] were outside looking at his [Kevin's] car. They had a warrant for his arrest. His brother [Bam-Bam] ran up the steps and ran back down and had a heart attack. They [the police] were the first ones to respond. We think the police should automatically come in and start giving CPR, but they don't and they didn't. They didn't do any of that. They just called the paramedics, the fire trucks, they didn't give CPR. The officers were walking through the house searching for Kevin, looking for whatever, and he was watching them do all of this.

With Kim's mention of a warrant for Kevin's arrest, we learn that Kevin's involvement with the criminal justice system did not begin with the 2005 murder of Sgt. McEntee. It began with a 2002 domestic assault conviction, landing Kevin on probation. Kevin had apparently violated his probation, placing officers outside of his grandmother's and great-grandmother's homes, both of which happen to be directly next door to each other. Before officers' arrival at those addresses, it has been suggested that they had located Kevin's little brother in the neighborhood and questioned him about Kevin's whereabouts. Kevin's great-grandmother reported hearing his brother, twelve-year-old "Bam-Bam," gasping for breath after having been chased home by the police in search of Kevin.[2] Shortly thereafter, Bam-Bam collapsed and lay dying from a congenital heart condition as officers reportedly "stepped over him" and continued their search for Kevin throughout the great-grandmother's house.

By all accounts, officers' failure to attempt to revive Bam-Bam occurred while Kevin purportedly watched from next door, peering through a window from inside of his grandmother's home that was perfectly aligned with a window displaying the inside of his great-grandmother's home. From two different locations, both Kevin and his great grandmother were left believing officers were more concerned with catching him than providing medical assistance to his brother, Joseph "Bam-Bam" Long, who later died. Consequently, hours later, Kevin emerged from a neighboring home to avenge his brother's death, which he saw as having been avoidable had officers intervened. With a 9mm, he circled the Meacham Park neighborhood and opened fired on Sgt. McEntee as he sat in his police cruiser, killing him after a total of seven shots to the head and upper torso.

> It was ironic the way it happened. At the time, I didn't know what Kevin had done. I was down here [pointing away from the scene] and I said, "Damn, those sound like gun shots." By the time I made it up here, the police was coming.

These are the recollections of Terrance. Just blocks away, Terrance remembered hearing numerous shots fired. While he had no knowledge of all that had transpired in the hours since having seen Kevin earlier that day, he sensed something was very wrong. Therefore, like others in the neighborhood, he followed the sounds of the gunfire and sirens and was stunned by what he learned.

Within minutes of Sgt. McEntee being shot, details surrounding the day's events spread like wildfire throughout the Meacham Park neighborhood. As the participants reminisced, many of them expressed shock, like Felecia, thirty-seven, who stated: "I was shocked . . . let me put it like this, you didn't have time to think, I just froze." In sum, no one could have anticipated Bam-Bam dying, let alone Kevin murdering Sgt. McEntee as a result. While some participants reported McEntee as having an unfavorable reputation in the neighborhood, particularly among black youth, no one wanted or fathomed such a gritty end for him. One participant, Travis, referred to it as a "lose-lose situation":

> It's very unfortunate that something like that happened because to me, per-sonally, it was a lose-lose situation. Kevin lost his life and his family and the police lost his life and his family.

As everyone—poor blacks and affluent whites, inside and outside of the City of Kirkwood—worked to make sense of Sgt. McEntee's murder and the events leading up to it, they would find themselves once again embroiled in another horrific incident. This time it would not be with a troubled black teen from Meacham Park who had already been entangled with the criminal justice system, but rather a middle-aged black entrepreneur who had no his-tory with the criminal justice system and who had seemingly lived a life that garnered respect from both the blacks in his neighborhood and the whites in Kirkwood Proper.

"THE TRUTH WILL COME OUT IN THE END": THE SHOOTING RAMPAGE ON KIRKWOOD'S CITY HALL

> He never said anything, not one inkling that he was going up there to do what he did. I mean nothing, absolutely nothing. He said, "Hey, man," but he was always like that. "Glory be to God, I love you, man. I finally caught you at home." We were at my house and Cookie's a big eater, so he said, "Man, I'm hungry." So we were sitting there, eating burgers, watching TV, and just talking about stuff. We graduated from high school together, we grew up together. We talked about City Hall a little, but he really didn't seem focused on it.

These were the final hours of Charles "Cookie" Thornton's life as described by Dwayne, fifty-four. Little did he know that this would be the last time he would see his friend alive. It would be only hours later that Cookie would descend on Kirkwood's City Hall in a deadly tirade. He had attended city council meetings numerous times before, often distraught and verbally ranting over what he perceived to be persisting injustices leveled against him. But never had he been moved to such violence until then—days after having learned that his last efforts to be heard and vindicated had fallen through. Cookie's federal lawsuit against the City of Kirkwood, allowing him the right to freely speak at public meetings, had been thrown out. At that juncture, with no legal recourse or channel for addressing believed acts of discrimination against the City of Kirkwood, it appeared that all had been lost.

For years, Cookie had been embroiled in a contentious relationship with the City of Kirkwood. Tension dates back to the 1991 annexing of Meacham Park. It was during this time that he reportedly landed a demolition contract with the city, whereby his company would level and clear Meacham Park's land to make room for the new shopping plaza, Kirkwood Commons. Though disputed, most believed this to be a quid pro quo agreement: Cookie would solidify the black vote in favor of the Meacham Park annexation in exchange for lucrative demolition contracts. Here is how Terrance explained it:

> Cookie's biggest problem was he was one of the proponents of the annexation with Kirkwood. Why? Because he was in the construction business and one of the things they [Kirkwood city officials] promised him was that he was going to get a piece of the construction project. They turn around, he don't get none of the contracts, he don't get none of the money.

Cookie's implied construction deal would have been consistent with Kirkwood's initial promise to support Meacham Park blacks and their businesses. As the annexation project would employ thousands—during the construction phase and well after—the City of Kirkwood promised them full priority regarding employment. This was one of several significant selling points in the move to annex. However, while many blacks were skeptical and did not trust white city officials, it has been suggested that many had full confidence in Cookie. After all, he was one of them—bred and reared in Meacham Park—and therefore, some thought him to be genuinely concerned and forthright regarding the future of the neighborhood. Mark, fifty, on the other hand, stood his ground. Unlike some, he refused to buy in to the land deals, despite Cookie's position, and said:

> No was my answer. I didn't want to sell and I still don't want to sell. But with Cookie, like I said, he had gotten on the other side of the fence for a while [in

agreement] Then when he came back, he was like, "Man, they're [Kirkwood] doing us wrong."

In sum, Cookie became one of Kirkwood's most influential black allies in the merging of the two communities. By all accounts, he was rather vocal regarding the benefits of annexing and excitedly looked forward to a partnership geographically and professionally with the City of Kirkwood. As Francis, sixty, recalled the relationship between Cookie and some city officials, she described him as "being in like Flynn at first." She continued:

> They [city officials] were like his best friends, they ate together, they'd come to his place, he'd go to their place. He had a big smile for them, they had a handshake for him. It was lovie dovie until that contract fell through.

In anticipation of his newfound business venture, Cookie ambitiously purchased trucks and other costly equipment for what he believed would be a massive undertaking for his construction company. He now needed to hire laborers and so forth. This would be his biggest and by far most profitable opportunity yet, and therefore money well spent. While Cookie envisioned his business as a significant part of the new redevelopment efforts, unfortunately, it proved to be no more than just that—a vision. City officials argued that Cookie was never promised a demolition contract and that such decisions were left to the discretion of the developers. In fact, when asked about the supposed contracts, former mayor Marge Schramm stated:

> I know we strongly urged that he be included in minority businesses—we did require a certain amount of work for minorities. But that's not just Cookie.[3]

Becoming clear almost immediately, there had been a grave misunderstanding of Cookie's supposed role as a contracted minority businessman. He did not receive the demolition contracts as expected, and consequently, he felt lied to and used by city officials. Dorothy, fifty-seven, too, believed promises were made and then broken, and here is how she made sense of the change in Cookie's temperament:

> I think that Cookie was promised a lot and that he was lied to. He was used and manipulated and once he figured it out, he became irate because he was hurt and disappointed. I think he really thought he could trust certain individuals and he just snapped.

Yet again, the City of Kirkwood, or Kirkwood Proper, appeared to be the greatest beneficiary in this project. With Cookie's support, they won the vote to annex Meacham Park—landing them the right to a significant portion of Meacham Park's land, the construction of a new shopping plaza, and millions in tax incentives—but they did so with Cookie's full support.

With no way of validating an official agreement between Cookie and Kirkwood city officials, written or verbal, what resonated most was Kirkwood's promise to include minority businesses and afford employment opportunities to blacks from Meacham Park, neither of which, many participants argue, happened. While a few participants suggested that Cookie did land one or two opportunities to work with developers before finally being dropped, and that several residents did gain jobs at the new shopping plaza, Kirkwood had established a trend: a white competitor received the bulk of the demolition work as did white citizens with jobs in the shopping plaza. In general, many participants did not believe that city officials followed through on what they hoped would address the loss of their black businesses and high rates of unemployment in their community. Instead, they perceived them as giving the appearance of inclusion to pacify them, all the while maintaining exclusion. Mark explained:

> They'll lead you along, they'll appease you, but in the end, they'll look the other way. They'll walk away.

Cookie came to the same realization. Like many of his neighbors, the annexation left him at a disadvantage, and even more so, given that he felt partly responsible for theirs. Mark continued to describe him as feeling as if he had no place:

> He couldn't run back to the neighborhood because he dealt with a lot of people and they had gotten rid of their property.

Cookie was embarrassed, and the more resistance he met from city officials in hopes of vindicating himself, the more enflamed he became.

With double the frustration of other Meacham Park blacks, Cookie took to protesting with a vengeance. Fixated with trying to make things right and exposing the perceivably unscrupulous, discriminative practices of city officials, he frequently expressed disgust. Becoming increasingly aggressive, he did so at city council meetings, on the street corners wearing placards, and by filing lawsuits. In return, he was met with thousands of dollars in citations, numerous arrests—one of which occurred at a city council meeting—and numerous failed lawsuits. Shamed, separated from his wife, with a preponderance of debt, and seemingly without other recourse for redeeming himself—his reputation, family, community, or business—on February 7, 2008, Charles "Cookie" Thornton left a suicide note on his bed stating, "The truth will come out in the end."[4] Scorned, bitter, and exhausted from years of feuding, he proceeded to Kirkwood City Hall for what would become his last and final stance with city officials. By his own account, Cookie had decided that the truth as he knew it would be best served through death—his own and that of those who represented a system that concealed that truth. Denise, sixty, explained:

> He [Cookie] targeted the mayor, he had targeted the commissioner. He was trying to get the lawyer for Kirkwood. You [Cookie] killed policemen, you killed innocent people, you killed people that were in charge of the city.

Therefore, as described by Denise, the world learned that a black fifty-two-year-old Meacham Park resident went on a shooting rampage at a Kirkwood City Council meeting, resulting in six dead, including himself, and two critically injured. Among those dead were a Kirkwood police sergeant and officer, two city council members, and the director of public works. Cookie was killed by responding officers. Among the injured were Kirkwood's mayor, Mike Schwoboda, and a *Suburban Journal* reporter. Seven months later Schwoboda would die from injuries sustained in the shootings at City Hall, and from cancer complications.

Cookie had grown tired; in his eyes, people and the system had persistently failed him. When conventional means to clear his name and make good on all that had happened became seemingly unavailable, he became unconscionably desperate and turned to murder. In an effort to make sense of this catastrophic end, St. Louis forensic psychiatrist Dr. John Rabun suggested:

> It may be because after years of being devoted or involved, the person starts to feel jilted or muscled out or maneuvered out ... anger can be cumulative ... when they feel wronged ... they can justify 10 different ways why it's right to kill somebody, even when it goes against their religious tradition. They hash it over and over again before they actually do it, until they have numbed themselves to it. If you obsess about something, you are turning it over thousands of times a day in your mind, and every time, you feel more comfortable turning thought into action.[5]

As Meacham Park gained national attention for the actions of Kevin Johnson and Charles "Cookie" Thornton, all thirty study participants experienced vicarious police contact—indirect police contact whereby citizens acquire knowledge of the police through the experiences of others.[6] Research shows such contacts as common among blacks, and blacks in Meacham Park are no exception. As blacks are likelier to encounter the police compared to their white counterparts, it is commonplace for them to share and exchange stories of those experiences with their family, friends, and neighbors. Through learned accounts or secondhand experiences, those listening and observing internalize police encounters as their own.

Blacks also come to experience vicarious policing through various media accounts, especially regarding police brutality.[7] For example, through footage of the Rodney King beating or perhaps coverage of the Trayvon Martin murder, blacks become further enthralled and involved with dispelling police aggression and perceived injustices within the criminal justice system (even when only pseudo law enforcement is involved). In essence, they become witnesses to or even survivors of such acts, and thus associate them with previous incidents and very real possibilities for future ones.

What blacks experience indirectly can be just as detrimental as encounters faced directly. It leaves them sensing that, criminality notwithstanding, what made other blacks vulnerable to aggressive policing may easily do the same for them. So while vicarious police contacts are just that, they are significant nonetheless; they negatively shape black perceptions of the police. Therefore, it is through what participants heard and saw regarding the police—prior to and especially following both incidents in Kirkwood—that they came to understand Kevin's and Cookie's murderous acts against them. They unanimously believed police harassment as having played a significant role in precipitating the actions of both.

Nevertheless, as many participants viewed police behavior as having in some way fueled these events, most made clear their disgust with the murders. In fact, seven older participants expressed great disdain for Kevin's and Cookie's shootings, and they chastised both men's earlier actions and involvement with police. For example, three participants characterized Kevin as a troubled youth. They talked about his association with other troubled individuals as well as a "less than admirable" history. In sum, they believed that Kevin's actions warranted police attention. As for Cookie, one participant spoke of complaints from neighbors. She suggested that it was not city officials—as often believed—that prompted contentious police interactions with him, but rather his neighbors calling in on him.

Generally, the participants attempted to be fair in their assessment of both tragedies. While they attributed excessive police behaviors to Kevin's and Cookie's actions, on some level they understood why the police initially sought both men out. Even so, those same participants made it clear that officers could have handled things differently. In other words, what participants learned and shared regarding Kevin's and Cookie's cases reflected a view of both men, in the end, as having been incited by aggressive policing. This was especially true for participants who had experienced involuntary police contacts or acts of police aggression themselves.

The participants frequently talked about these two cases, and collectively, they defined police-citizen interaction in the community of Meacham Park as negative. Despite specifically calling attention to Cookie, one participant (Francis) described the frequent conversations and the broader impact of those cases regarding race relations and inevitably policing relations:

> The wounds are still not healed. The citizens, the white and the black citizens, still have animosity for each other. The police had animosity, they don't like you and you don't like them. The people talk about it a lot. The residents in Meacham Park talk about the incidents and residents of Kirkwood talk about the incidents. He [Cookie Thornton] was a madman, that's what the white folks say . . . and the black folks say he did justice. So, that's conflict.

As dialogue and ill feelings persisted regarding these cases, the participants discussed what transpired moments before the tragedies, the role of police harassment in both tragedies, and finally, how they came to have involuntary police-citizen interactions of their own in the aftermath. Accordingly, the next section explores how a compilation of indirect police experiences, witnessed and shared throughout the neighborhood of Meacham Park, led to turning points in Kevin's and Cookie's decisions to kill.

Failing to Listen: Too Little, Too Late

As participants described what took place in the moments leading up to the tragedies, they seemed to be trying to make sense of Kevin's and Cookie's actions. By the time each incident occurred, both Kevin and Cookie had established histories with the local authorities. Kevin was on probation at the time and was being sought for a violation, while Cookie had faced countless citations and several arrests for disruptive behavior at city council meetings. Because many of the participants had experienced similar encounters with police, or knew someone who had, they sought to understand what led to the breaking point for both men. These accounts were not so much about justifying the actions of Kevin and Cookie, but rather about humanizing and contextualizing them. There were instances that could have potentially worked to deter the shootings but instead were lost because of pervasive disconnects between blacks in Meacham Park and the aggressive Kirkwood officers that policed them.

Kevin's Case. "It's so many people who are doing a lot of talking and not listening," said Romona Miller, the assistant principal of Kirkwood High School.[8] While she was not a resident of Meacham Park or a project participant, her involvement with the Kevin Johnson case is significant. She was one of few black educators in the district who regularly communicated with youth from the Meacham Park neighborhood. Additionally, she was Kevin Johnson's former biology teacher, and later, a character witness for him during the penalty phase of his trial.

One year prior to the murder of police Sergeant William McEntee, she reportedly went to the police with concerns regarding troubled interactions between McEntee and black youth in Meacham Park. She had received several complaints from students—one of whom was Kevin Johnson—and thought them to be serious enough to warrant a personal visit to the Kirkwood police station. Here is what she told the *St. Louis Beacon:*

> Before the Kevin Johnson case, I went to the police department and spoke to them. "Here are some of the things the kids are saying about a man named Mac," I told them. I didn't know his name was McEntee. I went as an educator.[9]

Miller reported numerous negative accounts regarding Sgt. McEntee in the neighborhood of Meacham Park. Kim recalled the kids saying "that he [McEntee] was mean and stuff like that." Denise characterized him as a bully and suggested tension between him and residents "because of the way he talked to and treated people." Francis reported hearing the same, but her statements indicated that some came to know McEntee positively. She explained:

He came to our meetings [Meacham Park Neighborhood Association]. He was very friendly and very informational. He was one person when he came to our meetings, but they said on the street, he was another.

Kirkwood Police Department had often been invited to give neighborhood crime reports, and McEntee had reportedly been the police representative on occasion. However, despite his involvement and the kindness some may have been privy to in those meetings, the sentiments on the street remained negative toward him. The word in the neighborhood was that McEntee not only corrected or chastened the youth, but was insolent toward them as well. Despite the favorable perceptions of a few, there remained an undeniable consensus in the Meacham Park neighborhood that McEntee was instigative and disrespectful. Jasmine, forty-two, reported:

I've heard rumors that he was supposed to been a racist and I don't think I ever had a run-in with him to actually know if that's true or not. I just heard that from others.

Since Jasmine did not know McEntee, she could not confirm whether he was racist. However, because she knew Kevin and she knew those sharing the stories, she admittedly shared the same accounts with others as though they had been her own.

Reports of McEntee's alleged impudence went beyond the Meacham Park neighborhood to no avail. The police reportedly never followed up on Miller's information, and instead acted, from her perspective, as if her visit never took place. She stated:

They never took any ownership that that had happened. They left it saying, "We'll check into it." I remember saying at the time, "Kirkwood is primed for a race riot."[10]

Miller's visit to the police station would prove to be a significant missed opportunity, one of many that could have changed the tide of what was to happen next. While there had been other attempts to intervene, Miller's arguably was one of the most crucial. Credible information was reportedly given to the police regarding one of its own, and yet it went unaddressed. In Francis's recollection of her efforts to work with Kevin, whom she identified as intelligent but headed in the wrong direction, she places the onus on the local police department for failing to follow up on its officers:

He was a very smart young man. You try to redirect them [young people], guide them, sometimes you don't ever reach them. It was just some things that contributed to that that perhaps could've been dealt with better.

Even though Miller's report stood disputed, particularly as in that instance it was communicated only between her and one officer, what cannot be disputed are the subsequent police reports submitted by the media. Black or white, involved or not, the entire St. Louis metropolitan area heard startling accounts from the press of the murder of a Kirkwood police sergeant and a young black male suspect from Meacham Park who was now at large. Instead of citizens' reports to police, it was now the police relaying information to citizens and seeking their help. Here is one example of an urgent all-points bulletin (APB) from a local TV station:

> A Kirkwood police sergeant died ... several hours after being shot at an apartment complex ... police say he was responding to a fireworks call ... a white Ford Explorer, was later found ... heavily armed officers raced to the scene ... police say he should be considered armed and very dangerous ... described as 5'7" and 160 lbs. . . . he has some tattoos pictured on the left ... County police have taken over the investigation.[11]

While most participants reported being shocked at learning that Kevin killed an officer, they were mostly concerned with the details surrounding the officers' actions. Since the police had an established history of negative interactions with their community, they wanted to know what the police did that pushed Kevin over the edge. As participants discussed officers' pursuit of Kevin and their response to the collapse of his brother Bam-Bam, they sought to understand how it all came together. Here are a few accounts of what they learned from one another:

> Barbara, fifty-three: What I understood is that he [Kevin] was upset because of his brother and I don't know the whole story. But he [Kevin] was saying that the officer didn't pay attention to his brother, who had a bad heart and he [Sgt. McEntee] could have saved him. It's very vague, very vague.

> Keith, twenty-two: I don't know detail-to-detail cause it's always different stories. From what I know, I guess Sgt. McEntee came looking for Kevin. I guess he [Kevin] was on house arrest. Kevin's little brother Bam-Bam collapsed, the grandma asked them to call 911, he [Sgt. McEntee] didn't and when Kevin seen him [Sgt. McEntee], they say he shot him.

> Mark: I wasn't there. But in general, I think about what I know about Bam-Bam. I was told that they [the police] picked him up and shook him and when

they put him down, he ran back to the grandmother's house and what I was told was that when he [Bam-Bam] went in, he collapsed.

Details from each of the stories differ. However, they are similar in that none of those participants were present, yet they all drew conclusions and worked to make sense of what transpired through bits of information shared throughout the community. So while they readily admit to learning the details of Kevin's case indirectly, they still discussed the events surrounding the case as if they had experienced them firsthand. We see how many participants internalized learned information and processed it as if it were their own through Ed's (fifty-five) account as well:

> The police was knocking on the door, telling them [the grandmother and brother] he had a search warrant. But I guess they figured he's [Kevin] going to run back to his [brother's] body. I was told Kevin was close by and could see what was going on. [The police] wouldn't even let them back in the house to make an ambulance call. They had to make it from the across the street. That was what the big discussion was all about, with how long did it take them [ambulance] to get there. And then after Kevin saw that, he heard the news that his brother had died. He looked at the time frame to where he sees his family outside the house, he looked at the time frame where the ambulance didn't come. You know I've had a lot of deaths in my family, but to see things happening, to try and protect . . . that was his younger brother. I don't know how a man could feel.

Despite learning this information from others, as Ed recalled the details, he internalized them, relived them, and consequently, experienced them by comparing Kevin's loss to his.

While most participants admitted to not knowing all the details surrounding Bam-Bam's death, they internalized what they learned. This case hinged on the death of a child, and that the police continued their search for Kevin as he lay dying; this was, for many participants, inconceivable. Similarly internalizing what she learned, another participant (Dorothy) was certain that officers should have been doing something other than searching for Kevin:

> I just think it's a tragedy, just an utter tragedy. Decency and humanity should stand when other things don't and being a servant, serving in a capacity of being a protector and someone that's looked at to be a help but here a child has collapsed in the doorway of his home and he's unconscious but yet you [police] just gone step over him.

Convinced that there are two sides to every story, Dorothy felt Kevin's family deserved the benefit of the doubt. Her empathy likely grew out of her own negative experiences with the police. Her "accumulative experience" negatively influenced her view of the police and predisposed her to think the worst of them.[12] This a common pattern among several participants. Kevin, too, went through this process: it was through all that he learned indirectly and experienced directly that he came to blame Sgt. McEntee for his brother's death.

Cookie's Case. Despite a history of reportedly bad encounters between Kevin Johnson and Sgt. McEntee, Kevin's final murderous act can be characterized as an impulsive killing: an impromptu act committed out of the sudden loss of Kevin's brother. The purported ongoing feud between Kevin and McEntee was sporadic, and thus, what the participants saw and heard regarding it was often ambiguous. By contrasts, disputes between Charles "Cookie" Thornton, city officials, and the police were overt and well known. For years, they manifested in very public ways through protests and other acts, and therefore were visible to the residents in Meacham Park and to many in Kirkwood Proper. One participant (Francis) witnessed much of it. She said:

> It lasted for a long period of time. [for] about ten years that was going on and it was getting hotter and hotter and there wasn't too much we could do to cool it off.

Another participant (Rodney, fifty-five) even suggested some people were going to city council meetings on purpose, just to see Cookie demonstrating.

> We went to see what Cookie was doing, cause he would have signs. It was like a joke, you know. But he meant what he was saying.

Rodney's reference to Cookie's displays as "like a joke" suggests he was nothing more than a rabble-rouser from the perspectives of those around him. If that is how his neighbors perceived him, how must the city council members have perceived him? It is no wonder that Cookie believed his complaints were not taken seriously. Cookie had spoken out for years against what he perceived to be injustices committed against him as well as other blacks in Meacham Park. His protests were certainly not a joke to him; he was literally fighting for his life. In his mind, he was fighting to restore his name, his character, and all that was lost to him as a result of perceived discrimination and manipulation by the City of Kirkwood. He was crying out, and by design, he did so in ways that could not be ignored—at least not visibly. Mark explained:

> Cookie did a lot of things, most things the right way. But he tried to get a lot of attention by wearing placards, trying to get people to back him. But a lot of people in Meacham Park didn't know how to think about Cookie because he is the one that kind of influence them to sell [their homes].

Cookie's efforts to gain support backfired. Reportedly, he had hoped that with a strong backing, he could pressure the local government into acknowledging their mistreatment of him, and thus make amends for it. Interestingly, the City of Kirkwood did offer to erase twenty thousand dollars worth of parking tickets and code violations they had levied against him—"if he agreed to be less confrontational."[13] However, this only enflamed him further. Their offer suggested that *he* was the one who needed to redirect his behaviors, when the point of his protests had been about having *them* own and change theirs.

Consequently, Cookie's protests persisted. Whereas Kevin felt wronged by the lack of intervention on the part of police, for Cookie, intervention—even by the chief of police—in hopes of dissuading him only intensified his actions. Tiffany, thirty-six, said it best:

> The city officials and the police are not accepting nothing. Basically, they saying they didn't do anything wrong. They don't know why Kevin killed Sgt. McEntee, they don't know why Cookie came into City Hall. It's kind of like they don't know why instead of saying, "We [city officials] probably didn't do everything that we should have done." They still don't want to accept responsibility for their actions.

Hence, as they did in the case of Kevin, participants continued sharing what they saw and heard regarding his actions. This is what Marsha, fifty-nine, witnessed:

> We were right there, we saw it, when he wore those signs. He'd be standing on the corner down there by Meramec and everything and you know them signs that go down the front and all the way down the back with a ball and chain on his leg and everything. I called my husband and said, "Baby, Cookie is standing up here on the corner with a sign hanging off of him, with a chain on his leg and all that stuff."

Francis recalled Cookie being arrested following a city council meeting. She stated:

> He [Cookie] went to a meeting and they handcuffed him for disturbing the Kirkwood City Council, handcuffed his hands behind his back and took him out by his collar, drug him down the steps and out and over to the police department.

Additionally, Denise recalled incidents in which Cookie had used props and gone on what seemed to be long tangents when allowed to speak in city council meetings.

> Every Thursday they had city council meetings, he would come up and do demonstrations and talk. They have an open mic time and we could be there for some other reason and here comes Cookie. He had signs and he would hand out bananas [to City Hall officials] and say, "If you all act like a bunch of monkeys, I'll give you a bunch of bananas."

As he continued expressing discontent with what he believed to be racism and failed promises by the local government, Cookie came to be regarded as a "thorn in Kirkwood's side." However, his actions had an inverse effect and did not compel people to join in and fight with him. Others became involved only to the extent of trying to change him. His pleas became spectacles. Where his initial intent was to highlight the differential treatment of blacks in the City of Kirkwood, instead he came to be labeled as deviant and was progressively treated as such. Cookie went from having a stellar reputation among blacks and whites throughout the City of Kirkwood to being characterized as obsessively disgruntled and insane. One of his great friends, Franklin McCallie, a retired principal of Kirkwood High School who happens to be white, released a statement to the press two days after the rampage. He remembered Cookie as:

> A vivacious, enthusiastic member of the Kirkwood Community. . . a full-time booster for young people's activities within the Meacham Park neighborhood and the wider Kirkwood community. He was one of the most out-going persons I ever met. My wife and I attended his wedding. I saw him often in the community. We hugged each time we met.[14]

Additionally, Karen, sixty-four, remembered his voicemail announcement being "Praise the Lord, hallelujah," and Felecia described him as "a respectful man in the neighborhood." She stated, "If he could help you, he would. If he could give you a job, he would."

Cookie had been known to employ black men in the Meacham Park neighborhood. When they could not find employment otherwise, he often gave them work to do while simultaneously teaching them the trade. Johnny, fifty-seven, was one of them. Here is what he said:

> Sometimes he [Cookie] tore down houses and stuff like that and when he got home, he did his paperwork and he'd tell me, "I'll call you when a job needs to be done and we'll go to work." If it was cold, we couldn't do asphalt and stuff like that, I understood that. So then he'd keep me something to do around the house. Then in March, April, May, we'd have lots of work. Now, I don't really have nobody to give me work. I just try to work for other people around here.

Furthermore, Cookie started and participated in several Meacham Park organizations, one of which was the Men's Breakfast Club. He had also established a good rapport with the youth in his community. Crystal, nineteen, recalled visiting his home when she was younger:

> He was always doing things when I was younger, like things for the kids. We could just go up there to his house and ride go-carts. He would let everybody take turns on the field across the street. He had a playground in his backyard.

The very two groups that Cookie spent time with, helped, and garnered respect from—black men and youth—are the same who experienced negative interactions with the police in their neighborhood. Thus, watching Cookie change from a seemingly God-fearing man, who met most with a big smile and a blaring "FAN-TASTIC!" when asked about his day, to being depicted as a seeming monster only furthered the racial divide and distrust. So as some participants felt obliged to celebrate him, to remember what he had come to mean to them, some whites were perceivably disturbed and angered by it. Here is how Mark explained it:

> The white folks don't want you to mention Cookie's name. It scares them. It frightens them, you understand? He shook their comfort level of what could happen if you got pushed over the edge and without any help, you pushed that man so far that you changed him. You changed him from a God-fearing man to wanting to paint him as a monster, and no matter who you believe or talk to, that was just not the same man that did what was supposedly happened.

It is in these overlapping exchanges that opportunities for closing the racial divide were lost. The participants witnessed Cookie's downward spiral through what they heard and saw. Consequently, they took notice of all the dynamics that changed him and of the response of city officials, the police, and the City of Kirkwood at large in their handling of him. Hence, ownership became a salient theme. Though at varying degrees, while the participants held Cookie responsible for inappropriate and unseemly behaviors, they also believed the City of Kirkwood persistently failed to accept any responsibility for fueling it.

Denials of perceived racial problems surrounding Cookie or otherwise, directly or indirectly, did not prove advantageous here, but rather catastrophic. It only furthered the effects of power in relation to differential treatment. Dominant structures and their actors work best at policing others and not themselves. By this, they benefit from not having to be cognizant of a consequence; that is, they face no pressure to make sensible decisions, to minimize tension that prove advantageous to those least powerful. Case in point: the strong arm of law enforcement excessively ticketing and citing Cookie in the neighborhood of Meacham Park—twenty thousand dollars' worth—reinforced the idea that the inclinations of government officials, and more directly, the police, were to be persistently aggressive when interacting with blacks.

So while Cookie displayed obsessive behaviors, likewise, the local government habitually ignored the long-reaching effects of segregating and isolating its disadvantaged black community. Kevin's and Cookie's murders should not be reduced to a couple of rare incidents or a few interactions simply gone awry. Rather, it is through all the details, the broken pieces, that we should understand these incidents in a broader sense. They are the products of preexisting dysfunction, of purposely constructed relationships whereby the advantaged and disadvantaged exist contrarily, with one reciprocally distressing the other.

As people are deliberately and inequitably matched up one against the other—the powerful and the powerless—so are the discomforts, knowingly and unknowingly. What makes for normalized pangs among those disadvantaged can inevitably becomes unexpected upsets for the advantaged. Individual distresses and clashes should have been anticipated. The relationship between Meacham Park and the City of Kirkwood—from the onset and at the highest level—was not only forged under adversarial circumstances, but was then pervasively neglected. This was evident, as Pete, fifty-nine, attempted to explain, with tears streaming down his face. Pete had been childhood friends with Cookie, as well as with several of the victims. Notice the irreparable shift he felt, even before being told what had transpired:

I was over in Illinois when my wife tried to get me by phone. When I got her, she said, "Don't come through the City of Kirkwood" and I thought "Cookie, what have you done?" I didn't know anything about it, nothing. That was just in my spirit, and people were blowing my phone up because they know that I usually go to the city council meetings. But that's not the travesty for me and my family. It's just that we had a personal relationship with every one of those people . . . [crying] . . . I'm sorry.

The Role of the Police and Harassment

Despite the fact that seven years have elapsed since Kevin Johnson shot Sgt. McEntee and four years since Cookie Thornton's shooting rampage at City Hall, participants easily and clearly remembered the details of each incident. Many participants even recalled where they were and what they were doing when each incident occurred. While recalling the shooting of Sgt. McEntee, Johnny stated,

> I was over my friend John's house watching TV when the news came on and I said, "Oh my goodness."

Another respondent, Ricky, fifty-six, said:

> [My wife and I] were at the Lake of the Ozarks on vacation and somebody called and told us that the FBI and the officers were using our driveway . . .

As Jasmine recalled the City Hall shootings, she, too, described her whereabouts:

> I remember being at home and it was a group of us sitting around the table and we were playing cards. One of my cousins called me and said turn the TV on, it was a shooting at City Hall. But at the time, she didn't know who it was. I turned the TV on and they didn't say any names at the time. So I called my mom and the first thing that came out of my mom's mouth was "Oh it wasn't nobody but Cookie." By the time I got off the phone with her, they [the news] said his name.

These are very specific details. Along with recalling where they were and what they were doing, participants recalled feeling shock when they learned about the incidents. While many of them said they knew about problems with the police that Kevin and Cookie had faced, none said they could have predicted that those interactions would take such a drastic turn. For example, while discussing Kevin's case, Jasmine stated:

I mean, I couldn't believe it. I have heard rumors about McEntee harassing Kevin and other guys. I've heard rumors.

Pam, twenty-one, also commented on Kevin's case:

I think personally there was animosity built up in Kevin. They [police] did use to harass him a lot and kind of pick on him and aggravate him.

As Pam commented on what she perceived to be "animosity" on Kevin's part, she sympathized with him. In fact, many participants took pity on Kevin, and the more they learned, the more they internalized it.

It had also been reported that Sgt. McEntee smiled at Kevin, as if to taunt him, following his brother's collapse. One participant (Kim, sixty-two) stated:

And after it happened, McEntee drove around the corner and Kevin was there. Something in his mind just triggered [it]. It wasn't a plot or anything, he [McEntee] just looked at him and laughed.

What Kim attempted to do is narrow things down to the precise moment Kevin decided to shoot. It is within this narrow time span that Sgt. McEntee allegedly smiled cynically at Kevin, and this was presumably only minutes after confirming his brother's passing. While a smile may appear to be a small matter in a rather broad range of events proceeding murder, it was repeatedly referenced as a salient one.

Many participants were not surprised that the story of Kevin and McEntee came down to a smile. In fact, hearing about it only reinforced similar experiences. Here is how it was discussed in Kevin's appeal to the Missouri Supreme Court:

Attempts to restart Bam-Bam's heart using CPR were unsuccessful (Tr.1187–89). An ambulance took him to a hospital where he was pronounced dead (Tr.1197–98). Sgt. McEntee and Nelson walked to No. 411 and told where the ambulance was taking Bam-Bam (St.Ex.80-T.32). Kevin had moved to the front window of No.411 and heard McEntee ask if he was in the house (St. Ex.80-T.33). Sgt. McEntee saw Kevin "standing in the window" and tapped Nelson's shoulder (St.Ex.80-T.33). "[T]hey both looked and they just started smiling" then got in their cars and left (St.Ex.80-T.33).[15]

Those same court transcripts continued:

Reaching the passenger window, Kevin saw Sgt. McEntee and stopped (St.Ex.80-T.44–45). McEntee saw Kevin; "he just started smiling" (St.

Ex.80-T.45). Kevin "flipped out," said "you killed my brother" and shot McEntee seven times (Tr.1299,1384–86;St.Ex.68; St.Ex.80-T.45).[16]

Like others, Kim is convinced that something beyond Bam-Bam's death made him snap; perhaps it was the reported smile. After all, she knew Kevin and watched him growing up in the community. She could not imagine him committing such an incomprehensible act unless provoked. Thinking about Kevin having to see that smile brought Kim to empathize with him.

The more details learned throughout the neighborhood, the more suggestive they became of police harassment. As they did with Kevin Johnson, participants empathized with Cookie and the role of police harassment in his case. Take Steve, twenty-two, for instance. He discussed what he heard concerning aggressive policing with Cookie:

> I heard about it. I mean, I figured they [police] was just picking on him, to keep giving him tickets on the vehicles he had and he had his own company. Why keep ticketing him if he trying to do something right? From a lot of people in the community, he was just fed up and went about it the wrong way.

Steve felt sorry for Cookie, especially as he had an excellent reputation in the community. Unlike Kevin, apart from parking violations and arrests stemming from his protests, Cookie had no criminal history. He had not been characterized as a "troubled" individual; rather, he had first been known by blacks in Meacham Park and whites in Kirkwood Proper as a reputable business man who went out of his way to help people. He often gave back to his community through volunteerism and service. From his and the participants' point of view, he was being targeted—and unfairly at that—by police. Almost one month following the murder of Sgt. McEntee, Cookie stated:

> They [city officials and police] know exactly where I'm going to be ... They arrest me right on the job and harass me right on the job. They just find ways to create these tickets. It's a vigilante-type situation.[17]

Cookie was referring to having been arrested while at a job site from which city officials had prohibited him. He showed up anyway, and from there, it is reported that he was taken into custody.[18]

Being arrested while working was one of many times Cookie felt targeted by city officials, and more specifically, the police. His property and vehicles were plastered with tickets, and he believed that he was constantly being confronted by the police directly or indirectly and could not catch a break.

Claiming to have had his civil rights violated by being "falsely arrested and falsely imprisoned," he described the toll these highly visible acts took on his character and ability to effectively serve the community:

> I had to resign from seven boards because I could no longer provide services to the city and be subject to racial discrimination and harassment at the same time. . . . I was on Project 2000 for eight years, but could not continue to serve with parents seeing me being arrested all of the time.[19]

Cookie's comments reflect a man feeling increasingly cornered. By *his* accounts, harassment had left him feeling stigmatized and, consequently, no longer recognizable as exemplary in the community. Again, calling attention to the extreme aggression he felt, he stated:

> I've had so many cases on the docket that I was once afforded my very own court date.[20]

Frequent and impromptu police contacts over parking violations, fines for incorrectly hanging business signs, failing to show correct work permits—totaling $18,450 to be exact—criminalized him. They limited his ability to perform tasks in the community, from earning a living to mentoring young black males through Project 2000.[21]

In trying to reconcile the shootings at City Hall with the man they once knew, many participants perceived police harassment as inciting Cookie. As in Kevin's situation, this explanation especially resonated with many of the participants because they themselves had experienced harassment in the community or knew someone who had. As a result, many saw Cookie's actions as extreme, but understandable.

Participants' stories of police harassment helped them to better make sense of the two tragedies, which they saw as related, despite their differences (e.g., Kevin had been on probation, while Cookie had not been), and as emblematic of poor police relationships in the community. Terrance stated:

> Look at what they did with Cookie and look at what they did with Kevin. To me, those are the exact same stories. Both of them [Kevin and Cookie] the same damn story. Regardless, the story ain't different. You got a fifty-somethin'-year-old man that ran up in the Kirkwood City Hall and shot up everything. There's a problem. That man [Cookie] always had a smile on his face. So any time you get a man with a smile on his face to let loose on City Hall, I don't care what you say, something else is wrong other than he crazy. It's the same song with Kevin.

Not being able to account for their actions would mean that both men were somehow abnormal, inhuman even. It would mean that they both were monsters, or "madmen" as they were often called in the media. In a predominantly black community, where the residents and participants already feel stigmatized, not being able to account for the horrific behaviors of those most like them would mean further stigmatization. As Kevin's and Cookie's experiences became the indirect experiences of those in the community, community members themselves felt stigmatized as abnormal or monstrous. Providing a context for and humanizing their heinous acts humanizes the whole community. Kim described how many residents felt following the shootings:

> People that knew people over here didn't feel like that. But on the average, we were just this little ghetto community of nothing over here and that's how some people viewed us. And that's just how it came out in the news and everywhere else. But it wasn't so.

As both cases gained national attention, participants became familiar with conversations and depictions of their community, locally and nationally, as "ghetto" and "dangerous." Outsiders viewed their community through the lens of Kevin's and Cookie's actions. Consequently, sharing information became a line of defense; the more they learned from one another in Meacham Park, the better equipped they felt they would be to fend off the backlash of differential actions toward them.

THE CRIMINALIZATION OF A NEIGHBORHOOD: INVOLUNTARY POLICE CONTACT IN THE AFTERMATH

Poor blacks and the communities they live in often face persisting social isolation, economic and political alienation, and aggressive policing. They find themselves contending with inescapable social injustices, which often translate to brushes with the criminal justice system, sometimes unwarranted. All of this leads to negative stigmatization.

It also leads to perceived differential treatment from various social agents (e.g., police) and the institutions they are linked to, which, in turn, leads to black distrust of said agents. Blacks fear that if one or two black people commit a crime, it becomes a criminal indictment on the entire race. Inversely, the successes and accomplishments of black persons—apart from sports and the entertainment industry—are treated as anomalous. They are the exception; stigmatization on the entire race is held constant. Under these circumstances, blacks tend to empathize with one another. The indiscretions of a few in-group members (Kevin and Cookie) incriminated the entire group (Meacham Park), so accordingly, the group collectively braced for a disparaging out-group (white) response.

Blacks in Meacham Park reportedly faced undue police contacts as a result of Kevin's and Cookie's crimes. While many of them—mostly men—had already experienced some form of police aggression, they believed it worsened following these events. They reported feeling *more* vulnerable while in contact and interacting with police. They believed the police treated them as if they expected them to do the same thing Kevin and Cookie had done—commit murder. They believed officers perceived and treated them as guilty by association.

Participants identified encounters with the police following both tragedies as turning points for increased police presence and aggression in the community. Here is how Tiffany described them:

> Ever since that shooting, it's like when they [police] come out here, it's like get ready for war, cause my son, he's one of the boys that hang on that corner and I'm constantly telling him, you need to be careful. I really believe that one of these officers are going to kill somebody's kid. They're [police] going to feel threatened and to me they're going to a have a reason why. They just on high alert. It's kind of like the old saying, when you say that a person is "trigger happy," right? It's like they're just waiting for something to happen, but that's just how they act.

While the City Hall shooting did not take place in the neighborhood of Meacham Park, the residents there still saw and felt the effects of it through the way the police behaved while around them. Similarly, Mark recounted:

> After those incidents, they [police] just seem to have a smug look, probably just needed a new police squad. With Kevin and Cookie, they needed a completely new squad because the ones that were left obviously were their [slain officers'] friends and they were bitter. But if I could get rid of anything it would be the stigma of the things that's happened. But only if the truth could come out because it [stigma] takes away from a life instead of adding to it. For that incident with Kevin, that night Kirkwood police was out. So many police came from out of other areas. They were walking around with riot guns, they were going in people's homes. They overstepped boundaries

that day. That night it looked like we were in a riot, and the night Cookie went up to City Hall, I was just leaving with my cousin from having a bite to eat here in Kirkwood Commons. The police came past there at about eighty, ninety miles an hour. It looked like a movie. There were so many police from everywhere.

Mark's concerns were clear. He did not trust the police and sensed what he perceived to be biases that would ultimately work against him and his fellow Meacham Park residents. He continued by also describing the scene outside of the house that Cookie shared with his mom:

I seen a bunch of cops go into Cookie's house. They went and searched his mom's house and marched up and down the street like soldiers.

Notice Mark's progression of thoughts: first he was afraid of residents being stereotyped and scrutinized as criminals, and then he alluded to police seeing the residents of Meacham Park as enemy combatants.

Participants not only shared very real memories about the police, what they looked like and the way they behaved in their community; they also provided insight into the long-term effects of having to face them. Though they were inwardly disturbed by what they experienced, it was outwardly apparent that these would become life-long memoirs of negative encounters with the police.

While some perceived their targeting to be a result of guilt-by-association, Dwayne experienced direct police contact. He was questioned by the FBI the night of the City Hall rampage, since he and Cookie were close friends. Dwayne described his experience:

It blew my mind. I couldn't believe it! I had the FBI come by my house, reporters interviewing me. I could not believe it! I could not believe it! You know they're [police and media] asking me, "When was the last time you saw him?" For a minute, wanting to know if he got the gun from me, you know, that kind of stuff. It's crazy. I couldn't believe it. I have never experienced anything like that. You got FBI coming up in your house. It makes you a little nervous you know. I just couldn't believe it!

This was a devastating experience for Dwayne. He had no criminal history. He described being in shock, especially as Cookie had been at his house not long before the shooting. He could not recall anything said or done that would have ever indicated Cookie's plans for City Hall. Nevertheless, he became part of the investigation and was scrutinized as if he had been involved or had known something about it. As Dwayne shared his account, he was visibly moved. The FBI's questioning was overwhelming; it was frightening. He could not separate this experience from his perceptions of Kirkwood police. There were so many law enforcement officers, local and federal, combing the neighborhood that they became one and the same and perceived negatively.

Valerie (Val, forty-four) also shared vivid accounts of perceived police harassment and believed it to be linked to hostility toward the community entirely:

> The police officer, she came down the street with his [Sgt. McEntee's] wife in the car. OK, you're a police officer, why you out here [Meacham Park] riding with his wife. [Are] you showing her where everybody lives? So you're making me think now [the police] are getting ready to do something. I saw both of them and I told. I filed a complaint. I called up the police. He [police] told me that he would get back with me. [*signaling the route they took*]. When she came down the street, this how it was. She made a U-turn on Alsobrook. This woman [police] made a U-turn and did me like this [*puts up the middle finger*]. I'm thinking, "What did I do to you [police]? What did I do to you for you to give me the finger?" She's still on the force.

In an already tense environment, such interactions make police-citizen relationships even more volatile. In fact, it put her on edge, believing that the police was planning some kind of retaliation. Just as the police were perceivably anticipating negative actions from them, the participants expected negative actions from the police. Such explosive circumstances cause all involved to feel threatened by each other and to be pressured into a draw. In such case, it comes down to managing who acts first, as they both feel threatened and want to be left standing. Val wanted to respond; she felt provoked and disrespected. However, she remained composed and instead reported it to the police. Now, two years later, she reported no follow-up to her complaint from the police but instead continued to feel insulted, angered, and threatened by the local police.

Another respondent (Rodney) attempted to explain what he believed to be police harassment due also to resentment. He described the seriousness of what he perceives Meacham Park young men now face following the murders of officers:

> I just understand these lil' young cats [young men], what they're going through. They're going through some hell of a shit. I'm telling you that since

that officer [Sgt. McEntee] got killed out here, it's a lot of defenses still, you know. It's a lot of, I want to say hatred.

Rodney is speaking of police cynicism and what that means for young men in Meacham Park. After all, it was a young man like them who killed the sergeant. He realizes the fallout for them is cause for concern. Rodney continues:

> Like I can put myself in their shoes. It's hard to do because I can't really say, but if I was a police officer and my best friend got killed, that would be a lot of animosity. Even though they got the guy that did it, I'd still have a lot of animosity every time I see somebody.

Rodney attempted to explain and make sense of police resentment. He referenced their loss as one of a best friend rather than a colleague. Being fair, he normalized the police's emotions and responses based on how he would feel if his best friend or partner was killed. However, as he seemingly empathized with officers on one hand, he affirmed what he believed to be retaliatory behaviors on the other. Rodney recalled St. Louis County police intervening days following the City Hall shootings.

> Yeah, they [St. Louis County police] took over for like a week or two to calm things down. Man, it could've went any kind of way. It could've gone crazy. I mean because you already had, with that incident right there, three Kirkwood policemen killed within three years. So I told one [St. Louis County police], I said, "It's a good thing ya'll came out here to keep Kirkwood police away because the same way they have guns, these lil' cats [young men] got guns. And now days, these cats ain't scared to shoot guns no more. It's on the news every day, them shooting at the police and everything."

In other words, he believed Kirkwood police to be tense, edgy, and ready to respond with force, and he believed that if pushed out of fear, not-so-law-abiding residents might be inclined to fire as well.

Consequently, many participants lacked optimism about police-citizen relationships in Meacham Park. With negative experiences and feelings shared between both the residents and the officers, a few participants were very pessimistic about the relationships improving. In fact, one respondent stated, "Eye for an eye, it'll never end." Many participants say that until Kirkwood police acknowledge and change their approach, they will remain suspicious and defensive of them. Val notes:

Yeah, it's gotten worse and you'd think they [police] would have woke up by the incident, what happened to Sgt. McEntee. You would have thought they would have woke up to the situation with Cookie Thornton. But no, they are still harassing.

Kevin's and Cookie's Defense Equals Meacham Park's Defense

Kevin's and Cookie's murderous acts were the indirect effects of a seemingly ill-fated relationship between Meacham Park and Kirkwood Proper left untreated. Having two socially opposed communities merge—a poor black one and an affluent white one—deserved much attention. Similarly, the relationships between Kevin and Sgt. McEntee and between Cookie and various city officials called for careful consideration. For years, neither of the troubled interactions were appropriately acknowledged or addressed, and consequently, preexisting racialized dysfunction between the larger two communities in the suburb trickled down to the individual interactions within it. It seems that the trend had been toward the minimal, if anything at all, as if to hope with time that perceivably insignificant matters would improve. Unfortunately, they did not, and instead, the approach to do nothing translated to endemic denial and avoidance by the dominant. Both denial and avoidance were critical factors in how incidents were (mis)handled preceding both tragedies. As with the issues from annexation, the extent of Kevin's and Cookie's problems were discounted, taken for granted, and thus, left unaddressed by those powerful enough to make a difference.

This is not to suggest that there was an absolute answer for preventing the two tragedies along the way. Rather, the goal here has been to examine associations and thus to call attention to effects of broader dysfunctions and the circumstances from which relationships emerge. In many respects, Meacham Park is a colony; it had been colonized by the City of Kirkwood. While British colonization proved beneficial for Great Britain and then later for what became white American settlers, their interactions proved historically catastrophic for natives, and to date, they continue to face hardships as they too are segregated and face persisting poverty, substance abuse, and other social ills uniquely resulting from who they are.[22] Likewise, annexation proved beneficial for the City of Kirkwood but not entirely for residents of Meacham Park.

At minimum, the blacks in Meacham Park are geographically cut off from the rest of the suburb. Their community is boxed in, leaving residents with limited options for getting in and out. Kevin and Cookie felt cornered, boxed in, with no options for getting out, and consequently turned to malice. While they should in no way be absolved, the patterns that provoked their behavior merit attention and consideration. If the mission is to understand why the tragedies occurred, it behooves us to examine the perceptions of this neighborhood, these men. No one can account for their decisions to kill better than them or those most like them.

CONCLUSION

Vicarious police experiences are powerful. As police harassment had been identified as inciting and maddening both shooters, it is through their stories and others shared among friends, families, neighbors, and the media that many of the participants came to reserve judgment and empathize with them. Since blacks, or more specifically, the residents of Meacham Park, are categorically stigmatized and face indiscriminate backlashes—despite their involvement—they are forced to defend themselves. Through vicarious experiences—what they see and hear—blacks come to identify and internalize each other's plights and empathize. By examining policing in the aftermath of tragedies, we are afforded greater insight into how the consequences of a few in a black community can easily become that of all, and have lifelong ramifications for additional black citizen-police interactions.

FIVE

The Road to Reconciliation

WHILE THE CITY OF KIRKWOOD—the poor blacks in Meacham Park and affluent whites in Kirkwood Proper—worked to move beyond tragedy in their community, they did so (re)evaluating their roles as its citizens. Back-to-back catastrophes, especially the City Hall rampage, had exposed years of avoidance for some and ignorance for others. It forced everyone, at varying degrees, to acknowledge persisting racial tensions between its citizens, local government, and police. Therefore, residents of the suburb, irrespective of race and class, found themselves more receptive to dialogue and change. Citizens wanted to know what, if anything, they could have done and could do in the future to ensure that like disasters never occur again. This demanded clarity by all, especially as the local government had repeatedly failed to understand or acknowledge the plight of the neighborhood it annexed. Furthermore, it was an opportunity for city officials to clarify the intentions of the local government and its enforcers, thus accounting for countless actions through the years that were perhaps misperceived by blacks in Meacham Park.

This chapter traces a shift in policing and race relations in the City of Kirkwood. Years of divisiveness and tension had taken a toll on this suburban community, resulting in the heinous deaths of citizens from its two factions—the poor blacks in Meacham Park and affluent whites in Kirkwood Proper—and change was now, finally, a real possibility. Shared crises dictated it as such.

The chapter is organized into two sections. The first discusses changes regarding black ATP and voluntary police contacts whereby the participants make contact with officers, gaining positive policing experiences. The second recounts the U.S. Department of Justice's (USDOJ) intervention and negotiation of race relations between the blacks in Meacham Park, city council, the whites in Kirkwood Proper, and the police. It discusses the meetings, propositions, and decisions as a mediation agreement was drafted and implemented between the neighborhood of Meacham Park and the City of Kirkwood.

WHEN BLACKS (DISS)LIKE THE POLICE

In the tragedy aftermath, dialogue became commonplace between the black neighborhood of Meacham Park and the affluent whites of Kirkwood Proper. Many conceded, to varying degrees, that years of contention between the two factions had been a result of constant miscommunication regarding the merging of the two municipalities.

With this in mind, a common misconception regarding blacks and the police needs addressing. Simply put and generally speaking, blacks do not hate the police. There seems to be a widespread notion that blacks' negative attitudes toward the police means blacks are in direct opposition to the police. This is not true: blacks do not categorically oppose the police. Rather, they oppose a particular *kind* of policing.

When the West Coast rap group N.W.A. graced the world with "Fuck tha Police," they were not dissing the police for the sake of being antagonistic. They were ridiculing a *form* of policing: the kind that appears to work in the best interest of all people, when in actuality, it is perceivably discriminative and disproportionately criminalizes black people. Here are the lyrics:

> Right about now NWA court is in full effect.
> Judge Dre presiding in the case of NWA versus the police department.
> Prosecuting attorneys are MC Ren, Ice Cube, and Eazy muthafuckin E.
> Order, order, order. Ice Cube take the muthafuckin stand.
> Do you swear to tell the truth the whole truth
> and nothin but the truth so help your black ass?
>
> Why don't you tell everybody what the fuck you gotta say?
>
> Fuck tha police
> Comin straight from the underground
> Young nigga got it bad 'cause I'm brown
> And not the other color so police think
> They have the authority to kill a minority . . .[1]

This black rhetoric regarding the police has become misunderstood, misdirected, and therefore lost in the greater social debate. Many would be inclined to identify this rap as a license to show blatant disregard and outright disrespect for the police and, by extension, the law, but some would argue the contrary. The rap depicts a trial where the police—as aggressors—stand accused similarly to disproportionate numbers of black men. These lyrics show the criminal justice system metaphorically through the perceptions of those most vulnerable to it.

"Fuck tha Police" caused concern. It is disconcerting and aggressive, perhaps leaving some readers/listeners appalled at the bluntness of the artists who wrote it. The Federal Bureau of Investigation (FBI) was certainly alarmed by it. In a blog post titled "The Politics and Provocation of N.W.A.," the *Huffington Post* wrote:

> When "Fuck tha Police" was at the height of its popularity, the FBI stepped in, claiming the song provoked violence against law enforcement. Focus on the Family, bent on curbing the group's influence, convinced assistant director of the FBI Milt Ahlerich to send a letter (now on display at the Rock and Roll Hall of Fame in Cleveland, Ohio) to Priority Records. Soon, the group was being banned and edited like mad. . . . "Fuck tha Police" lingered for six months until it was taken off the air, bringing the controversy surrounding N.W.A. to new levels.[2]

The widespread negative reaction suggests a true examination of black citizen–police relationships is difficult. Outrage at such an undeserved and absolute generalization should go both ways: unrestricted, unchecked aggression toward police by blacks should not be tolerated any more than unrestricted, unchecked aggression toward blacks by police.

While the police risk their lives daily—contending with overwhelming challenges across populations in ways that perhaps we cannot fathom—their quality and preservation of life should not be esteemed any higher than those who they serve. Yet, this is often what blacks fear happens: the lives and safety of the police are deemed more worthy of protecting than their own. In a business model, this sort of uneven valuing of needs would never hold up. Consider a restaurant: its viability is intrinsically linked to the satisfaction of its customers, and consequently, they are forced to review, update, or enhance their products and services as dictated by the social climate and its cliental (dieters, vegans, meat eaters, those needing delivery, those wanting to order online, etc.). To fail to do so means to compromise its sustainability: people are not inclined to patron businesses that afford them little to nothing to their advantage. This is the case with policing. Blacks are least likely to support it when policies and practices—still bearing resemblances to Jim Crow—perceptibly weaken their quality of life rather than improving it.

However, blacks' expressions of discontentment with the police, gentle or harsh, should not be interpreted as race-wide defiance of them. Such expressions apply only to aggressive policies—its creators, supporters, and enforcers—that allow for differential police treatment based on race and place. Like other marginalized groups (women, LGBT) and with numerous social issues, blacks do not take kindly to prejudices or discrimination; irrespective of criminality, it alters their livelihood, along with that of their families and communities. Therefore, it should be understood that as do their white counterparts, blacks look to the police for assistance. Even in this project, some participants expressed wanting to partner with them in preserving their community. However, when expected services from the police persistently wane in exchange for scrutiny, partnering becomes impeded. So as the police act perceivably suspicious of them, likewise, blacks distrust them.

Blacks are, consequently, reluctant to assist the police due to distrust. This is in effect a lack of confidence in a system that—even in the absence of crime— persistently punishes them. A feedback loop is in place. When blacks are less than enthusiastic to work with police, they face further defamation. The implications are then that blacks not only dislike the police, but in refusing to assist them, that they take to harboring criminals and supporting lawlessness.

Inferring that poor blacks are complacent with crime and criminals in their community further denigrates them in several ways. One, it sets a precedence whereby the dominant are free from having to acknowledge the actions of officers as *they* hindered potential partnerships. Two, it further masks the role of discrimination in contentious black citizen–police interactions, thus allowing for continued avoidance of action toward improving it. And three, such notions undermine the integrity of black citizens, implying a lack of morals or an inability by them to differentiate and choose right over wrong.

Therefore, as long as blacks perceive that they are subject to stereotypical ideas and suspicion (in theory and practice) that keep them situated on the wrong side of the criminal justice system, they remain less apt to team up with the police—no matter the circumstances. Perhaps this accounts for some participants' willingness to defend and show empathy toward Kevin and Cookie. Some of their responses did not have as much to do with Kevin's and Cookie's murders per se as they did with defending themselves and their

neighborhood as a result of them. As their community was perceivably typi-
fied by the media as anomalous to the City of Kirkwood, and as Kevin and
Cookie became stereotypically characteristic of the entire neighborhood,
some participants attempted to also safeguard themselves through rhetoric
that salvaged their own image.

To be clear, black empathy for those who have committed crimes is not an
endorsement for lawlessness. Take, for example, Marsha's (fifty-nine) sentiments regarding Kevin's case:

> I've known his grandmother. I know the four and five generations of families
> out here. But I've said I don't know whether I want to be home on the day
> he's executed or whether I want to be out of town. It scares me. I don't know
> what did or didn't take place, time frame wise, frame by frame, and I would've
> liked to have seen that part investigated. But nothing justified what Kevin
> did, absolutely nothing.

Marsha is one of many participants who expressed compassion toward Kevin
and Cookie *and* disdain for their actions. Frustration and confusion about
the surrounding circumstances and their feelings for the perpetrators or the
police do not trump their regard for the sanctity of life or the law.

In fact, despite blacks' distrust of the police, they still sought them out
and periodically expressed satisfaction with them prior to and following the
shootings. These accounts are significant since blacks are often posited as
hating the police, unwilling to work with them; thus they are blamed for
persisting crime and ineffective crime fighting in their communities. The
participants did reach out and partner with the police. However, sometimes
the participants' well-intentioned efforts to team up with local officers were
squandered as a result of negligence and insensitivity.

SERVICE CALLS AND VOLUNTARY POLICE CONTACT

While most of the participants in this project came in contact with the police
involuntarily or through what can be characterized as police-imposed circumstances, some reported instances where *they* contacted them. Fifteen
participants (eleven women and four men) reported calling the police,
thereby gaining direct voluntary experiences with them (see table 6). They
were mostly women and thirty years old or older. Men and the younger participants in this study were least likely to call them.

TABLE 6 Voluntary Police Contacts: Use of 911 Service Calls

	No. (N=30)	%
Dialing 911 to request police service on at least one occasion	15	50
Never dialing 911 to request police service	15	50

TABLE 7 Voluntary Police Contacts: Perceived Quality of Service from 911 Calls

Reported response to 911 calls	No. (N=15)	%
Satisfied with the quality of police service	11	73
Satisfied with the quality of police service, with previous direct, negative contacts	5	33
Satisfied with the quality of police service, *without* previous direct, negative contacts	6	40
Dissatisfied with the quality of police service	4	27
Dissatisfied with the quality of police service, with previous direct, negative contacts	4	27

Eleven of the fifteen participants (seven women and four men) were satisfied with the police and four were not. The eleven satisfied participants were over the age of fifty, with six of them reporting no previous negative experiences with the police. The four dissatisfied participants were below fifty years of age and all reported having had multiple previous negative contacts with the police. In sum, the participants who had not directly experienced the police negatively were likelier to think of them favorably following service calls compared to those who had (table 7).

When participants called the police, they usually did so as a result of an emergency situation or out of fear of victimization.[3] Service calls occur only as citizens need them and are requesting and expecting specific services. How well the services are provided often determines citizens' views of the police. For example, specific services were expected with the collapse of Kevin's little brother Bam-Bam. While the details remain unclear in terms of whether the family or police actually called for EMS, what is clear is that the police response came under scrutiny. What they perceptibly did or did not do in assisting Bam-Bam is what furthered participants' negative perceptions of them.

Regarding police calls, some participants identified improvements immediately following the annexation—from County Brown to Kirkwood Police Department—and again, following the shooting. While such instances were few compared to persistently negative reports at both junctures, they are important nonetheless. Service calls are one of several outlets whereby black citizen–police relations can be improved.

Satisfied with Service

Of the eleven participants who made service calls, seven women and four men reported being satisfied with officers' responses (see table 6). Six calls were for home burglaries, reported by three men and three women. Five calls were for other disturbances (noise, park/street lights, prank call, property damage), made by four women and one man.

The participants in this project called the police mostly in response to home burglaries. They shared details surrounding those burglaries and then followed up with whether they were satisfied or dissatisfied with the way police handled things. Dwayne, fifty-four, was one of them. After attending a mediation meeting between Meacham Park and the City of Kirkwood, he returned home to find a burglary in progress. He explained:

> I went home to change shoes or something and this little guy was trying to break into my house. When I pulled up in the driveway, I saw him walking on my property leaning over on my back sidewalk. He had a sawed-off shot gun. I called the cops and they were there just like that . . . caught the guy a couple of days later. We hadn't had any break-ins since they arrested that guy. But they caught the guy and come over with a line up and I had to go through this line up and pick this guy out. So they [police] handled it all the way through the process. They handled it, I was very impressed with the way Kirkwood handled the situation.

In Dwayne's case, not only was he pleased with the police for having caught the burglar, but he expressed satisfaction with officers' response time and overall attentiveness to his case. He is one of many participants who consistently acknowledged positives and negatives associated with policing. Despite having been wrongly scrutinized by them in the hours following the City Hall rampage, he still came to have a positive attitude toward them because of this encounter.

Francis, sixty, also called the police to report a burglary:

> Somebody broke in [my neighbor's] house. She came home and someone was in her bedroom and they jumped up and ran out the door. She ran over here and I called. She called the police and I called the police and they came right

away. They tracked their footprints all the way out her yard and everything. We [Francis and her neighbor's husband] were satisfied with their response and she was too. She went on and got an alarm on her house.

Like Dwayne, Francis and her neighbor were pleased with the police response, particularly as "they came right away." Again, police response times factor significantly in citizens' opinions of them. Ultimately, they can make the difference between life and death for citizens. Additionally, a quick response denotes "concern," while a slow response or no response communicates the lack thereof. Some participants even seemingly timed the police. For example, Pete, fifty-nine, compared response times for Kirkwood police to that of St. Louis County police (County Brown):

> The [Kirkwood] patrols are set up to where you can get multiple cars in a four to six minute range. St. Louis County [police] response time was in the twenty-minute range once a call was put in. So that's one plus.

The one "plus" identified by Pete refers to annexation. He noticed shorter response times after calling Kirkwood police than that of St. Louis County. In any case and as communicated by the participants in this project, immediate police response increased their confidence in the police.

Dorothy, fifty-seven, also expressed satisfaction with a police interaction. While recalling a service call to her home, she referenced the actions of one officer in particular as "commendable." She explained:

> I had an instance where somebody was calling my house and I found out who it was. They were hanging up and stuff like that all day long and I called the police department and talked to them about it and they told me what to do and I did it as far as contacting AT & T. Then they sent an officer out and I was explaining what was going on and there came this one nice gentleman [police], older fellow, and he was so nice about it and he actually, literally, went to that person's house, knocked on the door for me and told them that they needed to stop calling my house . . . that a police report had been made and if it didn't stop, they would have to be dealt with legally, you know. And I thought that was pretty good. He's always been a nice person, that particular officer. I can't remember his name, but I know him when I see him. He really took out time to address the problem and I thought that was pretty commendable.

Dorothy has also had negative policing experiences in the City of Kirkwood, many of which she attributes to racism. She shared numerous accounts, past and present, where she had unfavorable interactions, ranging from issues surrounding annexation to the local police. Despite the previous negative experiences, she could still be objective enough to see this experience as positive. The police simply having a quick response time and "being nice" spoke volumes for Dorothy. The calls stopped.

Officer Friendly. Most participants shared an "Officer Friendly" encounter, that is, an officer engaging in pleasantries ranging from waving and speaking while out patrolling to community participation.

Participants did not feel all police officers were bad. While many had unfavorable experiences and attitudes toward them, in general, they did not believe every Kirkwood officer to be unethical. Eighty-seven percent (twenty-six out of thirty) of participants acknowledged or admitted to at least one friendly or helpful experience with the police. This went for participants who reported having both negative and positive police encounters. The four participants who did not report any positive experiences with the police had the most frequent and most aggressive experiences with the police. Generally, they had nothing positive to say about them.

It is important to acknowledge, understand, and analyze the positive experiences reported by the participants. While the participants acknowledged times where the police were helpful and/or friendly, most of them did so dismissively and reluctantly as compared to the manner in which they shared the negative interactions. Also, where negative encounters were reported on participants' own initiative, positive experiences were reported only when directly prompted. Perhaps the negative experiences were easier to recall because there were more of them; also, negative experiences were their focus at the time given the recent tragedies.

When asked about friendly or helpful experiences with the police, some participants shared accounts of officers waving and saying hello and even engaging in very brief friendly exchanges while out patrolling. Most participants thought positively of the police when they waved or greeted them. In fact, when asked about police friendliness, Ed, fifty-five, stated,

> Just saying hello or waving, you know, pull up and "How you fellas doing?" They [police] aren't all bad.

For Ed, salutations show common courtesy, and having officers acknowledge him made him feel important and respected in his community. As blacks in Meacham Park often feel suspected and disregarded, greetings from the police make for great consensus-building.

Another participant (Jasmine, forty-two) described moments where she and officers engaged in a friendly exchange:

> There's a couple of them [police] I can speak to and I can joke around with. I might run into them at Wal-Mart or Quick Trip and they know me by name and we speak.

These instances are brief, but again very meaningful to citizens. Jasmine welcomes being able to joke around and share a laugh with officers. For her, being able to interact with the police in that way normalizes them. It levels the playing field, in the sense that for a moment, they seem more citizen-like rather than authority-like. Dwayne, on the other hand, expressed feeling safe in the community. He stated:

> In the mornings I see them [police]. You know, "How you doing?" "Happy Fourth of July," you know, I'm really impressed. I feel safe, they're out here. I feel they're more accessible on a personal basis. You can almost for sure wave one down at anytime and they'll stop and talk to you.

Being able to greet one another during patrols meant a lot to Dwayne as well. It communicated personal acknowledgement, which translated into personal "accessibility." In other words, these exchanges made him feel that if the police are personally available to speak to him, then they are more likely to be available to him in other ways beneficial to him. While Dwayne does not know for a fact how available the police would be to him, the fact that they take time to personally address him spoke volumes. In those instances, he perceived them as being kind and as a result, believed them to be approachable.

Lisa, thirty-four, also shared an account of kind policing. She described an officer being nice to her and her children. She stated:

> There's one police officer, he's such a sweetheart, he checked on us over the summer when our air was down. He used to come by check on the kids, talk to us, he came by brought James [her son] a flashlight. He [police] was James's buddy. I don't even know his name. I just call him my friend. He was just real close with the family.

These gestures were important to Lisa, especially as she is a single mother. She believed the officer acted out of genuine concern for her and her children, especially as his actions were self-initiated. In a community where the residents tend to be very distrusting of the police and often question their motives, Lisa embraced this officer as a friend and thought positively of him, despite numerous negative encounters. In this sense, differential policing was embraced, though only to the extent that it was not the usual behavior of officers as reported in Meacham Park.

With regards to youth, participants often spoke of them as having very tense exchanges/relationships with the police. However, even Carla, eighteen, the youngest participant in the project, provided a positive experience with the police.

> They [police] wave at us. I mean, they're cool. There are no sidewalks for real so we walk in the street. And they told us to get out the street. They just said, "Will you please not walk in the street, cars fly up and down the street. It's only twenty-five mph, but they do like ninety. So can you walk on the sidewalks from now on." And that was it.

This conversation about walking on sidewalks versus walking in the street is especially interesting. It is one of many areas of controversy in terms of how the police deal with the residents in Meacham Park, especially youth. Many participants referenced this issue or complained about the police handing out tickets to youth for walking in the streets. Take Tiffany, thirty-six, for instance. She told a somewhat different story:

> Like a couple of our kids got tickets for walking in the street. We never had sidewalks around here until they [Kirkwood] annexed, so a lot of people, especially the older people and like young people, they never walked on sidewalks so it took a minute to adjust. But officers were giving people tickets for walking in the street, not just warnings, they were just giving them tickets. My brother's ticket was a hundred or two. I think it was for loitering. I don't know what it was, so it would seem like the laws that they would never enforce were the ones that they would, you know, enforce in order to mess with people.

In Carla's instance, officers could have ordered these youth to the curb and punished them accordingly, but their choosing not to worked in their favor. The situation did not warrant aggression; appropriately, the officers displayed balance and restraint. Carla appreciated the break, perceiving them as going the extra mile by explaining the issue as a safety concern. This is an excellent example of how very little effort can make a big difference and police mannerisms can lead to favorable ATP, even among youth who can be their harshest critics.

Two participants reported having no negative experiences with the police. They shared friendly and helpful stories with ease. Francis was one of them. Apart from stories learned throughout the larger community, she personally had only positive experiences with the local police. As a result, she thought highly of them, stating:

> Well, when it comes to the Kirkwood Police Department, I've had nothing but plus relationships with them. I've not had anything that I could identify negative personally with my family or myself or my close neighbors. They've stopped and when we had the night out, they came here and they had lemonade and they had barbeque with us, you know.

Participants embrace officers getting involved and attending the several community events Meacham Park has throughout the year. Travis, forty-five, explained:

> Well, I met the chief of police at the area parade they [Kirkwood] have every year, and he was pretty cool and he introduced me to a couple of officers and they were OK, and I even got pulled over by one and just because of that, he let me go, gave me a warning and no ticket.

Travis felt good about meeting the chief of police and having him introduce him to other officers. This was a change from how many men have come to know the police in Meacham Park. In general, men spoke about knowing officers and becoming familiar with them through antagonistic involuntary contacts. Travis believed the positive encounter with meeting the chief set a precedent for future chance meetings, perceiving his warning to be a direct result of having previously met those officers under positive circumstances.

Some other participants also thought favorably of the Kirkwood police chief. Despite negative encounters with his officers, many perceived the chief himself to be well intentioned and generally responsive when confronted with problems regarding his officers. In fact, one participant (Kim, sixty-two) stated:

> Chief Plummer's pretty good about dealing with his officers. If you take it [complaint] to him, he will deal with it personally and he's pretty fair.

Likewise, Denise, sixty, shared positive sentiments concerning the chief of police:

I think he does a good job of responding to the riffraff that folks have about what happens with the police. I think he's right on with trying to keep the lines of communication going.

Some participants called attention to the chief's generous accessibility and willingness to extend himself to their community through acts such as donating food and money to needy families in the neighborhood—anonymously to most. These were personal acts of kindness, apart from the city government, and he did them requesting no attention.

Granted, the chief does not spend most of his time patrolling the neighborhood of Meacham Park. Therefore, his encounters with the residents of Meacham Park are few and less tenuous compared to that of the officers assigned there. However, as he is positioned at the core of city government, his efforts not only reflect positively on the police department but they bear implications for changing participants' perceptions and relationship possibilities with other city officials.

The chief was not the only one who garnered praise for community involvement; other participants expressed satisfaction with other police participation in community activities as well. Take Keith for instance. He spoke of officers actually assisting with setups for community events. He stated, "When we set up for the Meacham Park homecoming, they actually helped us take stuff out the car." Additionally, Denise discussed the role of the police at monthly community meetings:

> The policemen come to the meetings and make a report about what's happening in the community. That's a good thing, because in many communities, there is not a regular monthly communication between the police and the community.

In both cases, participants thought it wonderful to have the police involved. For them, it showed interest; it showed the police engaging in ways apart from the all-too-common traffic stops, pursuits, and other activities many of them are used to seeing and hearing about.

Accounting for participants' positive experiences and views of their local police is necessary. These not only counter the stereotype that blacks oppose the police, but they afford opportunities for identifying positive changes as well as improvements with police-citizen relationships.

As Meacham Park and the entire City of Kirkwood had to face very tragic situations, partly resulting from poor police-citizen relationships, several participants thought it important to state what they liked or saw as improvements with them since those occurrences. Ed, for example, stated:

> Seems like the police been reaching out more. Even the police chief has been here talking, trying to form some kind of relationship. That's good.

Marsha also weighed in:

> I've seen more of an effort since the [officer's death] and the city massacre. I've seen more of an effort and I contribute all that to the chief. I contribute every bit of it to him.

Similarly, Dwayne identified and described improvements made with the Kirkwood Police Department since first assigning patrols to Meacham Park. Again, prior to annexation, Meacham Park had been under the jurisdiction of the St. Louis County Police Department (County Brown). He said:

> Sound crazy to you when I say it. I think from what I see, they're [police] doing a much better job than I've seen them do since they've taken over this place, better than I've ever seen it. They've been personable.

One of the most salient messages from participants was that improvements have occurred with policing in Meacham Park since annexation and since the tragedies. The residents of Meacham Park are not opposed to policing and do not believe all police to be bad. In fact, despite negative experiences with them, some were empathetic toward them and worked to understand and be fair in their views of them. Jackie, thirty-four, summed those views best:

> Whenever you're dealing with the public, you gone have good cops, you gone have bad cops, but you can't put them all in the same category.

Dissatisfied with Service

Voluntary contacts (service calls) with police are perfect opportunities for police to counteract the perception that black citizen–police interactions are always negative. Since they are commissioned servants of the community, the onus is on the police to prove that they are capable of befriending and supporting citizens. When voluntary contacts with police go well, ATPs improve. Not surprisingly, when they go badly, ATPs worsen.

Of the fifteen participants who made service calls to the police, four of them were dissatisfied with the results (table 7). All four were women, and all had previously experienced negative encounters with the police. Some of these women made numerous calls to the police, reporting issues ranging from incidents with the police to property damage. The reasons for these participants' dissatisfaction varied and included delayed responses, no responses, no resolutions, and/or name-dropping with anonymous reports.

Jasmine spoke of police response time in Meacham Park compared to what she believed it to be in Kirkwood Proper. Based on observations and accounts from others in Kirkwood Proper, she stated:

> I think it's not just me because it's like when nothing's going wrong we're Kirkwood, but as soon as something happens, we're Meacham Park. And they, to me, the police act in a different way when they come out here. [For example,] they're responding to a kid fight or they're just riding through, they just act totally different than they do on the other side of the tracks [Kirkwood Proper], they respond, like they come quick. But they don't come quick out here. This is something I've seen for myself.

While she cannot prove that response times in Meacham Park are slower than in Kirkwood, she is convinced based on her own experience with slow response times as well as observations and information obtained from those she knows in Kirkwood Proper.

It is important to put police response times in perspective. Participants judged response times as good or bad relative to response times of their former police agency St. Louis County (County Brown) and to response times experienced by affluent whites in Kirkwood Proper. When comparing to the response times of County Brown, participants were satisfied. However, participants who thought about police response times in relation to Kirkwood Proper were dissatisfied. One participant, Lisa, came to have a negative ATP when the police did not respond at all. Lisa stated:

> It's just certain things I call the police for. I get tired of hearing the music you know. Music blasting at two o'clock in the morning and when I call the police, they don't come . . . I don't see them. I don't see them come and I think it's sad.

While Lisa's call to the police regarding peace disturbance was not an emergency, she was bothered nonetheless by what she believed to be a "no-show." She has several school-aged children whose ability to sleep was affected by the noise she reported, and the police's no-response made her feel ignored and distrusting of them.

Lisa is one of two participants who has contacted the police numerous times for assistance and one of several participants who has had involuntary experiences. She expressed satisfaction with only one of her interactions. Ironically, it was an involuntary contact during which the police reached out to offer assistance during a heat wave. However, regarding her voluntary interactions, Lisa stated unequivocally that the police did nothing to assist her. For example, she described being at the scene of a neighborhood fight involving her teenage daughters. Lisa needed and requested EMS service for her one of her daughters. She told the story:

> She had a big lump on her [her daughter's] hand and she was shaking real bad. I told her to sit down. The police were there, they had already been called by several people. So as I'm going up there, they're [the police] telling me to get away, get away. So I said, "Can you guys call the ambulance for my daughter, she has seizures," and they [police] told "me" to call the ambulance. I called on my cell phone four times for an ambulance for my daughter, nobody would send me an ambulance. I'm getting pissed and I started cursing. My daughter was sitting on the sewer shaking really, really bad and that's what I was worried about. I'm shaking too and I'm worried about me being pregnant and no ambulance coming. And so, it had been at least twenty-five minutes passed and I came back to the house and I called on the house phone." Can you [911] send me an ambulance, I think my daughter's having a seizure," and then they sent one.

Lisa was furious as she recalled this incident. It is important to note that this incident occurred after the murder of Sgt. McEntee, in the wake of community members' belief that the police did not respond adequately to the collapse and untimely death of Bam-Bam. In a scene including countless witnesses, a radio call to EMS would have been an ideal opportunity for responding officers to extend themselves to Lisa and her injured daughter. Instead, Lisa's account revealed that even when the police were present, participants still experienced delayed responses or no responses.

Participants' distrust of the police also hinged on their dissatisfaction with how they resolved (or didn't resolve) offenses committed against them. Jasmine called the police for an incident at her home and was dissatisfied with the way they handled it. She explained:

> There were some boys in the neighborhood that paintballed my house. I heard a noise outside and so when I opened my side door, from my backyard they were just shooting the paintballs and I hurried up and shut my door so I wouldn't get hit. I couldn't see who it was and I called Kirkwood police. Two officers showed up. The side of my house was orange, but my house is

blue. And they [police] told me that it was not property damage and that all I had to do was take a water hose and wash it off. They didn't take a report. They just asked me did I know who it was and I said no. But there was a young lady who had just left my house, one of my daughter's friends. Her car was paintballed. She ended up going to the car wash and called the police to let them know. She knew who it was and she told them [police] who it was. There had been problems with certain individuals who were paintballing people's homes. But they [the police] just came and saw the paint spots that were on the house and were like there's nothing they can do.

Like Lisa, Jasmine has had a history of negative interactions with the police. As a result, she has no confidence in them. The police's assertion that they could do nothing to address the paintballing of her house only furthered her distrust of them. Jasmine continued:

Right now, the way I feel about the police, there's no love lost between me and them. I could care less and do my best to stay out their way because I don't trust them after all the stuff I been through and things I've called them for. I felt like I didn't get any satisfaction, no results, I just don't trust them.

In another incident, Valerie (Val, forty-four) recalled waiting for a follow-up to a complaint she had filed with the police. She reported later spotting and confronting the officer who was to have followed up with her:

And one day, I saw him [police] because there was an incident out here [Meacham Park]. I ran into him. I said, "Do you know who I am, I made a complaint and you never got back with me." He said, "Right now I can't deal with that and I have to get back with you." [He] ain't got back with me yet. It was a year ago when that incident happened.

When she saw the officer, it was clear to her that he remembered her. Maybe the officer was too busy with the current situation to address hers. However, Valerie expected him to do what he promised to do, which was to follow up with her long before the new incident occurred.

These kinds of exchanges explain why participants do not trust the police and often believe them to not care about their problems. Valerie reported what she believed to be inappropriate behaviors by an officer in the community, but did not hear back from the officer who took her report. This became another significant opportunity lost by police. It would have been a great chance to dispel black perceptions of the police as lacking concern and refusing to police their own.

The participants' reports in this project—even amid some of the most negative experiences—make clear that they do not embrace lawlessness in their neighborhood. Like their white counterparts, the participants fear victimization and want to be policed in ways that protect them. When officers respond quickly and treat them as if their safety and comfort matters, black citizens think positively of them. However, when their victimization begins with or becomes compounded by policing that categorically treats them as the threat, they retain or gain negative ATP.

As with everything else, participants recognized that there are good and bad police (people). While they often depicted bad experiences with the police, that does not mean they would rather be without them. They are merely frustrated with the treatment or services sometimes received from them. Many blacks face harsh, insensitive, and substandard experiences through involuntary, vicarious, and voluntary policing. Their stories, taken together, make clear that they are interested in the kind of policing that reflects what they believe to be genuine concern and considerate exchanges, if even in the simplest ways. There can be no denial, disregard, or failure to act in exposing and eliminating discriminative politics, policies, and police personalities. Positive black citizen-police interactions are often undermined, thus hindering the quality of life for all, directly and indirectly.

Following the tragedies discussed in the last chapter, in an attempt to foster positive relationships and safeguard the suburb from further racially charged improprieties—black or white—the U.S. Department of Justice (USDOJ) stepped in. The next section explains the mediation process under federal government supervision whereby committees were formed and agreements made in hopes of improving the state of relations between poor blacks and affluent whites in the City of Kirkwood.

FEDERAL INTERVENTION

> You've got to sit down and look another human being in the eye and trust each other . . . Otherwise, it doesn't make a damn bit of difference.[4]

These were the timely words of the Kirkwood police chief, reported in the *Webster-Kirkwood Times* online, just days before the official signing of the City of Kirkwood Mediation Agreement.[5] The road to recovery had proven to be uphill. As black and white representatives of Kirkwood met at the roundtable and formally engaged in dialogue for almost two years, the likelihood for a peaceful resolve dwindled.

The mediation process as mandated by the federal government did not mean that the agreement in itself would consist of government directives, as the U.S. Department of Justice's (USDOJ) role was minimal. The division of Community Relations Services (CRS) authorized the process only as a voluntary one, meaning, they deemed mediation as necessary, but its tenants and outcome needed to be at the discretion of the city. The USDOJ served as a referee, providing a generic template for how this suburban community may reach a consensus through a non-specific process afforded to other racially/ethically divisive communities throughout the nation. However, many participants' optimism for change hinged on the federal government's function; that is, they hoped that they would be more hands-on with crafting the agreement, implementing it, and consequentially, holding the city liable for its ineffectiveness. Instead, the City of Kirkwood—its local officials, offices, and committee members—was left to its own devices.

Without federal-government enforcement, many of the participants feared continued denial, exclusion, and contentious policing. What initially looked like an ideal opportunity for reconciliation appeared to be more of the same: propositions and promises offered in word only. This approach had not worked previously and had been the reason for conflicts surrounding annexation. More directly, it had been the initial source of contention for Cookie. There would be no accountability for the city should officials fail to comply, and thus, efforts were often stalled as a result of double-talk. For example, early in the process, the mayor had been quoted in the press as saying, "We really don't have a race problem," and reportedly did not support federal mediation.[6] However, after coming under fire for his comments, he attempted to explain:

> When this first started, I wasn't an enthusiastic participant. But as it went on and the more we worked on it, I thought we as a community had to be proud that we stuck it out.... Not many communities would have participated in this. We really wanted to find out if we had any problems . . . I don't think we have a big race problem in our community. I think we found out (in the mediation) that we didn't have a real deep hatred of one another like in other places.[7]

This comment is indicative of the denial that kept key players, such as the Meacham Park Neighborhood Association president and residents, at odds or altogether out of the mediation process. After all that had transpired, some black and white citizens were angered by the continued refusal of some (such as the mayor) to see racial disparity as the source of contention. Reverend Scott Stearman of the Kirkwood Baptist Church, who happens to be white, weighed in by saying, "I have been very supportive of the mayor, but that just speaks of some denial."[8] In short, the mayor's statement and others like them undermined the process. If the lead city official—who happened to be the supervisor of the police chief and all other city officials—failed to see troubled race relations as a catalyst for disaster within the city, then the mediation process was believed to be without merit.

Simply put, participants doubted the integrity of the impending agreement or proposed practices and programs aimed at promoting racial diversity and cultural inclusion throughout the suburb. There were no consequences for failing to comply, and thus the blacks in Meacham Park seemingly found themselves again embroiled in negotiations with their local government. Similar to the annexation process, the move toward communal improvements rested on hope rather than accountability. Frustrated and discouraged, fearing things would not improve, Dwayne expresses how many participants felt about the mediation process:

> It was nothing. You're not going to uphold what's on it. There's nothing legally that says that you have to and there's nothing on it that the community [Meacham Park] agreed with. We're sitting here arguing over this document, wasting a lot of time over this document that means absolutely nothing. [Do] you think these people out here [Meacham Park] are so crazy until you can put a spin on them? It's not a law. You got people [the committees] that were basically not even from the neighborhood. You just got a bunch of citizens to say, "Oh wow, wouldn't it be nice if this could happen or if that could happen or the neighborhood was like this," and that's fine. Dialogue is always good, that's cool. But it means nothing. We're putting together this mediation agreement because Cookie wiped out City Hall, that's what it's really about. [White] citizens are afraid and scared. The good white people understand that "Hey, maybe there *was* a reason for him to get so angry. Oh my God, what made him [Cookie] do that?" These are the questions you [City Hall] have to answer, so to sugarcoat those questions, you come up with this agreement, where blacks and whites of Kirkwood could say [*in condescending tone*], "Oh, OK, my white neighbor and I are sitting down and we'll go have coffee every morning before we go to the office, make Kirkwood a nice little safe place" Bullshit! That's crazy.

Dwayne is one of several participants who tried to keep a balanced perspective. He offered praise and criticism on numerous issues for both his black neighbors in Meacham Park and the whites in Kirkwood Proper. However, as were other participants, Dwayne was visibly disturbed. In his opinion and that of other participants, what he thought could be an opportunity to turn things around, had vanished. It might be that he wanted change so intensely because of his relationship with Cookie; he had been one of Cookies' closest friends. Dwayne had consistently expressed hurt from the loss of lives at City Hall, including Cookie's. He badly wanted to see things improve so that the tragedy would not have seemingly occurred in vain.

Over two-thirds of the participants in this study did not support the mediation process. Their lack of support hinged on distrust of the local government: contradicting rhetoric and denials of racial tension from city officials, perceived exclusion during the process, and the overall belief that promises would be made on paper but not in practice. So while committees were formed and forums were held, there continued to be a sense of apathy and disconnect between Kirkwood and Meacham Park.

Nevertheless, on January 21, 2010, in accordance with a congressional mandate issued by the USDOJ, CRS, a mediation agreement was drafted between the City Team of Kirkwood (city officials) and the Community Team (black and whites citizens) of Kirkwood. This agreement was to bridge gaps and mend relations between Meacham Park and the larger part of Kirkwood (Kirkwood Proper). In essence, this agreement was to unite the City of Kirkwood, black and white, advantaged and disadvantaged. However, dissent remained. It seemed that the very passions that brought some together for dialogue and change had also fueled rifts between them in deciding, enacting, and ensuring said change.

Upon execution of the mediation agreement, more than half of the participants had not even read it, particularly the younger participants and those with a history of negative police contacts. The seven participants (two men, five women) who had read it were older, were more educated, owned homes in the community, and were socially and politically active in the community before the 1991 annexation. However, they too were split in their views about the process. Four of them (one man, three women) did not support the process or the final agreement, while the other three did.

CONCLUSION

It is important to remain cognizant of all that has transpired between the neighborhood of Meacham Park and the City of Kirkwood. Decades of differential treatment, shaped by race and place, have damaged this suburban community, and efforts to address the problems were not working, at least not from the perspective of many of this project's participants. Much work in forging new and improved relations between the people is needed. As there have been persistently overlapping layers of disparity in the neighborhood of Meacham Park, the solutions for resolving them are not simple and immediate, but rather complex and ongoing. Social consciousness without boundaries—endorsed and exhibited by social institutions and its actors alike—is key if true reconciliation is to ever be achieved, locally or nationally.

Conclusion and Discussion

> We [Meacham Park] got to have something different from every-
> body else. How come the rest of these people, these white people,
> they're not agreeing to it? Why should we agree to it and they
> don't have to?

THESE WERE THE WORDS OF ONE PARTICIPANT (Mr. Willie, eighty)
regarding the USDOJ mediation agreement. No other neighborhood in the
City of Kirkwood needed an agreement with the city's government except for
Meacham Park—its predominantly black neighborhood. This frustration
was shared by other blacks in Meacham Park.

As angered residents of Meacham Park raised questions and interjections
throughout a meeting with the committees that had forged the USDOJ
mediation agreement, the one statement that resonated most was that of a
black sympathizer (Jamal). He was not a resident of the suburb, but felt it
necessary to address the committees regarding the disparities of its black citizens. He said:

> I hope that you [Kirkwood] handle this situation right regarding Meacham
> Park, especially as it has received national attention . . . all eyes are watching
> and this is a perfect opportunity for Kirkwood to be a model, an example for
> other communities and cities in the nation.

He was right, the room was filled with countless members of the press and
interested citizens—observing what they perceived to be a historically significant moment in time that extended well beyond the City of Kirkwood
and the St. Louis Metropolitan area. I attended that meeting. It was the first
one following the implementation of the agreement and was held at City
Hall—the same chamber once filled with tirades, and in the end, raided by
Charles "Cookie" Thornton.

Four years later, in an effort to understand differential treatment as shaped
by race and place, we have come full circle. All eyes are still watching, and
this project presents opportunities for communities to address race- and

place-induced contention between blacks and the police. As the model in this project, the City of Kirkwood provide snapshots into a history of discriminative occurrences as perceived and recalled by black participants from the neighborhood of Meacham Park. The push for social change remains vital and ongoing and we need to pursue it with the same resolve we had following the Rodney King beating and the senseless murders of Amadou Diallo, Sean Bell, and countless others.

As Kevin Johnson awaits execution and Charles "Cookie" Thornton has already succumbed to his, this project offers a renewed effort to challenge white improprieties in race and place dialogue, such as the denials of racism by the mayor of the City of Kirkwood and juror B37 in the Trayvon Martin murder trial. Juror B37 told CNN's Anderson Cooper that she did not "think race had anything to do with this," and that "people are looking for things to make race play a part." Such statements make the mandate for race, place, and policing projects abundantly clear.[1] Here's what we have learned:

The introduction argues for more race, place, and policing dialogue, as its interactive effects continue to negatively impact the everyday lives of blacks nationwide. As society better understands the extent to which race and place shapes stereotypes and discrimination, it will endeavor to form and implement policies and practices that counteract these types of racism. The chapter examines discriminative ideas, policies, and practices stemming from the broader social sphere to narrower locales within it in hopes of increasing social awareness and furthering social change. Awareness is the vehicle for social change and thus, attention should not only be given to the differential treatment of blacks in urban spaces, but other places as well.

As I argue for the significance of all places, I do so accounting for contentious black citizen–police interactions in predominantly white places—the suburbs. Often race, place, and policing dialogue focuses on urban locations, inadvertently ignoring the experiences of blacks in other places.[2] Yes, literature shows disadvantaged blacks in urban areas are subject to aggressive policing but it also shows that its likelihood increases when they travel near or into upper-class, white spaces.[3]

While this study does not compare urban experiences to suburban experiences per se, in accounting for race-and-place effect and racial-threat theories, it creates a platform for analyzing black citizen–police interactions in urban versus suburban areas. The chapters of this book after the introduction connect the dots—a string of institutionalized agendas garnered by an inequality whose effects came to be disregarded and normalized for blacks.

Chapter 1 contextualizes the historical significance of race and place. Contentious black citizen–police interactions do not occur in a vacuum; they are the result of an established history, a legacy of race and place shaping stereotypes, situating and segregating blacks to certain places with differential policing. Blackness came to be regarded as deviant and was feared throughout U.S. history, and the literature traces a white need to restrict blacks to certain places and monitor their behaviors within them. To this end, the chapter also examines the inner workings of slavery that idealized blacks as "different" in this nation, giving way to the enactment of "black-only" laws (Slave Codes, Black Codes, Jim Crow) and "black-only" policing to ensure adherence to them.

As they do elsewhere, blacks in Meacham Park perceive themselves to be different and therefore treated as such by the police and affluent whites throughout the City of Kirkwood. This feeling of "difference," explored in race-and-place effect and racial-threat theory,[4] can be traced to historical "sundown towns" and the accompanying efforts to maintain predominantly white suburbs. I use spatial-assimilation and place-stratification theories,[5] to argue that a preference for white distance from blacks is how poor blacks and affluent whites came to be geographically situated in this project. Meacham Park is a one-way-in, one-way-out community. The participants reported feeling "quarantined" from the larger, more affluent parts of Kirkwood.[6] The entrance and exit to the community is also the intersection where the black and white populations meet. Additionally, this is the intersection where men and women reported seeing police cars regularly parked, and where black men reported being tailed and stopped as they entered or exited the community.

This study extends race-and-place effect in that the participants are not just black motorists passing through a white community; rather, they have the same residential status as the neighboring upper-middle- and upper-class whites.[7] They are all residents of the City of Kirkwood, an affluent St. Louis suburb, and yet, this enclave remains very segregated. This project affirms that place can mean very different things to different people. Suburban status does not afford the same luxuries to the blacks in Meacham Park as it does to the whites in Kirkwood Proper. Hence, urban experiences should not be the sole or immediate deferment for analyzing black disparity and injustice. The participants in this study were not protected by suburban status but rather became more vulnerable as a result of it. Consequently, I argue that it is where black and white spaces overlap—inevitably and unavoidably colliding with one another—that the true rigidity of inequality becomes apparent and test-worthy.

Chapter 2 discovers race and place to be inflexible in that the expectations for equitable and peaceful cohabitation among poor blacks and affluent whites in the City of Kirkwood are uncompromising. Because of the rigidity of race, class, and place, this suburb presents a unique opportunity for dismantling the three. I mostly defer to the narratives of participants and media to explain how two socially opposed communities came to be one—only in theory and not in practice. I contend that blacks, by mere fact of race and poverty status, became subject to the ambiguity of privilege or the lack thereof. Affluent whites in Kirkwood Proper not only maintain separation from them, but they do so while profiting from having adjoined themselves to them. The City of Kirkwood benefits economically and legally. They secured a steady flow of revenue by acquiring Meacham Park land and perceptibly increased the preservation and safety of its white neighborhoods by positioning themselves as regulators and police over those closest and most threatening to them: the blacks in Meacham Park.

This project's case study contributes to the literature because of its intersections of race, place, and policing in a socially indurate location—an affluent, white suburb. There is a long-standing history of tense race relations in this community, a contentious history that begins with the local government. Over half of the participants reported that they do not trust the local government in Kirkwood. For them, being annexed has meant manipulation, broken promises, and losing property to a white, wealthier community. A strip mall, Kirkwood Commons, now sits on two-thirds of the original community.

Through annexation, the participants of this study come to be subject to vicarious contacts and experiences under the jurisdiction of multiple police agencies; they also became more susceptible to direct, involuntary contacts as well (twenty-two of thirty participants). As Meacham Park's governance changed, so did its ordinances. Some of the regulations that residents were used to living under as an unincorporated community changed after annexation to the City of Kirkwood. Consequently, as the rules changed, becoming stricter, so did policing efforts and sanctions. For example, the younger participants in this study reported being harassed by the police. They reported being stopped, warned, and ticketed by police for walking in the streets rather than on sidewalks. For decades, Meacham Park did not have sidewalks. Therefore, walking in the streets was common; it was expected. The residents of Meacham Park needed to now become "Kirkwoodians" by adopting new rules, while simultaneously disassociating themselves with the former ones or the lack thereof.

While the police worked to enforce Kirkwood ordinances over the previous ones, aggressive policing ensued, along with citizens' negative attitudes toward them. This is consistent with the literature, especially as citizens' attitudes toward their local social and political structures are often reflected in their attitudes toward the police.[8] Political relationships significantly affect local police-citizen relationships. Dissension between a community and its local government likely means dissension between the residents of that community and its agents (the police) as well.

In its examination of how the police work to protect Kirkwood's interests, this project supports race-and-place effect as well as racial threat theory. Meacham Park is physically and socioeconomically characteristic of a disadvantaged inner-city community. Similarly, it has been identified as troubled and subject to criminal activity. Contrarily, it becomes unique in its closer proximity of disadvantaged blacks to wealthier whites, meaning their spaces overlap. In such cases, studies show that fear and safety become very real concerns for whites.[9] Consequently, black suburban status—as in the case of Meacham Park—gives way to heightened dominant fears, loss of communal identity, a new local government, changing police jurisdictions, and new, stricter rules. Therefore, it is amid the previous factors that this study becomes distinct. As a result, blacks are targeted more for police suspicion, and thus, subject to more aggressive policing when closer to whites than they are when at a distance.

Chapter 3 calls attention to involuntary police experiences. Seventy-three percent of the participants experienced direct contact with the police that they believed took the form of harassment. They experienced this contact through surveillance, stops, questions, frisks and searches, and arrests. These interactions occurred through involuntary contacts with the police and were more common among men compared to women and younger participants compared to older participants. Additionally, such interactions were likelier to occur with participants who had previous negative encounters with the police than with participants who had not. Participants with previous negative encounters also reported more acts of police aggression with each encounter, meaning each time they met with the police, their encounters escalated and worsened.

In a few cases, participants who experienced police disrespect also reported police engaging in unethical behaviors and even outright misconduct.

Participants reported physical brutality, falsified reports, and evidence planting. While both men and women who experienced multiple involuntary contacts with the police reported police misconduct, men reported the most incidents. Men reported use of excessive force, even while they were handcuffed and compliant. Participants who experienced physical brutality described being slammed, shoved, roughed up, or maced by the police while they were cooperating and already subdued. They believed the police acted aggressively toward them as a matter of grandstanding, or showing off their authority, and reminding them who was in charge. Two female participants also reported excessive force by the police. Two men, neither of whom had prior contact with the police, reported having had falsified police reports against them. One man with a long history of negative contacts with the police reported being "free-cased," or having drug evidence planted on him.

Chapter 4 examines the lives and tragedies of two men—Kevin Johnson and Charles "Cookie" Thornton. I find their stories intriguing and unique in that Kevin was young and had a criminal past while Cookie was older, more established, and did not have a criminal past. Despite their differences, they were perceived and treated the same: as black men from Meacham Park who, through a totality of negative neighborhood experiences, including escalating police encounters, became murderers. I argue that the more citizens feel harassed and provoked by police who seemingly face no consequences, the likelier they are to retaliate. To be clear, Kevin's and Cookie's actions were heinous and unacceptable and should not have occurred under any circumstances. Still, it matters that their actions were in response to their perception of the city's inability to rein in its officers and officials. We can establish and explore a context for their actions without exonerating or condoning them.

Chapter 5 finds that fifteen of the participants have experienced policing through voluntary contacts. In these cases, they came into contact with the police as a result of calling them or otherwise seeking assistance. More women reported voluntary police contacts than men. In this study, participants who placed service calls to the police did so by seeking their help with home burglaries, various neighborhood disturbances (e.g., noise, park/ street lights, prank calls), and property damage. Women and older participants were likelier to place such calls, be satisfied with police responses to their calls, and thus, have favorable perceptions of them. This was especially true for participants who reported only voluntary contacts; that is, their only experiences with the police were when they sought help from them.

Meanwhile, younger participants and those who reported negative experiences with the police were least likely to be satisfied following a service call. They reported delayed responses or no responses or resolutions following their calls. It is likely that their experiences and perceptions stemmed from involuntary contacts; after all, these participants were unchanging in their perceptions of the police, and therefore very critical of them. Hence, the experiences they gained from calling on them only exacerbated their negative perceptions of them. The literature suggests that it is in these experiences that voluntary police contacts, like involuntary contacts, can lead to negative perceptions of the police. Since citizens often call the police in emergency situations, the way officers respond can significantly affect their perceptions of them. Additionally, citizens may hold officers responsible for the occurrence of crime in their community or they may hold officers responsible for acts personally committed against them.

In general, I found that most participants agreed that not all police were bad. While there were many reports of negative experiences, most participants related times when they were satisfied with police and thought favorably of them. The few participants who did not share such sentiments were those who had experienced the most frequent and aggressive of police contacts. In general, they had nothing positive to say about the police. Again, they were the younger participants.

IMPLICATIONS

We want to clarify the vision. What are we trying to accomplish? We see the human condition in its fullness. How can we transform the present condition?

PASTOR BENNETT, COMMUNITY MEETING

Despite the mediation agreement, there continued to be a sense of apathy and disconnect between the larger part of Kirkwood and Meacham Park. Two-thirds of the participants did not feel their voices were well represented in the mediation process. Thus, my suggestions for improving police-citizen relations in the community rely on the participants' reports. Many expressed views of change and improvement consistent with three areas: political sensitivity, inclusion, and accountability.

While contentious relationships with the local police were the primary focus of this project, the onset of community dissension did not begin with them. Rather, it began with the local government. The dismantling of communal relationships—years of exclusion and distrust—was the result of systematic decisions made and maintained by local policymakers and their constituents. More broadly, persisting discriminative policies and practices at the national level also bear responsibility. After all, it is under federal directives and exampling that state and local governments take cues, spurring a domino effect. Therefore, as participants' needs mostly hinged on political change, it is there that I will begin recommendations and subsequently offer ideas for improving black citizen–police interactions.

Political Sensitivity

Pre- and post-annexation, there have been numerous justifications for adjoining Meacham Park to the City of Kirkwood. By admission, countless individuals ranging from former mayors to members of the press called attention to the community's long-standing history of disparity. At minimum, the City of Kirkwood recognized Meacham Park's need for better public services and an improved infrastructure. The fact that it once lacked basic amenities such as indoor plumbing and sewer systems—a stark contrast to other neighborhoods surrounding it—demands careful examination. Similarly, the persistently mounting dissension between Meacham Park's black disadvantaged population and Kirkwood's local government—before, during, and after losing a significant portion of its community—fundamentally calls for sensitivity. Hence, *true* examination is needed to understand how Meacham Park came to be socially destitute compared to others, as well as how and why it persisted and resulted in recurring communal controversy.

At the humanitarian level, most participants expressed a need for what they perceive to be *true* racial and cultural awareness and sensitivity: social and political acknowledgment and awareness by local policymakers that their roles, decisions, and practices matter, not only to the advantaged members of Kirkwood, but even more so to those disadvantaged in Meacham Park. In essence, this means the local government, its representatives and cooperating constituents, must become and remain cognizant of systematic discrimination, as it has historically been at the root of *national* black and white contention. Meacham Park and the City of Kirkwood are not the exception; the annexation has not been quarantined from broader racial tension, but it is rather a symptom of it. As evident in chapter 1, many participants voiced their thoughts of racial insensitivity and discrimination from a historical perspective. Take Mark's words for instance: "That's gone on in our history . . . for hundreds of years." So while some residents see persisting racial conflicts between Meacham Park and Kirkwood as symptomatic of our nation's history, often those in lead positions, seemingly working to resolve such problems, do not. Instead, some key players continue to address it as nonexistent, "not that bad," or as having occurred only by happenstance. Solely addressing such disputes at the community level—as if they are somehow separate from society at large—impedes true awareness and undercuts the depth at which healing and resolution can take place.

Consequently, the City of Kirkwood, or rather its members, committees, and offices, must *first* be open to comprehending the dynamics of power and privilege—their origin and everyday manifestations through policies and practices nationwide—and then, *second,* must be willing to situate, examine, and attempt to resolve such conflicts even as its structures and practices are a result of it.

Political Inclusion

While many participants expressed apathy toward participating or associating themselves with the local government, they did so as a result of what they perceived to be a political shut-out or a continuum of systematic disregard by virtue of economic disadvantage, little voting power—even if all of its residents turned out to vote—and a dearth of government representation compared to its affluent white counterparts. Hence, services and programs as *they* see necessary for sustainability in *their* community, such as a youth center and youth programs housed in their neighborhood, along with another entrance/exit to the community, have yielded little attention and no action. In short, inequitable political influence and differential treatment between the two communities—Meacham Park and the City of Kirkwood—have not really changed since the time of annexation. If change is to take place, the City of Kirkwood must be receptive to the needs of *all* residents and neighborhoods—black and white—in practice. The local government must attend to the interests and overall inclusion of blacks in Meacham Park just as much as that of influential whites in Kirkwood Proper.

Take, for instance, the City of Kirkwood's 2014 city council election. Alongside of three Kirkwood incumbents emerged Jayson Thornton, a young black certified public accountant and viable candidate from Meacham Park. As a third-generation Meacham Park resident, with a wife, two daughters, and a resilient commitment to families and neighborhoods throughout the City of Kirkwood, his candidacy represented an invaluable opportunity for political inclusion.[10] This election embodied, for some Meacham Park residents, a hopeful break from years of political gridlock, similar to President Barak Obama's first election with blacks nationwide. It was through Thornton's candidacy that many—residents and nonresidents—gauged Kirkwood's commitment to racial progress and healing. Every St. Louis media outlet provided coverage, with Thornton as Kirkwood's headliner. In the end, some were left to ponder the state of Kirkwood's commitment to change when he lost his bid for city council with a little over 18 percent of the vote, while the three incumbents maintained theirs with a collective 75 percent of votes.

This had been a rare chance for political representation among Kirkwood's most alienated faction—an opportunity to have an elected official living inside and alongside of blacks in Meacham Park. Furthermore, no other resident from Meacham Park could impact the whole of Kirkwood; Jayson Thornton's influence ran deep. As the nephew of Charles "Cookie" Thornton, he undeniably reminded many—even if in name alone—of lives lost at City Hall. For Meacham Park, Jayson Thornton's being an elected official would have symbolized immeasurable change: the long-awaited evidence of social and political progress—inclusion, redemption, and reconciliation—amid Kirkwood's persisting rhetoric of such.

Running on the slogan, "One Kirkwood, Moving Forward," Jayson Thornton's decision to enter the race can be likened to extending an olive branch, a commitment to social cohesion on behalf of his family (the Thorntons), his neighborhood (Meacham Park), and his city (Kirkwood). If the City of Kirkwood is to ever become one and truly move forward, it must add up the costs for political exclusion. It must critically examine the motives of local government—irrespective of economics—for acting in a manner that is counterproductive for Meacham Park. Given that groups of youth, particularly young black men, are hanging out throughout the neighborhood with nothing to do and heavily surveilled by police, what would it cost the City of Kirkwood to provide supervised space or a staffed recreational center in the neighborhood? There are several facilities and activities available to youth on the white, affluent side that black youth rarely commute to. As such is the case, it is incumbent upon elected officials to consider the dynamics of its two groups—poor blacks and affluent whites—and within that context, account for why there is a lack of engagement from Meacham Park youth. Is it possible that traveling farther into Kirkwood, outside of their neighborhood, could mean additional disparagement for them by some white citizens, or more directly, the police? The findings of this study certainly suggest so.

Moreover, let us employ cultural awareness and racial sensitivity, while considering the taunt of a twelve-year-old black girl as a passerby yelled, "You're a monkey!"[11] during her walk from school to meet her mother at a local Kirkwood coffee shop, or the comment of a middle-aged black man during a community meeting:

> I feel a lot safer at three o'clock in the morning walking through Meacham Park then I do walking through north Kirkwood.

These are everyday experiences—in addition to misguided political decisions and influences—that leave blacks ostracized in the City of Kirkwood. In response to her sixth-grade daughter's encounter, Antona Smith responded to the press by stating:

> I am the only black person at the coffee shop. I'm the only black person in downtown Kirkwood. There are subtle things. You may be given a look. People make assumptions. You can just tell by their looks, like what's she doing here ... Kirkwood is very much an insular place ... It's very much a white experience.[12]

Black youth from Meacham Park come to be excluded from this "white experience," and consequently they become disinterested in facilities and programs in Kirkwood Proper. For example, the black kids in Meacham Park prefer roller-skating over ice-skating. This is indicative of a cultural disconnect; one of many, seemingly minor, yet significant instances where the City of Kirkwood does not account for its diverse populations. This translates into political punishment for failing to assimilate to the preferences of Kirkwood's whites, and therefore, being omitted by default from city planning and appropriation. An example of how this pans out in everyday terms is Kirkwood's decision to renovate its current recreational center, located on the affluent side, while providing no space for those located in Meacham Park.

For the sake of self-examination, the City of Kirkwood must ask itself, what are the costs for providing equal consideration to the interests of its diverse population? Do those costs outweigh community dissonance and ongoing racial tensions? Or do they simply become part of the toss-up between economics and political influence? In order for positive change to occur, the City of Kirkwood has to be considerate of *all* residents—poor blacks and affluent whites—in fiscal decisions and policies. The default should not be providing for its privileged citizens, but instead, also rendering fair consideration and allowances to those who are underprivileged. Implementing a form of the Weed and Seed Program in Meacham Park was certainly a start. The Meacham Park neighborhood pushed for it in hopes of tackling improprieties, particularly as it allows residents to report crime anonymously, without having to make direct contact or interact with the police or other emergency workers. Interestingly, not only did the local government approve the program, but by comparison to other Meacham Park requests, it acted on it almost immediately. Consequently, this allows for more policing in the neighborhood, initiated by citizens and later followed up by law enforcement. As the program serves to protect the residents, all actions taken in this community should not solely reflect crime fighting. Instead the local government should be similarly responsive and receptive to other requests, rather than having them lag in time or go unmet.

In sum, Kirkwood's government must be unambiguously "of the people, by the people, and for the people."[13] Its elected officials must be *truly* representative of its citizens—a reflection of diverse persons and *their* neighborhoods. Through strategic planning, Kirkwood's government should lead the change toward racial and cultural inclusiveness, moving the entire city—its departments and constituents—to take *everyone's* needs into consideration.

Political Accountability

While advancing social justice can be unifying and advantageous to the whole of society, likewise, it can be disruptive and unsettling. It forces us to challenge the status quo and break from dated practices in an effort to enact new, cohesive ones. As Kirkwood's local government moves toward more racially inclusive policies and practices, it must explicitly disallow its representative persons and departments to continue them. In general, the mission must be the same as Thornton's campaign slogan, "One Kirkwood, Moving Forward." A commitment to stay the course must resonate through action; safeguards must be put in place, as to avoid even seemingly well-intentioned officials, committee members, employees, and inevitably, citizens from deviating from them.

While establishing the Citizen Action Center as a place to report, track, and address concerns to the city is a start, in and of itself it does not ensure answerability. The administration and its management, across departments, must be committed to fairness, and therefore, relevant policies and practices should be transparent, not assumed. For example, diversity training for all government workers—elected, employed, or volunteering—should be mandatory. At best, people may behave insensitively without realizing it. For example, every semester, I can count on one or two students referring to diverse groups as "Coloreds" and "Orientals." Generally speaking, I believe they are well-intentioned students. As a result, I have had to proactively address these issues as classroom etiquette in course syllabi and lecture, particularly with undergraduates. As my courses, and more broadly, campus and society-at-large lend themselves to diverse interactions, it is incumbent upon me as an educator to dissuade often uninformed, unintentional conflict. Similarly, it is the responsibility of Kirkwood's administration to take proactive and retroactive measures in educating its members, in their initial hiring and, later, in professional development, thus establishing a precedent for accountability and for consequences in the case of deviation.

Kirkwood's Human Rights Commission (HRC) cannot and should not be solely responsible for ensuring cultural sensitivity. While this division of government is designed to address human rights issues, it cannot fully account for and is not responsible for reprimanding *all* improprieties. Racial and ethnic biases often fall below the radar, and discrimination may occur subtly and unrecognizably. Furthermore, professional cultures where employees indirectly or directly feel compelled to protect one another may then impede reports and investigations. This is commonly the case in policing. Though disputed at times, "the code of silence" and outright denial is real, pervasive, and persistent. Discriminative actions are often unfounded and unaddressed, resulting in underreporting or no reporting by both employees and citizens. This is what happened with information regarding Kevin and Sgt. McEntee. Disconcerting interactions that had been reported to the police were reported but disregarded. So offices like the HRC can lead the charge, making clear through policies and practices that discrimination is intolerable, efforts for eradicating it are nonnegotiable, and violations are punishable. But shared government responsibility and accountability is how *all* citizens' can come to be fairly respected and protected. This is a considerable undertaking and requires widespread support.

Such a joint effort, with increasingly judicious government oversight, is what will improve black citizen–police interactions within the City of Kirkwood and the neighborhood of Meacham Park.

Improving Policing, Advancing Black-Citizen Relations

My suggestions for immediately improving black citizen–police relationships in the Meacham Park community derive from the participants' perceptions. As participants shared numerous accounts of what they believed to be instances of the police showing little or no regard for them, likewise, they also provided instances of feeling respected by them. They experienced the latter in two ways: when officers were courteous with them, and when the officers were unpretentiously involved in their community.

Officers should work to be more courteous or friendly while out patrolling the Meacham Park community. While this solution may seem superficial, it is an immediate response in an often-contentious environment. Officers should make an effort to greet members of the community by waving, simply saying hello, or pausing for casual conversation. Part of changing negative perceptions means officers taking time to be nice through simple, kind gestures and extending themselves through greetings and casual conversations as a matter of practice. Participants reported feeling favorable toward officers who engaged them in this way.

Even when police stops occur, being courteous or considerate is important. In fact, research suggests that courtesy "strengthens in the public's mind the image of the police as a positive force" and is likely to be reciprocated by citizens.[14] As male participants complained about officers' initial approach of them, they explained that officers' voice tones and choice of words were offensive. Conversely, they also made clear that when officers approached them with a greeting and friendly tones, they felt respected. Granted, not all stops may allow for such simple words, gestures, or acts of kindness, but doing so as a matter of practice, rather than always slowing down and suspiciously gazing at individuals without speaking, would show officers in a different light.

Additionally, community involvement works to improve police-citizen relationships.[15] Police officers should continue to involve themselves in community programs and increase their involvement where and when possible. This should be done in three ways: continued participation in preexisting programs; increased involvement in the form of enacting new programs or adding to existing programs; and increased assistance to residents in need.

Participants who frequently attended neighborhood association meetings embraced police presence and took pleasure in their community reports. Through these reports, they felt connected to and aware of community activities. Participants also reported police involvement at local parades and celebrations, and even at the hotdog program for children in the park. In these instances, the police were reported as helping, assisting, and conversing with community members. In one instance, a respondent was thrilled with having met the chief of police at a parade and then having him introduce him to other officers. It made him feel important. The police should continue participating in such venues and increase their participation in programs where they have not. Doing so may provoke immediate change in police-citizen relationships.

The department should also involve itself by enacting or following through on newly proposed community programs and activities. Per the mediation agreement, increasing foot patrols, when possible, was proposed as advantageous to police-citizen relations in Meacham Park. Research shows that foot patrols decrease citizens' fear of crime, which translates to favorable attitudes toward police.[16] However, male and female participants, young and old, reported seeing officers only patrolling in vehicles and not on foot in Meacham Park. Because many participants, mostly those with no negative history or the least amount of police history, embrace the idea of improving relations through increased community involvement and the use of foot patrols, being consistent and following through on proposed ideas is crucial.

Additional programs or efforts by the police department, as suggested in the mediation agreement, are: increase minority recruitment for the Police Explorer Program; work with local agencies and volunteers to help youth attend college or procure internships or employment; assist volunteers and schools with getting expelled students involved in volunteer work; partner and coordinate with local agencies and youth to creating a local court for high school youth; create new initiatives to extend and attract more participants to the "Ride-Along Program"; place more emphasis on the Police Chaplain Program by forging relationships through the churches in the community; participate in the city's automatic complaint program; increase the number of block captains, extend Night Out Events and the Police Pancake Supper; provide speakers for events and school tours of the police department; increase the weight on department evaluations regarding discriminatory behaviors; review departmental policies with all employees; work with citizens on diversity issues/events when asked; commit to hiring qualified personnel indiscriminately; increase efforts to fight crime through two-person car patrols; establish a satellite office on a trial basis; and provide more diversity training for block captains.

Though numerous actions were proposed through the mediation agreement, there has been no real accountability in ensuring the creation, continuation, or extension of those programs—at least so far as my participants are aware. Though the agreement calls for oversight by both the Advisory Committee and ultimately requires the Kirkwood Human Rights Advisory and Awareness Commission (HRC) to annually report and publish actions taken with the previous programs, such reports can be subjective. Additionally, though the residents of Meacham Park are most affected by the implementation of proposed programs, they are unlikely to read about actions taken with them in an online report. Residents in Meacham Park are most interested in tangible actions as they see, hear, and know them to take place in their community. So, for instance, reporting that the Police Explorer Program increased from two youth to three means very little and is likely to have little impact on residents in a community where many are leery of the local government and its promises. Likewise, establishing a police substation—infrequently manned by police and inaccessible to residents—will not improve community relations. Creating, continuing, or extending police programs that do not allow for meaningful interactions between citizens and police only reinforces the perceived need to heavily police blacks rather than develop cohesive community relationships with them.

This too is the case with the implementation of the Weed and Seed Program. The "weed" aspect affords Meacham Park residents opportunities for anonymously reporting neighborhood improprieties via mail to encourage more police oversight and intervention in their community. However, the "seed" portion wanes in that there are no concrete efforts to embed and nurture improved direct citizen-police exchanges in their neighborhood. Given the amount of distrust and apathy with regards to bureaucratic meetings, reports, and overall structural effectiveness, continuing to respond in ways contrary to knowing and understanding the community the agreement is supposed to serve is indicative of a persistent cultural disconnection.

Moreover, as reporting actions taken with programs may provide some transparency, it does not account for impact. There is no real way of measuring the success of implemented or continued programs, which goes back to the very heart of accountability. As programs take place, the city or the HRC may state the number of participants, but the agreement in itself does not call for or detail a specified course of actions for measuring the effectiveness of having had those participants. Beyond stating that the committee "may convene at any time and choose to modify, amend, or dissolve the agreement" (Advisory Committee and Dispute Resolution Process section), there is no outlined plan for assessment, and thus, no "real" way of knowing whether the programs are doing what they were intended to do.

Another area of concern is the suggested diversity training for block captains. While participating in such training programs might be useful and advantageous in forging relationships, again, it seems that such programs would be equally beneficial if specified, mandated, and continuously conducted and reassessed similarly for the Kirkwood Police Department as well as all other city employees and committee members. As there is a history of strained relations between Meacham Park and the City of Kirkwood government—hence the mediation agreement—diversity training should be proposed and mandated for all Kirkwood City officials and employees. As cases in point, the tragedies of Kevin Johnson and Cookie Thornton do not reflect contention between Meacham Park and its block captains but rather tension with the city government and its officials. Therefore, diversity training should not be proposed on a voluntary basis for those least likely to contribute to poor community relations, but, rather, it should be mandated and ongoing tangibly for those likeliest to be implicated in persisting conflicts in Meacham Park.

Assisting members of the community who may be in distress is another way police could be more involved. Such instances may or may not warrant a service call; some may simply require more time or effort subsequent to one. Participants reported satisfaction with the police when they checked on them during heat waves and in other instances where they did not place calls. They also reported favorable feelings toward them when they vigorously worked to resolve their issues following calls.

In sum, police-citizen relationships may benefit tremendously from police courtesy and departmental training that encourages it along with attention to diversity (i.e., mandatory diversity workshops, hiring more minority officers); increased community involvement through actual programs or the enactment of new ones; a show of genuine concern by officers extending themselves to help, assist, or explain things to residents; and increased government commitment, consistency, and accountability regarding officers' behaviors and their delivery of relevant community programs and activities. More directly, officers should be policed in tandem with citizens. The local administration must institute and reaffirm police directives, implement routine assessments, and be willing to make swift, critical changes regarding employment and programs in hopes of progressing black citizen relations.

This project found the programs and activities proposed through the Department of Justice mediation agreement either as having not occurred as initially suggested or as inadequately publicized in the community of Meacham Park. Generally, the details surrounding them were superficial. They were articulated as vague ideas, allowing room for evading direct criticism. By doing this, the City of Kirkwood undermined its commitment to change, and justified distrust among the residents of Meacham Park. Furthermore, the mediation agreement expired in January 2013. It was determined by the mayor and other city officials that the city had accomplished the tenants of the agreement, and in similarly uncertain terms as the agreement, it (City of Kirkwood) had decided to move forward with additional programming as it deemed necessary.

Moreover, attention should be given to broader sociological issues and implications in Meacham Park and nationally. As low-income communities are often crime-ridden, improving the economic status of its residents could translate to a decrease in crime, and thus to better relations with the police.[17] After all, research shows crime or the fear of crime as significantly influencing citizens' perceptions of the police. Hence, as crime or the fear of crime decreases in a community, favorable attitudes toward the police increase.[18]

Additionally, research shows that the choices and experiences of blacks in marginalized communities often hinge on survival.[19] Tackling issues such as unemployment and a lack of relevant youth programs and facilities in the community is equally significant in changing and improving the overall culture of the community. Therefore, employment-training programs and opportunities should be made available to the residents of Meacham Park and similar communities. As there were proposed programs targeting youth employment, so too should there be programs made available for adult employment.

Also needed is a plan that addresses youth recreation. The youth in disadvantaged neighborhoods benefit from having recreational centers with structured programs and supervision actually located in their community. While there are recreation centers or other facilities for youth in larger, affluent communities, disadvantaged youth in Meacham Park and like communities often do not take advantage of them due to the distance, lack of transportation, or a cultural disconnect in the programming. Instead, they are more inclined to "hang out" locally. Hence, to keep youth from hanging out on corners, violating curfews, and potentially engaging in inappropriate activities that attract police attention, programs and activities such as midnight basketball or lock-ins in a structured, supervised setting should be made available to them. Since all youth cannot and may not work for various reasons, having a neighborhood facility and activities for youth would work to decrease possible improprieties as a result of idle time.

And last, as blacks are disproportionately underemployed, unemployed, disadvantaged, and therefore isolated, they often do not have transportation to events (e.g., Police Nights Out) in the larger parts of their suburban communities. This has certainly been the case in the neighborhood of Meacham. Consequently, including them in events may mean publicizing them in their neighborhoods, making transportation available to those interested in attending, or alternately hosting events in their community. In other words, black residents may attend regularly scheduled events if they know about them, have in some way(s) been included in them, or have a way to get to them. Ideally, this is about eliminating reasons for why black residents may not attend by providing numerous outlets for why and how they can. This should be the logic to follow with all programs and activities where the goal is to promote unity and inclusion among all citizens.

Taking Advantage of Critical Opportunities

We all have spheres of influence and those kinds of things are powerful. If I don't get out and talk to people I don't see every day, I don't get the real story cause the guys that I talk to, that see me all the time and come up and pat me on the back will tell me what they know I want to hear. You gotta get to the people that's gone make you a little uncomfortable.

A CITY OF KIRKWOOD EMPLOYEE AT A COMMUNITY
MEETING, 2014

Some of the implications of these findings are limited by my research design. While qualitative research of this kind can produce depth, my sample size and respondent population limit my conclusions. More diversity by age—particularly the inclusion of those under eighteen—would be useful in that research suggests that negative contacts and negative perceptions of the police often become established during youth. Similarly, it would be interesting to compare the experiences of the few whites in such communities to determine whether their experiences mirror those of black residents. Additionally, this study also lends itself to future comparisons for disadvantaged, white populations with regards to police interactions. It would benefit the literature to know how their experiences compare to those of blacks. What do police-citizen interactions look like for poor white populations that live near or in white wealthier communities? Do they experience aggressive policing similarly to blacks by virtue of class and place, or do they benefit from close proximity to their wealthier counterparts as a result of race?

And finally, though five participants reported wanting to see more black officers added to the force, none of the participants discussed officers' race as making a difference in their experiences or perceptions. In other words, the participants in this study did not communicate whether they preferred black officers over white or vice versa. In general, they merely seemed to want fair, respectable policing in their community, regardless of officers' race. Hence, in future studies, it would be helpful to consider symbolic representation and to know whether that is the general consensus among black populations, or if the race of officers matters in how blacks interact with them and perceive them.

Overall, the data obtained from this project, and more specifically from this community, allows for additional dialogue and analysis where community context may dictate differential policing and provides insight into black relationships with the police in the suburbs. It offers details of what those relationships look like, how they came to be formed, and how they are maintained through everyday interactions. By relying on interview research, I afforded disadvantaged blacks an opportunity to describe their experiences with the police in a suburban community. Additionally, I furthered race, place, and policing dialogue by challenging ideas about inner-city communities as monolithically black places and the crux of racial disparity and differential experiences. It is my hope that the findings discussed here will become applicable in ways that will make for better police-citizen relationships in the neighborhood of Meacham Park, the City of Kirkwood, and other areas where tense black citizen–police relations persist.

EPILOGUE

As of 2014, the City of Kirkwood is six years removed from the initial shock and horror of numerous perceptibly racially induced shootings, and the local government has decided it no longer needs a mediation agreement. The city is better and continues to work toward healing. It now has a black deputy mayor; an increased number of black police officers and city employees relative to its overall black population; much-needed access to groceries within closer proximity; the removal of a restrictive covenant prohibiting "Malay's and Negroes" from residing in any homes, unless they were servants; and a group of fifteen to twenty black and white citizens who continue to meet monthly in hopes of furthering racial unity.[1]

Meanwhile, across Greater St. Louis, roughly fifteen minutes north of the interstate, the City of Ferguson appears peaceful as well. Its streets are clear of Mike Brown, Jr., protests and marches, rubber bullets, tear gas, looting, and burning buildings. While some business owners seek funding in hopes of rebuilding their establishments, other businesses display messages of love, hope, unity, and peace through artistry. The city is purportedly on the road to recovery; Darren Wilson is no longer employed with the Ferguson police department and a new civilian review board is finally underway.

Like Kirkwood in the wake of its tragedies, the Ferguson government remains somewhat baffled as it searches for various ways to heal and improve their city. The City of Kirkwood has reportedly offered to assist them. An MSNBC article suggested that faith leaders were communicating across both communities, and that there was "talk of political leaders joining together."[2] Gestures that work to mend fences or forge new relationships are honorable and very much needed, as long as those efforts are practical and advanced by persons and parties believed to be receptive, akin, and exemplary of true racial inclusion and diversity.

In truth, things are not always as they seem. The degree to which diversity *truly* advances and the citizens find *actual* solace and satisfaction in Kirkwood's and Ferguson's efforts can be misrepresented. Despite media-driven talking points and pleasantries from mayors and other elected officials, there remains persisting racial and class disparity among citizens and a continuance of black citizen distrust for local governments and city officials.

At a community healing meeting in Kirkwood two months prior to Michael Brown's shooting in Ferguson (August 9, 2014), a young man expressed disgust with the progress of things. Despite the previously mentioned city improvements, he called everyone in attendance on the carpet by asking, "How many people in this group have invested time inside of Meacham Park?" Except for one attendee, who happened to be a resident of the Meacham Park neighborhood, the group appeared taken aback and was unresponsive. Furthering his point that people constantly say they support change and racial inclusion, while subtly and perhaps unknowingly still contribute to persisting black isolation, he added:

> We're coming together trying to do all of this and that, but we got people who ain't never even been inside of Meacham Park. How is that gone change anything? More meetings and more meetings, right?!?

For some, efforts toward improving the state of racial disparity in Kirkwood still pale in comparison to what is believed to be *real* commitment. Taken as another example, the appointment of a black deputy mayor did little for the community. Some black citizens in Meacham Park clearly stated that he was not *their* choice for an elected official or new political appointee, while reiterating that *their* preference for government representation (Jayson Thornton) did not come to fruition.

Relying on politically timed, vague rhetoric, reporting, and decision making to gauge the state of affairs, in hopes that conflict will eventually just fade away, does not work. By contrast, a true picture will be drawn by those whose everyday lives are affected. Hence, the government's decision to end the mediation agreement and suggest that *they* (elected officials) will continue to work toward healing in and of itself does not advance racial harmony—especially if this "work" is done mostly in meetings. Ending the agreement undermined the role and significance of the Human Rights Commission and some Meacham Park residents. Both parties found that adherence to the agreement was ambiguous, and recommended that it be extended; but Kirkwood's elected officials overrode concerns and eliminated it.

Unfortunately, citizens fear similar contradictions in Ferguson. As a protestor infuriatingly put it, "We are sick and tired of smoke and mirrors." They believe racial injustice to be widely systemic and indicative of local governments—key decision makers and enforcers (police)—across the St. Louis region. Consequently, the St. Louis City and County have already been charged and condemned in its overall mistreatment of black citizens. That is, sentiments of persisting differential practices that became even more exacerbated with the grand jury's failure to indict Darren Wilson. This explains the outcry of citizens from Ferguson and other communities.

To this end, at the first city council meeting following the Brown shooting, Ferguson residents and citizens broadly made clear to the mayor and city council that they were not going away, that strategies to wait them out or institutionally wear them down would ultimately lose. At best, civil unrest appeared dormant, ready to reemerge with greater fury and prove even more catastrophic, as happened after failure to indict Wilson. Meanwhile, the meeting grew more intense by the minute, with residents disrupting the agenda of the mayor and city council by exclaiming "There will be no more business as usual" in the day-to-day operations. Refusing to stand down or compromise on numerous demands, another citizen stated, "Since we [blacks] live uncomfortable daily, so will you [decision makers]. You will not rest, until we can."

The deafening tone of disadvantaged blacks perceiving themselves institutionally cornered and defenseless must be heeded. Historically, many have witnessed the enactment and enforcement of insensitive, discriminate policies that left countless populations increasingly vulnerable and unprotected. This is analogous to the world watching countless, mostly black, law-abiding citizens, angered by perceived injustices, being met by government-sanctioned and seemingly unchecked, militarized police.

It is in these very poignant encounters that I conduct race, place, and policing research as lived and understood by black citizens. I have been on the ground in Ferguson, seeing the rules of protesting frequently changed. Such changes left peaceful citizens unable to manage how and where they could protest, mischaracterized as nonpeaceful violators, and thus, inescapably subject to aggressive policing and arrests. In those moments, the sense on the ground was that the world was watching but not stepping up to stop it. And so for days, innocent black people in Ferguson were publically victimized—continuously confronted with aggressive, indefensible words, tones, and actions—at the hands of countless police, there under the auspices of defending against a few "threatening" citizens. Many people from around the world saw images depicting these events, but I account for what they often do not see—similar, everyday contentious black citizen–police interactions in disadvantaged communities. The newly dubbed "ground zero," the epicenter for protests and citizen-police standoffs against the backdrop of a burned-out QuikTrip, is not exclusive to Ferguson. Rather, it is or can become applicable to numerous places, without notice, where people of color—irrespective of criminality—are historically and stereotypically typecast and treated as *threatening*.

Keep watching. Think critically. Wherever societal tension emerges—swiftly and spontaneously morphing at the hands of frantic, inconsolable citizens—social change is certain. Our role(s) in advancing it—for better or worse, welcomed or unsolicited—will forever be noted in print, pictures, media footage, maybe policies, or at minimum, social media. Be thoughtful and strategic as *you* determine your position.

APPENDIX

STUDY PARTICIPANTS

Name	Age	Gender	Interview Location
Barbara	53	Female	Neighbor's house
Carla	18	Female	Home
Crystal	19	Female	Home
Denise	60	Female	Home
Dorothy	57	Female	Home
Dwayne	54	Male	Neighbor's house
Ed	55	Male	Neighborhood gathering
Felecia	37	Female	Home
Francis	60	Female	Home
Jackie	34	Female	Neighbor's house
Jasmine	42	Female	Home
Jeremy	29	Male	Neighbor's house
Johnny	57	Male	Neighbor's house
Karen	64	Female	Home
Keith	22	Male	Phone
Kim	62	Female	Home
Lisa	34	Female	Home
Lola	59	Female	Neighbor's house
Mark	50	Male	Library
Marsha	59	Female	Home
Mr. Willie	80	Male	Home
Pam	21	Female	Home
Pete	59	Male	Home
Ricky	56	Male	Home
Rodney	55	Male	Neighbor's house
Steve	22	Male	Home

Terrance	38	Male	Neighbor's house
Tiffany	36	Female	Home
Travis	45	Male	Neighborhood meeting, Turner School
Valerie (Val)	44	Female	Home

NOTES

INTRODUCTION

1. Brunson and Weitzer 2011.
2. McCartney and Dillon 2012.
3. Ibid.
4. Fritsch 2000.
5. Doyle and Fisher 2012.
6. Botelho 2012.
7. Ne Jame 2012.
8. Washington 2012.
9. Thompson and Wilson 2012.
10. Referring to small areas with high rates of crime as "hot spots" and then implementing aggressive proactive strategies to curtail them, also referred to as "hot spot policing," derived from several urban-crime theorists and works: Pierce et al., 1988; Sherman et al., 1989; Weisburd et al. 1993.
11. Meehan and Ponder 2002.
12. The following exemplary studies chronicle black experiences that shape ATP: Brunson and Miller 2006a; Brunson and Miller 2006b; Brunson 2007.
13. Massey and Denton 1993, 70.
14. Blalock 1967.
15. See the following: Terrill and Reisig 2003; Phillips and Smith 2000; Bass 2001.
16. Smith and Holmes 2003.
17. Meehan and Ponder 2002.
18. Ibid.
19. City of Kirkwood 2012.
20. Corrigan 2008a–d.
21. See the following: Brunson and Miller 2006a; Brunson and Miller 2006b; Terrill and Reisig 2003; Meehan and Ponder 2002; Kane 2002; Websdale 2001; Reisig and Parks 2000; Anderson 1999; Anderson 1990; Cao et al. 1996.

1. Bass 2001.
2. Ibid.
3. Turner et al. 2006; Roth 2010; Williams 2004; Hadden 2001.
4. Williams 2004, 39–44.
5. Williams 2004; Hadden 2001.
6. Williams 2004.
7. Ibid.
8. For example, in 1671, the Charlestown Town Watch (slave patrol) was created in South Carolina, "consisting of the regular constables and the rotation of six citizens" (Williams 2004, 49).
9. Williams 2004, 40.
10. Websdale 2001.
11. Ibid.
12. Williams 2004; Hadden 2001.
13. Websdale 2001.
14. T. Wilson 1965.
15. Ibid., 66.
16. Bass 2001; T. Wilson 1965.
17. Bass 2001, 160.
18. Ibid., 161.
19. Adams and Sanders 2004; Woodward 1966.
20. Wright 1937, 277–78.
21. Loewen 2005, 4.
22. Ibid.
23. Ibid., 80.
24. Ibid., 25.
25. Ibid., 12.
26. Ibid., 25.
27. Ibid.
28. Quoted in ibid., 67.
29. Ibid., 277.
30. Ibid., 3.
31. Ibid., 173.
32. Ibid., 68–69.
33. Ibid., 74.
34. Ibid., 95.
35. Ibid., 93.
36. Ibid., 79.
37. Schneider and Phelan 1993.
38. Loewen 2005, 79.
39. Ibid.

40. Molotch and Logan 1987, 194.

41. Wilkes and Iceland 2004; Massey and Denton 1989; Massey and Denton 1993.

42. Ibid.

43. Ibid.

44. Charles 2003; South and Crowder 1997.

45. Charles 2003, 175.

46. While there are numerous explanations for suburban segregation, I rely on the two broader perspectives (i.e., spatial assimilation and place stratification models); they encompass the others. See Charles 2003.

47. Charles 2003; Logan et al. 1996; Alba and Logan 1993.

48. Iceland and Wilkes 2006; Charles 2003; South and Crowder 1997; Logan et al. 1996; Alba and Logan 1993.

49. Studies also show positive effects with regards to nativity, language, and predominantly white suburban residency, particularly with Hispanics (Logan et al. 1996; Alba and Logan 1993; Alba and Logan 1991). These factors reflect the "cultural" assimilation aspect of the spatial-assimilation model, that is, minorities' ability to comfortably interact or adapt to the white majority with regards to length of time spent in the United States and English proficiency (Alba and Logan 1991). It is often here that spatial assimilation lends itself to in-group/out-group neighborhood preferences, at least to the degree of forming ethnic enclaves (Alba and Logan 1991). Meaning, people live in areas where their neighbors are most like them culturally and away from communities where people are least like them.

50. Farley et al. 1978.

51. South and Crowder 1997; Alba and Logan 1993.

52. Alba and Logan 1993, Alba and Logan 1991.

53. Logan et al. 1996, 854.

54. Feagin and Sikes 1994.

55. Rice 1996; Logan et al. 1996, 854.

56. Schneider and Phelan 1993, 270.

57. Logan et al. 1996.

58. As place stratification hinges on racial prejudices and discrimination and is most consistent with explaining minority group residential segregation, particularly for blacks (Logan et al. 1996), spatial assimilation contends that residential integration increases for minority individuals as socioeconomic and cultural acculturation increases. Again, relying on 1980 census data comprised of 3.5 million Hispanics, 2.8 million non-Hispanic blacks, 1.0 million Asians, and 35.4 million non-Hispanic whites, Logan et al. (1996) examined minority access to predominately white suburbs across eleven U.S. metropolitan areas where they found both perspectives applicable. They found places of residency to be stratified by socioeconomic status and race. Socioeconomic acculturation (spatial assimilation) shaped neighborhood composition, but so did race as disproportionate, differential patterns and practices (place stratification) appeared indicative of systematic neighborhood segregation. In sum, residential mobility can be linked to both socioeconomic status

(spatial assimilation) and to differential residential patterns for minorities (place stratification).

59. Farley et al. 1994, 753.

60. Bobo and Zubrinsky 1996.

61. Farley et al. 1994, 751.

62. Iceland and Wilkes 2006.

63. Feagin and Sikes 1994.

64. After eliciting 1,134 interviews (734 whites, 400 blacks) where 85 percent of the white respondents and eleven black respondents lived in the Detroit suburbs, Farley et al. (1978) found a majority of blacks preferring suburban integration and perceiving it as a way of balancing racial interaction. Farely et al. (1978) quoted one respondent's view of integration as, "It might make it better to get along with white people" (328). In general, the blacks in this study believed a racial balance would decrease chances for racial hostility, while simultaneously exposing their children to diversity and increasing racial harmony (Farley et al. 1978).

65. Alba and Logan 1993; Alba and Logan 1991.

66. In addition to asking open-ended questions, Farley et al. 1978 showed white respondents. In response to a picture of even with just one black household and fourteen white, 25 percent of white respondents expressed discomfort with the prospect of having black neighbors. Consistent with racial (Smith and Holmes 2003) and group threat (Blalock 1967) theories discomfort for white respondents increased in accordance with the numbers of prospective black households.

67. Farley et al. 1978.

68. "Ignorance of the housing market" does not influence residential segregation. See Farley et al. 1978, 342.

69. Ibid., 342.

70. Ibid., 338.

71. Inasmuch as whites' initial answers reflected a willingness to integrate, in-depth details elicited through a series of techniques revealed the opposite. This study affirmed the significance of race and place in that black residential integration determines neighborhood desirability for whites. Thus, as whites are the dominant group, it is through their perceptions of blackness (i.e., subordinate, dangerous) that residential segregation persists, irrespective of social status. See Farley et al. 1978.

72. See Bobo and Zubrinsky 1996. In fact, when facing suburban integration, whites preferred integrating with Asians over other minority groups. Also see Charles 2003.

73. Bobo and Zubrinsky 1996.

74. Ibid.

75. Ibid, 890. Researchers found 8.3 percent of 481 blacks, 8.6 percent of 476 Hispanics, and 6.1 percent of 281 Asians in opposition to living with whites.

76. Ibid.

77. Ibid.

78. See Smith and Holmes 2003; Blalock 1967.

79. See Farley et al. 1994. They also found white comfort levels with blacks as improving with younger, and thus, more liberal generations, though still persistently affected by racial biases.

80. Bobo and Zubrinsky 1996.

81. Farley et al. 1978, 343.

82. Chambliss 1994; Meehan and Ponder 2002; Alpert et al. 2005.

83. Ibid.

84. Chambliss 1994.

85. Ibid.

86. Ibid., 179.

87. Alpert et al. 2005, 423.

88. Ibid.

89. Meehan and Ponder 2002.

90. Ibid., 415–16.

91. Meehan and Ponder 2002; Gelman et al. 2007.

92. Meehan and Ponder 2002.

93. Ibid.

94. Gelman et al. 2007, 820.

95. Meehan and Ponder 2002; Gelman et al. 2007.

96. Warren et al. 2006.

97. Lundman and Kaufman 2003.

98. Warren et al. 2006.

99. Alpert et al. 2005.

100. Overall, researchers determined that black men eighteen to twenty-two years of age are most vulnerable to police stops locally and on the highway. Importantly, researchers make clear that speeding behaviors were virtually the same for both black (7.40 percent) and white (6.70 percent) respondents, and yet, the percentage of stops for blacks compared to that of whites by local and state police remained disproportionate. See Warren et al. 2006, 721.

101. Researchers also asked (1) whether respondents felt their stops were legitimate, and (2) whether they believed officers to have behaved appropriately during stops. See Lundman and Kaufman 2003.

102. Ibid., 207.

103. Fine et al. 2003.

104. Ibid., 152.

105. Ibid.

106. Weitzer 2000.

107. While residents differed in their reasoning for why differential treatment existed, black residents attributed it to "simple racism" (Weitzer 2000, 136). Whites, on the other hand, discussed black criminality as justification (Weitzer 2000, 137–38). Similarly, a few black residents mentioned the idea of black criminality. But in instances where they did, they discussed it as an inexcusable explanation. Black residents also suggested "stereotypes and racialized expectations" as reasons for differential treatment (Weitzer 2000, 138).

108. They believed the white residents of the affluent neighborhood to be treated much better than those of the lower-class black neighborhood. The white affluent neighborhood (i.e., Cloverdale) was presumed to be crime-free compared to the black, low-income, crime-infested community (i.e., Spartanburg). Consequently, the police generally dealt with the white affluent residents reactively and the black disadvantaged residents proactively (Weitzer 2000:143).

109. Weitzer 2000, 151.

110. Wilson 1978.

111. Anderson 1990.

112. The poor black and predominately white affluent neighborhoods (i.e., Northton and Village) are adjoining; the residents frequently cross paths. They shared streets; they shared space. Consequently, the myriad of circumstances, particularly as faced by disadvantaged blacks, become transparent as they are socially isolated and left to deal with the effects of gentrification. Changing landscapes, where poor blacks and affluent whites, exists side-by-side make for overt clashes due to distinct races and classes. Additionally, black disadvantage becomes more apparent as they are dependent upon the businesses and services of the predominantly white, affluent neighborhood as well as subject to the disappearance of what Anderson refers to as "the Old Heads"—that is, the absence of black role models as well as underemployment. Subsequently, such neighborhoods become further destitute; they succumb to drugs, teen pregnancy, and black-on-black violence. See Anderson 1990.

113. Anderson 1999.

114. Ibid., 33.

115. Ibid., 10.

116. Websdale 2001.

117. Anderson 1999.

118. They spoke candidly about a local black man gunned down by the police. Recalling previous incidents of police brutality, residents expressed feelings of contention toward the police.

119. Websdale 2001, 193.

120. Brunson and Miller 2006a; Brunson and Miller 2006b. Also see Brunson 2007.

121. Brunson and Miller 2006a; Brunson and Miller 2006b.

122. Websdale 2001; Anderson 1999; Anderson 1990.

123. Brunson and Miller 2006a; Brunson and Miller 2006b.

124. Brunson and Miller 2006a, 539.

125. Ibid., 544–45.

126. Brunson and Miller 2006b, 623.

127. Ibid., 622.

128. Through these accounts, it is clear that as the police used proactive tactics to make contact so did the young men also—in an attempt to avoid contact. Young men were able to discuss how they negotiated and avoided unwarranted police contacts in their community by avoiding certain places and people (ibid., 625). In some

instances, avoidance worked to decrease police suspicion and contact; in most, however, police harassment remained the same. See Brunson and Miller 2006b, 622.

129. Brunson and Miller 2006a; Brunson and Miller 2006b.

130. Brunson 2007, 72.

131. Miller and Davis 2008; Brunson and Miller 2006a; Brunson and Miller 2006b; Nihart et al. 2005; Fine et al. 2003; Taylor et al. 2001; Hurst and Frank 2000; Browning et al. 1994.

132. Fine et al. 2003; Browning et al.1994.

133. Nihart et al. 2005; Fine et al. 2003.

134. Brunson 2007; Brunson and Miller 2006a; Brunson and Miller 2006b; Fine et al. 2003; Taylor et al. 2001; Hurst and Frank, 2000; Hurst et al. 2000; Leiber et al., 1998; Chesney-Lind and Sheldon 1998.

135. Brunson 2007; Brunson and Miller 2006a; Brunson and Miller 2006b; Mastrofski et al. 2002; Fagan and Davies 2000.

136. Brunson 2007; Brunson and Miller 2006a; Brunson and Miller 2006b; Smith and Holmes 2003; Bass 2001; Chambliss 1994.

137. Brunson 2007; Brunson and Miller 2006b; Kane 2002; Anderson 1999, 1990; Klinger 1997.

138. Brunson and Miller 2006a; McDonald and Chesney-Lind 2001.

139. Fine et al. 2003; Robinson and Chandek 2000; Bush-Baskette 1998; Visher 1983.

140. Websdale 2001; Anderson 1999; Anderson 1990.

141. Albrecht and Green 1977.

142. Anderson 1990.

143. Albrecht and Green 1977.

144. Weitzer and Tuch 2004; Bordua and Tift 1971.

145. Miller and Davis 2008; Brunson 2007; Rosenbaum et al. 2005; Weitzer and Tuch 2004; Weitzer and Tuch 2005; Feagin and Sikes 1994; Browning et al. 1994.

146. Weitzer and Tuch 2002.

147. Decker 1981.

148. Miller and Davis 2008; Homant et al. 1984; Koenig 1980; Smith and Hawkins 1973; Block 1971.

149. Reisig and Parks 2000; Reisig and Giacomazzi 1998; Sampson and Bartusch 1998; Cao et al. 1996; Davis 1990; Murty et al. 1990.

150. Cao et al 1996.

151. Dean 1980; Smith and Hawkins 1973.

152. Robinson and Chandek 2000; Freudenberg et al. 1999; Anderson 1999; Anderson1990; Klinger 1997; Walker et al. 1996; Homant et al. 1984; Koenig 1980; Furstenberg and Wellford 1973.

153. Murty et al. 1990; Maxfield 1988; Thurman and Reisig 1996; Reisig and Correia 1997; Radalet and Carter 1994.

154. Carr et al. 2007; Brunson and Miller 2006a; Brunson and Miller 2006b; Fine et al. 2003; Browning et al. 1994.

155. Dawson 1994; Benson 1981.

156. Weitzer and Tuch 2004; Kane 2002; Holmes 2000.

157. Brooks and Jeon-Slaughter 2001; Wortley et al. 1997; Hagan and Albonetti 1982.

158. Brunson and Miller 2006a, 2006b; Terril and Reisig 2003; Meehan and Ponder 2002; Kane 2002; Websdale 2001; Reisig and Parks 2000; Anderson 1999, 1990; Cao et al. 1996.

159. Akers and Sellers 2004; Kane 2002; Bass 2001; Anderson 1999; Anderson 1990; Klinger 1997.

160. Cao et al. 1996.

CHAPTER 2. BLACK FACES IN WHITE PLACES

1. NPR 2000.
2. Corrigan 2008a.
3. Speer et al. 1998.
4. Ibid.
5. Ibid.
6. Ibid.
7. Ibid.
8. Corrigan 2008b, para. 19.
9. Speer et al. 1998.
10. Ibid.
11. Freivogel 2010a.
12. Ibid.
13. Ibid., para. 43–44.
14. Corrigan 2008a, para. 15–16.
15. Kohler 2008.
16. Ihnen 2009.
17. Ibid.
18. Corrigan 2008c.

CHAPTER 3. THE POLICE MAKING CONTACT

1. Corrigan 2008c, para. 20–21.
2. Ibid.
3. Ibid.
4. Ibid.
5. Ecology: Park and Burgess 1925; social disorganization: Shaw and McKay 1942.
6. Wilson 1987.
7. Sampson and Wilson 1995, 38.

8. Hinojosa 1997.

9. *Chicago Tribune* 2002.

10. CNN 1998.

11. Meehan and Ponder 2002.

12. Brunson and Miller 2006a.

13. Lamberth 1998.

14. Weitzer and Tuch 2004; Tyler and Huo 2002; and Bordua and Tift 1971.

15. Brunson 2007; Brunson and Miller 2006a; Brunson and Miller 2006b; Smith and Holmes 2003; Bass 2001; Chambliss 1994.

16. Brunson and Miller 2006a; Brunson and Miller 2006b.

17. Fine et al. 2003.

18. Meehan and Ponder 2002.

19. Tyler 2006; Fagan et. al. 2011.

20. Butler 2012.

21. Fagan et. al. 2011, 8.

22. Gau and Brunson 2010, 258.

23. Alpert et al. 2005.

24. Ibid.

25. Gelman et al. 2007.

26. Chesney-Lind and Pasko 2004.

27. Maher 1997.

28. Brunson and Weitzer 2011.

29. Richie 2012.

30. Brunson and Miller 2006a.

31. Richie 2012.

32. Brunson 2007; Brunson and Miller 2006a; Brunson and Miller 2006b; Smith and Holmes 2003; Bass 2001; Chambliss 1994.

33. Brunson and Miller 2006a; Brunson and Miller 2006b.

CHAPTER 4. THE TRAGEDIES OF KEVIN JOHNSON
AND CHARLES "COOKIE" THORNTON

1. Genius 2014.

2. Cooperman 2008b.

3. Cooperman 2008a.

4. Associated Press 2008.

5. Quoted in Cooperman 2008a.

6. Miller and Davis 2008; Brunson 2007; Rosenbaum et al. 2005: Weitzer and Tuch 2004; Weitzer and Tuch 2005; Feagin and Sikes 1994; Browning et al. 1994.

7. Weitzer and Tuch 2002.

8. Quoted in Freivogel 2010b.

9. Ibid.

10. Ibid.

11. KSDK 2005.

12. Brunson 2007, 72.

13. Deere and Moore 2008.

14. McCallie 2008.

15. Missouri Supreme Court 2012.

16. Ibid.

17. Murphy 2003.

18. Ibid.

19. Ibid.

20. Ibid.

21. Ibid.

22. PBS 2014.

CHAPTER 5. THE ROAD TO RECONCILIATION

1. MetroLyrics 2014.

2. Quoted in Vidal 2012.

3. Reisig and Parks 2000; Reisig and Giacomazzi 1998; Sampson and Bartusch 1998; Cao et al. 1996; Davis 1990; Murty et al. 1990.

4. Kirkwood police chief, quoted in Hannon 2010.

5. City of Kirkwood, 2014a and 2014b. The U.S. Department of Justice initiated a mediation agreement between the City of Kirkwood and the neighborhood of Meacham Park. It was intended to bring city officials and black and white residents together in hopes of bridging the racial divide. Both communities were tasked with coming together, reaching a consensus on programs and activities that would promote equality, unity, and harmony.

6. Freivogel 2011.

7. Ibid.

8. Ibid.

CONCLUSION AND DISCUSSION

1. Brown and Hutchinson 2013.

2. Brunson and Miller 2006a; Brunson and Miller 2006b.

3. Meehan and Ponder 2002.

4. Race-and-place effect: ibid.; racial-threat: Smith and Holmes 2003.

5. Spatial-assimilation: Charles 2003; Logan et al., 1996; Alba and Logan 1993; place-stratification: Alba and Logan 1993; Alba and Logan 1991.

6. Websdale 2001, 37–39.

7. Meehan and Ponder 2002.

8. Dawson 1994; Benson 1981.
9. Meehan and Ponder 2002; Smith and Holmes 2003; Anderson 1990.
10. Jayson M. Thornton 2014.
11. Singer 2014.
12. Ibid.
13. Abraham Lincoln Online 2014.
14. Wadman and Ziman 1993.
15. Stewart 2007.
16. Kelling et al. 1981.
17. Websdale 2001; Anderson 1999; Anderson 1990.
18. Cao et. al. 1996.
19. Websdale 2001.

EPILOGUE

1. City of Kirkwood 2012.
2. Seitz-Wald 2014.

REFERENCES

Abraham Lincoln Online. 2014. "The Gettysberg Address." Abrahamlincolnonline.org. www.abrahamlincolnonline.org/lincoln/speeches/gettysburg.htm (accessed January 2, 2015).

Adams, Francis, and Barry Sanders. 2004. *Alienable Rights: The Exclusion of African-Americans.* New York: HarperCollins.

Akers, Ronald, and Christine Sellers. 2004. *Criminological Theories: Introduction, Evaluation, Applications.* 4th ed. Los Angeles: Roxbury Publishing.

Alba, Richard D., and John R. Logan. 1991. "Variations on Two Themes: Racial and Ethnic Patterns in the Attainment of Suburban Residence." *Demography* 28(3): 431–53.

———. 1993. "Minority Proximity to Whites in Suburbs: An Individual-Level Analysis of Segregation." *American Journal of Sociology* 98(6): 1388–427.

Albrecht, Stan L., and Miles Green. 1977. "Attitudes toward the Police and the Larger Attitude Complex: Implications for Police-Community Relationships." *Criminology* 15(1): 67–86.

Alpert, Geoffrey P., John M. MacDonald, and Roger G. Dunham. 2005. "Police Suspicion and Discretionary Decision Making during Citizen Stops." *Criminology* 43(2): 407–34.

Anderson, Elijah. 1990. *Streetwise: Race, Class, and Change in an Urban Community.* Chicago: University of Chicago Press.

———. 1999. *Code of the Street: Decency, Violence, and the Moral Life of the Inner City.* New York: W. W. Norton.

Associated Press. 2008. "Gunman Left Note with a Warning." *Washington Post,* February 9.

Bass, Sandra. 2001. "Policing Space, Policing Race: Social Control Imperatives and Police Discretionary Decisions." *Social Justice* 28(1): 156–76.

Benson, Paul R. 1981. "Political Alienation and Public Satisfaction with Police Services." *Pacific Sociological Review* 24(1): 45–64.

Blalock, Hubert M. 1967. Toward a Theory of Minority-Group Relations." New York: Wiley.

Block, Richard L. 1971. "Fear of Crime and Fear of the Police." *Social Problems* 19 (Summer): 91–101.

Bobo, Lawrence, and Camille L. Zubrinsky. 1996. "Attitudes on Residential Integration: Perceived Status Differences, Mere In-group Preference, or Racial Prejudice?" *Social Forces* 74(3): 883–909.

Bordua, David J., and Larry L. Tift. 1971. "Citizens' Interviews, Organizational Feedback, and Police-Community Relations Decisions." *Law and Society Review* 6: 155–82.

Botelho, Greg. 2012. "What Happened the Night Trayvon Martin Died." *CNN Justice,* May 23, www.cnn.com/2012/05/18/justice/florida-teen-shooting-details (accessed June 2012).

Brooks, Richard, and Hackyung Jeon-Slaughter. 2001. "Race, Income, and Perceptions of the U.S. Court System." *Behavioral Sciences and the Law* 19(2): 249–64.

Brown, Stephen, and Bill Hutchinson. 2013. "B37's Fellow Jurors in Trayvon Martin Trial Bash Her for Leading Country to Believe Spoke for Them." *Daily News,* July 17.

Browning, Sandra L., et al. 1994. "Race and Getting Hassled by the Police: A Research Note." *Police Studies: Int'l Rev. Police Dev.* 17: 1.

Brunson, Rod K. 2007. "Police Don't Like Black People: African-American Young Men's Accumulated Police Experiences." *Criminology and Public Policy* 6(1): 71–101.

Brunson, Rod K., and Jody Miller. 2006a. "Gender, Race, and Urban Policing: The Experience of African American Youths." *Gender and Society* 20(4): 531–52.

———. 2006b. "Young Black Men and Urban Policing in the United States." *British Journal of Criminology* 46(4): 613–40.

Brunson, Rod K., and Ronald Weitzer. 2011. "Negotiating Unwelcome Police Encounters: The Intergenerational Transmission of Conduct Norms." *Journal of Contemporary Ethnography* 40(4): 425–56.

Burgess, Ernest W. 1925. "The Growth of the City." In *The City,* by Robert E. Park and Ernest W. Burgess. Chicago: University of Chicago Press.

Bush-Baskette, Stephanie R. 1998. "The War on Drugs as a War against Black Women." In *Crime Control and Women: Feminist Implications of Criminal Justice Policy,* edited by S. Miller, 113–29. Thousand Oaks, CA: Sage Publications.

Butler, Paul. 2012. "Don't Antagonize Those Who Could Help." *New York Times,* September 20.

Cao, Linqun, James Frank, and Francis T. Cullen. 1996. "Race, Community Context, and Confidence in the Police." *American Journal of Police* 15(1): 3–22.

Carr, Patrick J., Laura Napolitano, and Jessica Keating. 2007. "We Never Call the Cops and Here Is Why: A Qualitative Examination of Legal Cynicism in Three Philadelphia Neighborhoods." *Criminology: An Interdisciplinary Journal* 45(2): 445–80.

Chambliss, William J. 1994. "Policing the Ghetto Underclass: The Politics of Law and Law Enforcement." *Social Problems* 41(2): 177–94.

Charles, Camille Zubrinsky. 2003. "The Dynamics of Racial Residential Segregation." *Annual Review of Sociology* 29: 167–207.

Chesney-Lind, Meda, and Lisa Pasko. 2004. *The Female Offender: Girls, Women, and Crime.* Thousand Oaks, CA: Sage Publications.

Chesney-Lind, Meda, and Randall G. Sheldon. 1998. *Girls, Delinquency, and Juvenile Justice.* 2nd ed. Belmont, CA: Wadsworth Publishing.

Chicago Tribune. 2002. "Convictions Overturned in Louima Abuse Case." March 1.

City of Kirkwood. 2010. "Meacham Park: A Neighborhood with History and a Growing Future." City of Kirkwood, MO, www.kirkwoodmo.org/com-dev/meacham-intro.htm (accessed January 2010; website has been updated and this page no longer exists).

———. 2012. "History and Demographics." City of Kirkwood, MO, www.kirkwoodmo.org/content/For-Visitors/1355/history-demographics.aspx (accessed January 2, 2015).

———. 2014a. "Human Rights Commission Mediation Agreement." Kirkwoodmo.com, www.kirkwoodmo.org/mm/files/Mediation%20Agreement.pdf (accessed January 2, 2015).

———. 2014b. "Human Rights Commission 2013 Annual Report." Kirkwoodmo.com. www.kirkwoodmo.org/mm/files/HumanRights/2014/HRC%20-%20End%20of%20Year%20Report%20for%202013.pdf (accessed January 2, 2015).

CNN. 1998. "5 N.Y. Cops Face Federal Charges in Haitian Torture Case." CNN website, www.cnn.com/US/9802/26/police.torture (assessed November 28, 2014).

Cooperman, Jeanette. 2008a. "The Kirkwood Shootings: Why Did Cookie Thornton Kill?" *St. Louis,* April 24, www.stlmag.com/Why-Did-Cookie-Thornton-Kill/ (accessed January 2, 2015).

———. 2008b. "The Kirkwood Shootings: Kirkwood, Meacham Park, and the Racial Divide." *St. Louis,* April 25, www.stlmag.com/The-Kirkwood-Shootings-Kirkwood-Meacham-Park-and-the-Racial-Divide/ (accessed January 2, 2015).

Corrigan, Don. 2008a. "Part 1: Meacham Park: A History of American Change." *Webster-Kirkwood Times,* March 21.

———. 2008b. "Part 2: Black Power Movement Affected Meacham Park." *Webster-Kirkwood Times,* March 21.

———. 2008c. "Part 3: Tragic Fire Spurred Kirkwood Interest in Meacham Park." *Webster-Kirkwood Times,* March 21.

———. 2008d. "Part 4: Meacham Park Annexation Ideas Failed in the 1970s." *Webster-Kirkwood Times,* March 21.

Davis, James R. 1990. "A Comparison of Attitudes toward the New York City Police." *Journal of Police Science and Administration* 17(4): 233–43.

Dawson, Michael. 1994. *Behind the Mule: Race and Class in African American Politics.* Princeton, NJ: Princeton University Press.

Dean, Deby 1980. "Citizen Ratings of the Police: The Difference Police Contact Makes." *Law and Policy Quarterly* 2(4): 445–71.

Decker, Scott. 1981. "Citizen Attitudes towards the Police: A Review of Past Findings and Suggestions for Future Policy." *Journal of Police Science and Administration* 9(1): 81–87.

Deere, Stephan, and Doug Moore. 2008. "Charles Lee 'Cookie' Thornton: Behind the Smile." *St. Louis Post-Dispatch,* May 4.

Doyle, John, and Jonan Fisher. 2012. "Police in Sean Bell Shooting Get Canned." *Daily News,* March 24.

Fagan, Jeffrey, and Garth Davies. 2000. "Street Stops and Broken Windows: Terry, Race and Disorder in New York." *Fordham Urban Law Journal* 28(2): 457–504.

Fagan, Jeffrey, Tom Tyler, and Tracey Meares. 2011. "Street Stops and Police Legitimacy in New York." Paper presented at the "Crime Decline" conference, John Jay College of Criminal Justice, New York, September 22–23, 2011.

Farley, Reynolds, et al. 1978. "Chocolate City, Vanilla Suburbs: Will the Trend toward Racially Separate Communities Continue?" *Social Science Research* 7(4): 319–44.

———, et al. 1994. "Stereotypes and Segregation: Neighborhoods in the Detroit Area." *American Journal of Sociology* 100(3): 750–80.

Feagin, Joe R., and Melvin P. Sikes. 1994. *Living with Racism: The Black Middle-Class Experience.* Boston: Beacon Press.

Fine, Michelle, et al. 2003. "Anything Can Happen with Police Around: Urban Youth Evaluate Strategies of Surveillance in Public Places." *Journal of Social Issues* 59(1): 141–58.

Freivogel, William. 2010a. "Kirkwood's Journey: Separating Myths and Realities about Meacham Park, Thornton, Part 2." *St. Louis Beacon,* February 7.

———. 2010b. "Kirkwood Talks About Racial Disparities, But Doesn't Listen, Say Black Educators." *St. Louis Beacon,* February 7.

———. 2011. "Kirkwood's Journey: Nearly Three Years Later, Some Are Still Looking for Answers." *St. Louis Beacon,* January 26.

Freudenberg, Nicholas, et al. 1999. "Coming Up in the Boogie Down: The Role of Violence in the Lives of Adolescents in the South Bronx." *Health Education Behavior* 26(6): 788–805.

Fritsch, Jane. 2000. "The Diallo Verdict: The Overview; 4 Officers in Diallo Shooting Are Acquitted of All Charges." *New York Times,* February 26.

Furstenberg, Frank, and Charles Wellford. 1973. "Calling the Police: The Evaluation of Police Service." *Law and Society Review* 7(3): 393–406.

Gau, Jacinta M., and Rod K. Brunson. 2010. "Procedural Justice and Order Maintenance Policing: A Study of Inner-City Young Men's Perceptions of Police Legitimacy." *Justice Quarterly* 27(2): 255–79.

Gelman, Andrew, Jeffrey Fagan, and Alex Kiss. 2007. "Analysis of the New York City Police Department's 'Stop-and-Frisk' Policy in the Context of Claims of Racial Bias." *Journal of the American Statistical Association* 102(479): 813–23.

Genius Media Group Inc. 2014. "Trapped." Genius.com, http://genius.com /2pac-trapped-lyrics (accessed January 2, 2015).

Granderson, LZ 2012. "Why Black People Don't Trust the Police." *CNN Opinion,* March 22, www.cnn.com/2012/03/22/opinion/granderson-florida-shootings /index.html?iref = allsearch (accessed November 28, 2014).

Hadden, Sally E. 2001. *Slave Patrols: Law and Violence in Virginia and the Carolinas.* Cambridge, MA: Harvard University Press.

Hagan, John, and Celesta Albonetti. 1982. "Race, Class, and Perceptions of Criminal Injustice in America." *American Journal of Sociology* 88(2): 329–55.

Hannon, Dennis. 2010. "Mediation Agreement Called First Step toward Better Race Relations." *Webster-Kirkwood Times,* February 19.

Hinojosa, Maria. 1997. "NYC officer Arrested in Alleged Sexual Attack on Suspect." CNN, August 14, www.cnn.com/US/9708/14/police.torture/ (accessed January 2, 2015).

Holmes, Malcolm D. 2000. "Minority Threat and Police Brutality: Determinants of Civil Rights Criminal Complaints in U.S. Municipalities." *Criminology* 38(2): 343–68.

Homant, Robert J., Daniel B. Kennedy, and Roger M. Fleming. 1984. "The Effects of Victimization and the Police Response on Citizen Attitudes toward Police." *Journal of Police Science and Administration* 12(3): 323–27.

Hurst, Yolander J., and James Frank. 2000. "How Kids View Cops: The Nature of Juvenile Attitudes toward the Police." *Journal of Criminal Justice* 28(3): 189–202.

Hurst, Yolander, James Frank, and Sandra Lee Browning. 2000. "The Attitudes of Juveniles toward the Police: A Comparison of Black and White Youth." *Policing: An International Journal of Police Strategies and Management* 23(1): 37–53.

Iceland, John, and Rema Wilkes. 2006. "Does Socioeconomic Status Matter? Race, Class, and Residential Segregation." *Social Problems* 53 (2): 248–73.

Ihnen, Alex. 2009. "Street Barricades in the Crosshairs: St. Louis City Fire Chief May Offer Momentum Needed to Open Streets."*nextSTL,* October 16, http://nextstl.com/2009/10/street-barricades-in-the-crosshairs-st-louis-city-fire-chief-may-offer-momentum-needed-to-open-streets/ (accessed November 28, 2014).

Kane, Robert. 2002. "The Social Ecology of Police Misconduct." *Criminology* 40(4): 867–96.

Kelling, George L., et al. 1981. "The Newark Foot Patrol Experiment." *Washington, DC: Police Foundation:* 94–96.

Klinger, David A. 1997. "Negotiating Order in Patrol Work: An Ecological Theory of Police Response to Deviance." *Criminology* 35(2): 277–306.

Koenig, Daniel J. 1980. "The Effect of Crime Victimization and Judicial or Police Contacts on Public Attitudes toward the Local Police." *Journal of Police Science* 8(4): 243–49.

Kohler, Jeremy. 2008. "As City Recovers, Racial Tension Remain." *St. Louis Post-Dispatch,* February 15.

KSDK. 2005. "Suspected Killer of Kirkwood Sergeant Still at Large." Multimedia KSDK, http://archive.ksdk.com/news/local/story.aspx?storyid=81487 (accessed January 2, 2015).

Lamberth, John. 1998. "Driving While Black: A Statistician Proves That Prejudice Still Rules the Road." *Washington Post,* August 16.

Lieber, Michael J., Mahesh K. Nalla, and Margaret Farnsworth. 1998. "Explaining Juvenile Attitudes toward the Police." *Justice Quarterly* 15(1): 151–74.

Loewen, James W. 2005. *Sundown Towns: A Hidden Dimension of American Racism*. New York: New Press.

Logan, John R., and Molotch, Harvey L. 2007. *Urban Fortunes: The Political Economy of Place*. Berkeley: University of California Press.

Logan, John R., et al. 1996. "Making a Place in the Metropolis: Locational Attainment in Cities and Suburbs." *Demography* 33(4): 443–53.

Lundman, Richard, and Robert Kaufman. 2003. "Driving While Black: Effects of Race, Ethnicity, and Gender on Citizen Self-Reports of Traffic Stops and Police Actions." *Criminology* 41(1): 195–220.

Maher, Lisa. 1997. *Sexed Work: Gender, Race, and Resistance in a Brooklyn Drug Market*. Oxford: Clarendon Press.

Massey, Douglas S., and Nancy A. Denton. 1989. "Hypersegregation in US Metropolitan Areas: Black and Hispanic Segregation along Five Dimensions." *Demography* 26(3): 373–91.

———. 1993. *American Apartheid: Segregation and the Making of the Underclass*. Cambridge, MA: Harvard University Press.

Mastrofski, Stephen D., Michael D. Reisig, and John D. McCluskey. 2002. "Police Disrespect toward the Public: An Encounter-Based Analysis." *Criminology* 4(3): 519–52.

Maxfield, Michael G. 1988. "The London Metropolitan and Their Clients: Victim and Suspect Attitudes." *Journal of Research in Crime and Delinquency* 25(2): 188–206.

McCallie, Franklin. 2008. "Retired Kirkwood High Principal McCallie Releases Statement about Shooting, Cookie Thornton." *Kirkwood-Webster Times,* February 8.

McCartney, Anthony, and Raquel Maria Dillon. 2012. "Rodney King, Whose Beatings Led to LA Riots, Dies." AP, *The Big Story,* June 17, http://bigstory.ap.org/article/rodney-king-whose-beating-led-la-riots-dies (accessed November 28, 2014).

McDonald, John M., and Meda Chesney-Lind. 2001. "Gender Bias and Juvenile Justice Revisited." *Crime and Delinquency* 47(2): 173–95.

Meehan, Albert, and Michael Ponder. 2002. "Race and Place: The Ecology of Racial Profiling African American Motorists." *Justice Quarterly* 19(3): 399–430.

MetroLyrics. 2014. "Fuck Da Police." Metrolyrics.com, www.metrolyrics.com/fuck-tha-police-lyrics-nwa.html (accessed January 2, 2015).

Miller, Joel, and Robert C. Davis 2008. "Unpacking Public Attitudes to the Police: Contrasting Perceptions of Misconduct with Traditional Measures of Satisfaction." *International Journal of Police Science and Management* 10(1): 9–22.

Missouri Supreme Court. 2012. *Brief of Appellant: Kevin Johnson, Jr. vs. State of Missouri*. Missouri Courts, www.courts.mo.gov/sup/index.nsf/9f4cd5a463e4c223862 56ac4004a490f/90296917d780480b86257ad500017129/$FILE/SC92448_ Johnson_brief.pdf (accessed November 28, 2014).

Murphy, Kevin. 2003. "A Thorn in Kirkwood's Side." *Webster-Kirkwood Times,* August 15.

Murty, Komandri S., Julian B. Roebuck, and Joann D. Smith. 1990. "The Image of the Police in Black Atlanta Communities." *Journal of Police Science and Administration* 17(4): 250–57.

National Press Club (NPR). 2000. "Cardinal Roger Mahoney." Live web cast, May 25, www.npr.org/programs/npc/2000/000525.rmahony.html (accessed January 2, 2015).

Ne Jame, Mark. 2012. "A Deadly Combination: Guns and Stand-Your-Ground." *CNN Opinion,* April 30, www.cnn.com/2012/04/30/opinion/nejame-guns-stand-your-ground/ (accessed November 28, 2014).

Nihart, Terry, et al. 2005. "Kids, Cops, Parents and Teachers: Exploring Juvenile Attitudes toward Authority Figures." *Western Criminology Review* 6(1): 79–88.

Park, Robert E., and Ernest W. Burgess. *The City.* Chicago: University of Chicago Press.

PBS. 2014. "Indian Country Diaries." Native American Public Telecommunications, PBS.org, www.pbs.org/indiancountry/challenges/ (accessed January 2, 2015).

Phillips, Tim, and Phillip Smith. 2000. "Police Violence Occasioning Citizen Complaint: An Empirical Analysis of Time-Space Dynamics." *British Journal of Criminology* 40(3): 480–96.

Pierce, Glenn L., Susan Spaar, and Lebaron R. Briggs. 1988. *The Character of Police Work: Strategic and Tactical Implications.* Boston: Center for Applied Social Research, Northeastern University.

Radalet, Louis A., and David L. Carter. 1994. *The Police and the Community.* New York: Macmillan.

Reisig, Michael D., and Mark E. Correia. 1997. "Public Evaluations of Police Performance: An Analysis across Three Levels of Policing." *Policing: An International Journal of Police Strategies and Management* 20(2): 311–25.

Reisig, Michael D., and Andrew L. Giacomazzi. 1998. "Citizen Perceptions of Community Policing: Are Attitudes towards Police Important?" *Policing: An International Journal of Police Strategies and Management* 21(3): 547–61.

Reisig, Michael D., and Roger B. Parks. 2000. "Experience, Quality of Life, and Neighborhood Context: A Hierarchal Analysis of Satisfaction with the Police." *Justice Quarterly* 17(3): 607–30.

Rice, Willy E. 1996. "Race, Gender, Redlining, and the Discriminatory Access to Loans, Credit, and Insurance: An Historical and Empirical Analysis of Consumers Who Sued Lenders and Insurers in Federal and State Courts, 1950–1995." *San Diego L. Rev.* 33: 583.

Richie, Beth E. 2012. *Arrested Justice: Black Women, Violence, and America's Prison Nation.* New York: New York University Press.

Robinson, Amanda L., and Meghan S. Chandek. 2000. "Differential Police Response to Black Battered Women." *Women and Criminal Justice* 12(2–3): 29–61.

Rosenbaum, Dennis P., et al. 2005. "Attitudes toward the Police: The Effects of Direct and Vicarious Experience." *Police Quarterly* 8(3): 343–65.

Roth, Mitchel. 2010. *Crime and Punishment: A History of the Criminal Justice System.* Belmont, CA: Cengage Learning.

Sampson, Robert J., and Dawn J. Bartusch. 1998. "Legal Cynicism and (Subcultural?) Tolerance of Deviance: The Neighborhood Context of Racial Differences." *Law and Society Review* 32: 777–804.

Sampson, Robert J., and William Julius Wilson. 1995. "Toward a Theory of Race, Crime, and Urban Inequality." In *Race, Crime, and Justice: A Reader,* edited by Shaun L. Gabbidon and Helen Taylor Green, 177–90. New York: Routledge.

Schneider, Mark, and Thomas Phelan. 1993. "Black Suburbanization in the 1980s." *Demography* 30(2): 269–79.

Seitz-Wald, Allen. 2014. "How a Community Near Ferguson Rebuilt after Racial Violence." MSNBC.com, www.msnbc.com/msnbc/lessons-ferguson-its-neighbor-the-south (accessed January 2, 2015).

Shaw, Clifford R., and Henry D. McKay. 1942. *Juvenile Delinquency and Urban Areas.* Chicago: University of Chicago Press.

Sherman, Lawrence, Michael Buerger, and Patrick Gartin. 1989. *Repeat Call Address Policing: The Minneapolis RECAP Experiment.* Washington, DC: Crime Control Institute.

Singer, Dale. 2014. "Racial Taunt against 12-Year-Old Girl Stirs Concerns in Kirkwood." St. Louis Public Radio, May 12, http://news.stlpublicradio.org/post/racial-taunt-against-12-year-old-girl-stirs-concern-kirkwood (accessed January 2, 2015).

Smith, Brad. W., and Malcolm D. Holmes. 2003. "Community Accountability, Minority Threat and Police Brutality: An Examination of Civil Rights Criminal Complaints." *Criminology* 41(4): 1035–64.

Smith, Paul E., and Richard O. Hawkins. 1973. "Victimization, Types of Citizen-Police Contacts, and Attitudes toward the Police." *Law and Society Review* 8(1): 135–52.

South, Scott J., and Kyle D. Crowder. 1997. "Escaping Distressed Neighborhoods: Individual, Community, and Metropolitan Influences." *American Journal of Sociology* 102(4): 1040–84.

Speer, Lonnie, Bill Jones, and Garnet Thies. 1998. *Meacham Park: A History.* St. Louis: n.p. Available at the Kirkwood Historical Society.

Stewart, Eric A. 2007. "Either They Don't Know or They Don't Care: Black Males and Negative Police Experiences." *Criminology and Public Policy* 6(1): 123–30.

Taylor, Terrance, et al. 2001. "Coppin' an Attitude: Attitudinal Differences among Juveniles toward Police." *Journal of Criminal Justice* 29(4): 295–305.

Terrill, William, and Michael D. Reisig. 2003. "Neighborhood Context and Police Use of Force." *Journal of Research in Crime and Delinquency* 40(3): 291–321.

Thompson, Krissah, and Scott Wilson. 2012. "Obama on Trayvon Martin: 'If I Had a Son, He'd Look like Trayvon.'" *Washington Post,* March 23.

Thornton, Jayson M. 2014. "One Kirkwood, Moving Forward!" Jaysonthornton.com, www.jaysonthornton.com/index.html (accessed January 2, 2015).

Thurman, Quint, and Michael D. Reisig. 1996. "Community-Oriented Research in an Era of Community-Oriented Policing." *American Behavioral Scientist* 39(5): 570–86.

Turner, K. B., David Giacopassi, and Margaret Vandiver. 2006. "Ignoring the Past: Coverage of Slavery and Slave Patrols in Criminal Justice Texts." *Journal of Criminal Justice Education* 17(1): 181–95.

Tyler, Tom R. 2006. "Restorative Justice and Procedural Justice: Dealing with Rule Breaking." *Journal of Social Issues* 62(2): 307–26.

Tyler, Tom R., and Yuen Huo. 2002. *Trust in the Law: Encouraging Public Cooperation with the Police and Courts.* New York: Russell Sage Foundation.

Vidal, Juan. 2012. "The Politics and Provocation of N.W.A." *Huffington Post,* August 6, www.huffingtonpost.com/juan-vidal/the-politics-and-provocat_b_1748784 .html (accessed January 2, 2015).

Visher, Christy A. 1983. "Gender, Police Arrests Decisions, and Notions of Chilvary." *Criminology* 21(1): 5–28.

Wadman, Robert C., and Stephen M. Ziman. 1993. "Courtesy and Police Authority." *FBI Law Enforcement Bulletin* 62: 23–26.

Walker, Samuel, Cassia Spohn, and Miriam DeLone. 1996. *The Color of Justice: Race, Ethnicity, and Crime in America.* Belmont, CA: Wadsworth.

Warren, Patricia, et al. 2006. "Driving While Black: Bias Processes and Racial Disparity in Police Stops." *Criminology* 44(3): 709–38.

Washington, Jesse. 2012. "Trayvon, My Son, and the Black Male Code." *Huffington Post,* May 24, www.huffingtonpost.com/2012/03/24/trayvon-martin-my-son-and_1_n_1377003.html (accessed January 2, 2015).

Websdale, Neil. 2001. *Policing the Poor: From Slave Plantation to Public Housing.* Boston: Northeastern University Press.

Weisburd, David, et al. 1993. "Contrasting Crime General and Crime Specific Theory: The Case of Hot Spots of Crime." *New Directions in Criminological Theory: Advances in Criminological Theory* 4: 45–70.

Weitzer, Ronald. 2000. "Racialized Policing: Residents Perceptions in Three Neighborhoods." *Law and Society Review* 34(1): 129–55.

Weitzer, Ronald, and Steven Tuch. 2002. "Perceptions of Racial Profiling: Race, Class, and Personal Experience." *Criminology* 40(2): 435–56.

———. 2004. "Race and Perceptions of Police Misconduct." *Social Problems* 51(3): 305–25.

———. 2005. "Determinants of Public Satisfaction with the Police." *Police Quarterly* 8(3): 279–97.

Wilkes, Rima, and John Iceland. 2004. "Hypersegregation in the Twenty-First Century." *Demography* 41(1): 23–36.

Williams, Kristian. 2004. *Our Enemies in Blue.* Brooklyn, NY: Soft Skull Press.

Wilson, Theodore B. 1965. *The Black Codes of the South.* Tuscaloosa: University of Alabama Press.

Wilson, William Julius. 1978. "The Declining Significance of Race." *Society* 15(5): 11–21.

———. 1987. *The Truly Disadvantaged: The Inner City, the Underclass, and Public Policy.* Chicago: University of Chicago Press.

Woodward, Comer V. 1966. *The Strange Career of Jim Crow.* New York: Oxford University Press.

Wortley, Scot, John Hagan, and Ross Macmillan. 1997. "Just Des(s)erts? The Racial Polarization of Perceptions of Criminal Injustice." *Law and Society Review* 31(4): 637–76.

Wright, Richard. 1937. "The Ethics of Living Jim Crow." In *Justice Denied: The Black Man in White America,* edited by William M. Chance and Peter Collier, 270–81. Berkeley, CA: Harcourt, Brace.

black citizen-police relationships, 191; effects of, 162–63; improvements, suggestions for, 200–204; template and timeline in United States, 14

Black Codes, 14, 19, 21–22, 34, 189

black migration, 61–62

blackness, perception of, 33, 96, 99–100, 189, 216n71

black-on-black violence, 41, 134, 218n112

"black-only" laws. *See* Black Codes; Jim Crow laws; Slave Codes

"black-only" policing, 189

black-on-white violence, 134. *See also* racial threat theories

black police officers, 206, 207

black rhetoric, 165–68

black settlements, original, 58

black-white suburban segregation, 27, 31

boys/men, and negative ATPs, 44–45

Brian (Meacham Park resident), 1–2, 3, 4, 7

Brown, Michael, Jr., 207, 209

Bruder, Thomas, 100

Brunson, Rod, 42–44, 127

brutality, physical, 9, 114, 192; and community policing, 42; and gendered experiences, 127–28; and Jim Crow laws, 22–23; police misconduct, 124–29, 218n118; and racialized policing, 100; slave patrols, 20; against women, 127–28; youth populations, 127

Butler, Paul, 109

buyouts, and home loss, 67–68

Cao, Linqun, 47

Carla (Meacham Park resident), 174

causation models, 26

census data, residential segregation/integration studies, 33

centralization, 26

Chambliss, William, 35

Charles, Camille, 27

Charlestown Town Watch, 214n8

Chicago, IL, 24

Chocolate City, 96–97

citizen perceptions, narratives, policing experiences. *See* local government, perceptions of

citizen-police interactions, 41–42; negative interactions, 143; and police ride-along observations, 35–36

citizen surveys, 38–39

citizen watch, 214n8

city official, Kirkwood, 13, 15

City Team of Kirkwood, 184

class, as individual-level variables, 44

Cloverdale, 40, 218n108

clustering, 26

Code of the Street (Anderson), 41

Collins, Michael, 100

community conditions, as contextual-level variables, 45

community context: and ATPs, 47; significance of, 40

community development: Meacham Park, 49, 61–63; and political process, 29

community events, police involvement in, 175–76

community improvements, police services, 89

Community Relations Services (CRS), 182, 184

Community Team of Kirkwood, 184

contemporary residential mobility, 25–34

contextualization of crime, 99–100

contextual variables of ATP, 44, 45–47, 47

County Brown (St. Louis County Police Department), 88–90, 169, 171, 177, 178

crime: fear of, 44, 45, 89–90, 204; in Meacham Park, 95–104; "originals" and "implants", 96; in suburbs, 93–95

crime of place/race of place, 100–101, 104

crime reporting, 98–100, 145

criminality, 14, 55, 91, 210, 217n107; and crime reporting, 98–100; and racial bias, 100; and racialization of place, 100

criminalization, 22, 157–63

criminal justice system, and ATP individual-level variables, 44–45

CRS (Community Relations Services), 184

Crystal (Meacham Park resident), 126–28, 131–32, 151

cultural acculturation. *See* acculturation

cultural assimilation aspect, 27, 66, 215n49

cultural insensitivity, 47

cultural loss/disruption, 66

police voice, 35, 37
police with attitudes (PWA), stop-question-frisk policing, 119–20
policing experiences, 11, 190; history of, 19–25; internalization of, 46; Meacham Park, 15, 48; negative experiences, 193; positive policing experiences, 15, 170–72, 170–77; racialized experiences, 85; as social control, 34–44; and social injustice, 12; stop-question-frisk policing, 112–18. *See also* attitudes toward police (ATP)
policing of blacks: historical overview, 17–19; policing of slaves, 20
political accountability, 198–200
political alienation: and ATPs, 46–47; black vote, 22; as contextual-level variables, 44, 45; and criminalization, 157–58
political inclusion, 195–98
political sensitivity, 193, 194–95
Ponder, Michael, 36
positive policing experiences, 15; "Officer Friendly" encounters, 172–77; satisfaction with service calls, 170–72
post-annexation, 76–91; Kirkwood Police Department, 169; local government, 91; ordinances and laws, 84–91; and police response times, 171, 178; St. Louis County Police Department, 169
postemancipation laws, 21–22
prejudice, inherent structural, 17
preservation of place, 55
property appropriation, 18, 68–75
public housing, 96–97
PWA (police with attitudes), 119–32

Quinette Cemetery, 58

Rabun, John, 141
race, as individual-level variables, 44
race-and-place effects, 7–8, 11, 189, 216n71; accounting for, 188; historical contextualization of, 189; historical contextualization of emergence of, 48; misconceptions, 11; policing shaped by, 100; "race-and-place inclusive", 10; research, 9–19, 29, 47–48; shaping interactions, 27; support of, 191

race of place, 100, 104–5
racial balance, 216n64
racial bias/ideas, 28, 100, 217n79
racial denigration, 100, 167
racial disparity, 183, 189, 208, 218n108, 218n112
racial divide, 9, 152, 222n5
racial/ethnic inequality, 27, 28, 31
racial injustice, systemic in local governments, 209
racial insensitivity, 47
racialization, 22, 31, 85, 100, 217n107
racially/ethnically diverse community, preferences for, 33
racially segmented housing markets, 28–29
racial profiling, 5, 9, 14, 19, 34–39, 46, 48, 100
racial threat theories, 11, 22–23, 33, 47, 55, 84, 134, 188, 189, 191, 216n66, 217n79
racism, denials of, 188
reconciliation possibilities, 15; (diss)like for *form* of policing, 165–68; dissatisfaction with service calls, 177–81; federal intervention, 181–84; overview, 164–65; satisfaction with service calls, 170–77; service calls and voluntary police action, 168–81
redlining, 29, 66
residential integration: and aggressive policing, 48; attitudes toward suburban integration, 31–34; barriers to, 27–29; race-and-place effects on, 216n71; spatial assimilation model, 215n58
residential mobility, 25–34, 29, 215–16n58
residential segregation, 215n58, 216n68, 216n71; attitudes toward suburban integration, 31–34; challenging, 30–31; hypersegregation, 26–29
residents, Kirkwood, 13
residents, Meacham Park. See narratives, Meacham Park residents
respect/disrespect, 119–23, 144, 191–92
response time, police, 171, 178
Ricky (Meacham Park resident), 89–90, 129–30, 153
Riverio, Heraldo, 6
Rodney (Meacham Park resident), 35–36,

Weitzer, Ronald, 40
white affluent neighborhoods: and aggressive policing, 48, 218n108; and assimilation, 66; and crime, 95, 98, 218n108; dependence upon, 218n112; and differential treatment, 41, 196; distrust of, 76; and social disconnect, 55. *See also* Kirkwood Proper
white dependency and control, 66, 218n112
white distance preferences, 189
white flight, 27, 32, 61–62
white supremacist groups, 24
white supremacy, and Jim Crow laws, 22
Wilson, Darren, 207, 209
Wilson, William Julius, 41

Women's Community Club, 62

youth microaggressions, 40
youth populations: harassment, 105, 107, 113; and McEntee, 144–45; and negative ATPs, 44; negative perceptions of police, 193; physical brutality, 127; and police resentment, 160–61; and police suspicion, 102–3, 117–18, 144; and policing, 98; and positive police interactions, 174; recreational programs and facilities, 79, 197, 204–5; and Thornton, 151. *See also* Johnson, Kevin

Zimmerman, George, 5–6